SO-AJK-386

Life and Philosophy of
LORD SWĀMINĀRĀYAN

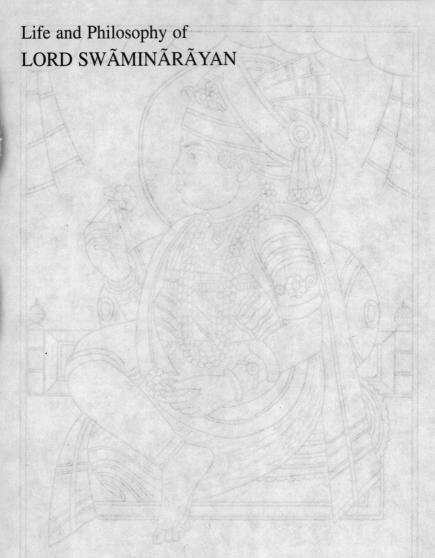

1. Shree Swāminārāyan

Life and Philosophy
of
LORD
SWĀMINĀRĀYAN
1781-1830

by H. T. Dave

Edited by Leslie Shepard

Foreword by Sir Charles Cunningham
C.B.E., K.B.E., C.V.O.

LIFE AND PHILOSOPHY OF LORD SWĀMINĀRĀYAN (English)
By H. T. Dave
Edited by Leslie Shepard
Foreword by Sir Charles Cunningham (C.B.E., K.B.E., C.V.O.)

Inspirer: HDH Pramukh Swāmi Mahārāj

Presented by:
Bochāsanwāsi Shree Akshar Purushottam Swāminārāyan Sansthā
Shāhibaug, Amdāvād - 380 004. India.

Publishers:
SWĀMINĀRĀYAN AKSHARPITH
Shāhibaug, Amdāvād - 380 004. India.

4th Edition:
June 2000. Copies: 4,000 (Total Copies: 8,000)

Copyright: ©Swāminārāyan Aksharpith
This book is published by Swāminārāyan Aksharpith. Material from this book cannot be used without due acknowledgement to Swāminārāyan Aksharpith, Shāhibaug, Amdāvād. For any reprints the written permission of the publishers is necessary.

ISBN: 81-7526-082-3

Price:
Rs. 50-00

Published & Printed by
Swāminārāyan Aksharpith
Shāhibaug, Amdāvād - 380 004

At the lotus feet of my Guru

SWÃMI SHREE YAGNAPURUSHDÃSJI

who inspired me into this life and

SWÃMI SHREE JNÃNJIVANDÃSJI

who moulded my life

FOREWORD

No one who has visited India, for however short a time, or who has known, however slightly, Indians who have settled in this and other countries can fail to have been impressed by the way in which the technological, industrial and commercial skills of the twentieth century have been accepted and indeed advanced – without any apparent loss of interest in the traditional cultures and religions of the Indian subcontinent. In the great nuclear research establishment in Bombay examples of Indian art are displayed; and I have listened there to Indian music and watched traditional Indian dances. In the manufacturing centres, as in the villages, religious practices are faithfully observed. In the towns and cities of this country in which Indians have settled, the culture which they have brought with them has been maintained in spite of the Western challenges it has had to face, and provision has been made for the continuance of the worship to which they have been accustomed.

We have seen recently, in a very striking way, how this ability to draw strength from cultural and religious continuity can help in facing the unpredictable trials of modern life. When nearly thirty thousand people were suddenly expelled from Uganda and had to come, often penniless, to start a new life in Great Britain their calmness and dignity, their readiness to accept hardship, the uncomplaining way in which so many of them who had known success and prosperity began again at the bottom of the ladder, impressed us greatly. It was evident that they had been sustained by a deep religious faith which had enabled them to accept adversity and to rise above it. They continued to practise that faith, helped by those of the same religion who were already living here, in remote resettlement centres and in the many areas all over the country to which they went.

This new edition of the Life and Philosophy of Shree Swāminārāyan helps us to understand these things. Many - perhaps most - of those who came here from Uganda were Hindus belonging to the branch of that religion which he founded in the nineteenth century and by whose teachings and precepts their lives are still governed. The book's distinguished author has now made these available to us in a form which enables us to understand, in a way that would not otherwise have been possible, the beliefs and attitudes not only of those who have recently arrived but also of the other members of the Swāminārāyan Hindu Mission who were already living here. Of the many hundreds of thousands who belong to this faith all over the world some thirty thousand are now our fellow citizens in Great Britain. So the publication of the book is timely.

We may perhaps welcome it for three reasons.

First, it is an account of a philosophy - and of the life of its founder - which is interesting and important in itself. The doctrine and the precepts which it outlines differ, of course, in many ways from those of the Christian faith. But they have a fundamental similarity in the belief in an omnipotent divinity who becomes incarnate for the redemption of mankind. In other respects the two religions diverge widely; but it is not, perhaps, presumptuous to say that one important part of the Swāminārāyan teaching could be summed up in the Christian beatitude: "Blessed are the pure in heart, for they shall see God." What is important, however, is not that we should analyse the similarities and the differences but that we should try, at a time when religious co-operation is being increasingly and rightly encouraged, to have a better understanding of what other people believe in. To that end the book makes a notable contribution.

Second, we now live in what it is fashionable to call a multi-racial society; and we have many agencies, and much good intent, to promote better race relations. But surely the key to good relations is understanding; and too few of us, to whatever race we belong, have tried hard enough to achieve that understanding. In this book we have a key to a better comprehension of the attitudes, the outlook, the beliefs, of thirty thousand people - and the number will grow - with whom we are living and working. It is a key of which hopefully many will make use.

And third, the book is of interest because of the circumstances in which Shree Swāminārāyan lived and worked. In the nineteenth century India into which he was born, traditional moral standards had in many cases been abandoned; crime and violence were common. His teaching was directed - and successfully directed – to the reversal of these trends; and he earned the gratitude of those who were then responsible for the government of India for his achievement. Today we live in a world in which violence is all too prevalent and in which many are concerned by the prevailing moral standards - or the lack of them. May we not have something to learn from the record of Shree Swāminārāyan's life and faith?

That faith is very much alive today; and those who profess it are conscious of their social as well as of their religious obligations. They have a strong sense of social duty - as those who were settled here showed by their support for the Ugandan refugees. There are many other ways in which, in our troubled times, advantage can be taken of it. Mr Dave's book, by helping us to understand the religious basis of it, will make it easier for all of us to seek out such ways and to follow them. I hope that it will be widely read.

SIR CHARLES CUNNINGHAM

PREFACE TO FIRST EDITION

Swāminārāyan was one of the early architects of the development of an Indian religious renaissance. During the days when India was in chaos, and the British were acquiring a dominion, Swāminārāyan made a way for non-brāhmins to become religious teachers.

Swāminārāyan's gospel, *Shikshāpatri,* is a code of moral rectitude in life, and during his lifetime he weaned away from violence, drinking and other vices the people of Gujarāt, Kāthiawār and U.P.

Swāminārāyan's movement was characteristically Indian, both in origin and inspiration.

Shree Dave has done distinct service to the religious literature of India in writing this book.

Bhāratiya Vidyā Bhavan
Chaupatty Road
Bombay 7
11 March 1967   K. M. MUNSHI

NOTE TO THIRD EDITION

H.T. Dave's Life and Philosophy of Lord Swāminārāyan has received widespread interest from both scholars and casual readers. It was first published in 1967. The second printing was undertaken by the British publishers George Allen & Unwin Ltd in 1974.

This third edition is being presented by Swāminārāyan Akshar Pith, India, the publishing arm of Bochasanwāsi Shri Akshar Purushottam Swāminārāyan Sanstha. In this work, minor changes in presentation have been made to help readers.

Firstly, the glossary has been expanded and a section introducing Swāminārāyan and general Hindu Scriptures has been added. Dialectic marks have been omitted, and replaced with a much simplified pronunciation system, which although having many drawbacks will at the same time eliminate major flaws in enunciation. The Sanskrit and Gujarāti long 'a' (અ, આ) has been written as 'ā', and is said as 'aa' as in; *art, cart, heart, after, basket, car*. Scholars will see this simplicity as lacking. Our humble apologies.

                                        - Swaminarayan Aksharpith

ACKNOWLEDGEMENTS

This is a revised and enlarged edition of a work first published in March 1967.

Many small errors have been corrected, and the text carefully edited to meet the standards of British publication. In addition, the material of the opening chapters has been rearranged and supplemented in order to clarify the philosophical basis of the subject for readers outside India. Finally, a completely revised translation of *Shikshāpatri*, the basic code of Shree Swāminārāyan, has been given in full, in place of the former extracts.

I am deeply conscious of my own limitations in attempting an exposition of such a unique philosophy. A complete understanding of the symbolic manifestation of the Absolute in Personal Form is possible only after complete Brahmanisation; all I can present here is a general exposition of the history and basic characteristics of a vast and subtle truth. It is only by the divine inspiration and grace of my Guruji, His Holiness the most revered Swāmi Shree Jnānjivandāsji, that I have been encouraged to attempt this task.

The life of Shree Sahajānand Swāmi has been elaborated by His various learned disciples in their works, in particular Satsangijivanam, Harileelākalpataru, Shree Hari Digvijay and others in Sanskrit, *Shree Harileelāmritam, Bhaktachintāmani, Shree Haricharitrachintāmani, Ghanshyām-Leelāmrita Sāgara* in Gujarāti, and various others in colloquial Hindi (Vraja) language. I have only selected some of the most outstanding events of His life which bring out His redemptive features of piety and compassion, and avoided over elaboration, since even the greatest details would not give a comprehensive idea of His working on this earth.

I am deeply indebted to all who made the first edition of this work possible; their kindness and wisdom sustain the present edition.

The late Dr K. M. Munshi, then President of Bhāratiya Vidyā Bhavan, Bombay, kindly wrote the Preface. I had the privilege of working under him when he was Home Minister to the Government of Bombay.

My gratitude goes to Shree M. R. Gopālāchārya, M.A., Nyāyavedānta Vidwān Panditaratna Panditarāj, the Head of the Vāni Vihār Vidyālaya, who took great pains to examine the manuscript of the first edition and gave valuable suggestions. I am grateful to the late Shree T. A. Dikshitārji, the Head of the Sanskrit Department of Bhāratiya Vidyā Bhavan, who also read the manuscript and was kind enough to make some important suggestions.

I also reaffirm my debt to His Holiness Shree Pramukh Swāmi, (Swāmi Shree Nārāyanswarupdāsji), the President of Shree Akshar Purushottam Sansthā, Bochāsan, who kindly consented to publish the work for and on behalf of the above Sansthā. I also acknowledge my indebtedness to many others who directly or indirectly helped and inspired me in the preparation of the work.

This second edition was commissioned at an auspicious period, on the occasion of the opening of a Shree Swāminārāyan Temple in London, England, by His Holiness Swāmi Shree Jnānjivandāsji (Yogiji Mahārāj), who visited England with his saints for this purpose in May 1970. Since then, to the sorrow and grief of his devotees all over the world, Shree Yogiji Mahārāj returned to his divine abode Akshardhām, on Saturday 23 January 1971.

This revised work will be a tribute to his unique grace, and a memorial to his divine inspiration.

During the preparation of this new edition I have been greatly indebted to his spiritual successor His Holiness Swāmi

Shree Pramukh Swāmi (Shree Nārāyanswarupdāsji) for his generous encouragement.

I am immensely grateful to Mr Praful R. C. Patel and other members of The Board of Trustees of the Swāminārāyan Hindu Mission, London, for all their labours in the difficult work of making this new English edition possible.

I am also grateful to Mr Leslie Shepard who has fully edited this edition.

H. T. DAVE

Shree Pramukh Swami (Shree Nārāyanswarupdāsji) for his generous encouragement.

I am immensely grateful to Mr Pratul R.C. Patel and other members of The Board of Trustees of the Swaminarayan Hindu Mission, London, for all their labours in the difficult work of making this new English edition possible.

I am also grateful to Mr Leslie Shepard who has fully edited this edition.

H.T. DAVE

CONTENTS

PART TWO

ILLUSTRATIONS

PART ONE

1 The Divine Quest

The holy land of our Bhāratvarsha or Āryāvarta[1] has been hallowed continually through the ages by the Lord's avatārs, sages, seers and bhaktas. The divine boon granted by Shree Krishna in *Shrimad Bhagawad Gitā*, to bring about a spiritual revival whenever righteousness waned or the cause of Dharma dwindled, has kept the spiritual morale of the people always uplifted. The glory of India is not simply in her industrial development, material welfare, or nuclear progress, but in the maintenance of her spiritual heritage. A nation survives only if its spiritual power is constantly reborn, to withstand and transform the onslaughts of agnostics, atheists, and materialists. In the history of India there has always been a descent of this power in innumerable avatārs (Avatār hyasankhyeyāhā) manifesting and revitalising the spiritual and ethical life of our people.

Hindu philosophy is based on the *Vedas*, scriptures which are recognised as inspired truths. The ultimate aim of Vedāntic philosophy is to show a way of life, to inspire people to shed mundane attachments, and to transmigrate into supramundane regions.

Our Vedic texts, Puranas and other sacred writings declare self-realisation to be the main aim of human life, to be reached through the pathway of one's duties or Dharma in this life.

---

[1] Bhāratvarsha, the kingdom of Bhārata, mentioned in the *Rig-Veda*; Āryavārta ('Land of the Āryans'), the territory between the Himālaya and Vindhya mountains, is mentioned in Manu-Sanhitā.

The law of Becoming is the central idea of Aryan culture. It teaches, nay insists on endeavour, self-discipline and asceticism in order to realise the Supreme Self in this life.'[2] Krishna Dvaipāyana Vyās, the Amshāvatār of Lord Vishnu and the greatest exponent of Brahma Vidyā, the Knowledge of God, says:

Buddhindriyamanahprānan janānam asrjat prabhuhu
Mātrārtham cha bhavārtham cha hyātmane kalpanāya cha

(The Lord has given us Buddhi, Indriyas, Manas, and Prānas[3] to enjoy sensuous pleasures within the limits prescribed by scriptures, and to secure nobler births here or elsewhere and finally to attain salvation.)

Asceticism does not necessarily involve withdrawal from the world. One who lives a good life, without attachment to the twin currents of desire and fear, happiness and misery, honour and insults, etc., who has focused his mind and senses on the divine, is a yogi or ascetic. Whereas one who is tied to the desire for pleasures of the senses is a bhogi or worldly man. The subtle state of desire for pleasures of the senses is vāsanā, and it causes continued births and deaths.

There is a great purpose in the creation of this Universe of innumerable jivas (individual souls).

The Universe as the Leela Vibhuti (play of divine power) exists not for pleasure but for the moulding of the soul into a mukta (one liberated from worldly experience).[4]

The creation of the Universe and its sustenance are for the ultimate release of the jivas. To those jivas who, however, could not attain release during the sustenance period of the Universe, and who had passed through innumerable yonis (physical births), Pralaya (dissolution after completion of a

---

[2] Munshi, Dr. K. M., The Fundamentals of Āryan Culture, Bombay, 1939.
[3] Intellect, Senses, Mind, and Vital Currents.
[4] Srinivasachari, P. N., The Philosophy of Vishishtādvaita, Adyar, 1943.

cosmic cycle) gives them ample rest.[5]

Rite Jnānān na muktihi [6]

and

Nānyaha panthāha vidyate ayanāya [7]

These Shrutis imply that without knowledge Mutki is not attained. It is only by realisation of God that death can be transcended.

This divine quest is the fascination of Vedāntic philosophy, for it does not merely involve intellectual enquiry. That is only the beginning. It must culminate in spiritual realisation through the development of intuitional meditation. Whilst it is proper to honour the inspired scriptures of the great religious geniuses of the past, the integrity of knowledge depends upon sharing that wisdom by inner realisation instead of mere repetition of scriptures.

Even though there are various schools of thought in interpretation of scriptures, there is a concurrence in their ultimate aim, which is approach to and realisation of God.

Confusion sometimes arises because of the complexity of Hindu concepts of God, and the varying interpretations of the different philosophical schools. Unlike other religions such as Christianity, which are content with relatively simple distinctions between God and man, the Hindu philosophical schools distinguish many subtle aspects of God and cosmic evolution, as well as the spiritual nature of man. Many of the special terms employed in Sanskrit cannot be translated into exact English equivalents. A detailed exposition of these terms lies outside the scope of the present work, but some basic terms have been given approximate English translation in the course of the text, and a Glossary of terms has been provided at the end of the book.[8]

---

[5] Vachanāmrit, Kāriyāni 1.
[6] Hiranyakeshiyashākhā Shruti.
[7] Shvetāshvatara, A. 3-8.
[8] See also the Chart of Cosmic Evolution, with notes, on page 274.

It will be easier to understand the unique contribution of Shree Swāminārāyan to Hindu religion if we first review briefly the five main schools of thought in Vedāntic philosophy, which were equally concerned with the need to seek the ultimate Reality of God (Purushottam) through study and realisation.

ADVAITA. This school was founded by Shree Shankarāchārya who flourished in the sixth century AD. He propounded the cult of Kevala Advaita or absolute monism. According to Shankar, Brahman (cosmic aspect of God) is without parallel, has no form, and exists as abstract consciousness or knowledge. Māyā or ignorance is an illusory principle responsible for the appearance of the phenomenal world and the individual souls (jivas) and their collective entity as Ātman. When the veil of Māyā is removed by proper awareness, jiva reverts to the original state of Godship from which it was apparently separated. For Shankar the world is an illusion, like a dream which dissolves in the waking state, the state of knowledge. What is real is eternal, and what is not eternal is not real. Since the world is not eternal it cannot be real. However, for those with an empirical state of mind, Shankar proposed an emanation of God as Ishwar or Sagun Brahman, to whom worship could be offered before the veil of Māyā was dissolved. Because of this conception of God as an absolute abstraction, neither real nor unreal (which he says were the distinctions of empirical mind), Shankar has been called Buddha in disguise, rendering the existence of God intangible.

VISHISHTĀDVAITA. This school was founded by Shree Rāmānujāchārya who was born in the year AD 1027. The absolute monism of Shankar, although complying with many of the demands of reason, fails to satisfy the cravings of the heart. Shankar commands respect because of his learning rather than his approach to God. Rāmānuja, the protagonist of theistic Vedānta, propounded qualified monism – that God is real and independent of the souls and world, which also have real existence. According to Rāmānuja, jiva, Ishwar and Māyā are eternal. Jiva and Māyā are not to be identified with Brahman or Ishwar, but collaterally sustain God as His body, while God, as their indweller, sustains them, since without God their separate existence is not possible. God is therefore one and without parallel as in Advaita, but since jiva and Māyā also exist with Him as His body, God is said to exist with two adjuncts as qualified Brahman. His oneness is not, however, impaired by such adjuncts. Rāmānuja laid down that God exists in five different modes: (1) *Parā*, the highest, residing in Vaikuntha (the divine abode) with a body of divine purity (sattva), accessible only to liberated souls; (2) *Vyuha*, with four forms, viz. Aniruddha who creates, Pradyumna who sustains, and Shankarshan, who destroys; the fourth form Vāsudev is the form of worship; (3) *Antaryāmin*, dwelling within jivas and witnessing their actions, good or bad, but not affected by them; (4) *Archā*, dwelling within images or images; (5) *Vibhāvas*, incarnations on earth. Rāmānuja claims that God is full of compassion for those jivas who crave to be redeemed, and responds to their call by manifesting as avatār on earth. Rāmānuja recognises three classes of jiva: (i) the nitya jivas who dwell eternally in Vaikuntha, the vicinity of God; (2) the muktas, liberated from bondage through devotion; (3) the jivas bound in the cycle of births and deaths as the result of their karmas (actions), who will not be redeemed so long as they perform karmas with ego. Freedom comes to the jiva through the inner craving of devotion, the consciousness of his nature and his relationship to God; in this eventual salvation he enjoys ānand, the bliss of Brahman.

SHUDDHĀDVAITA. This school of pure Advaita was founded by Shree Vallabhācharya, who was born in South India in AD 1401. Vallabha propounded that Brahman is God and jiva; Kāla and Prakriti (time and primal nature) are eternal but have no separate existence from Brahman. Jiva exists when the bliss of Brahman is obliterated. Vallabha refers to God as fire and the jivas as the sparks of fire. Whereas Shankar claims that the world is an illusion and that God manifests in many forms through the help of Māyā, Vallabha believes that manifestation is merely Divine Will, and the world is therefore the expression of His Leela or sport. Vallabha emphasises the divinity of Shree Krishna; jivas who serve Him with intense devotion are liberated, and sport with Him in Goloka, His divine abode. According to Vallabha, the world and the jivas are regarded as emanations of the chit (pure consciousness) and sat (pure being) respectively, whereas Akshar, the immutable Brahman, is the emanation of anand or bliss, which is limited as distinct from the ultimate divinity of Purushottam.

DVAITA-DVAITA. The creed of Dvaita and Advaita, or dualistic non-dualism, was propounded by Nimbārka, a Telugu brāhmin, who flourished in the eleventh century AD. According to Nimbārka, jiva, Ishwar and Jagat (the world) are distinct. Because of the independent reality of Purushottam, Ishwar differs from the dependent jivas and Jagat in attributes and nature, yet jiva and Jagat are also identical with Brahman, inasmuch as they could not exist independently. In this paradox of difference and non-difference, jiva is compared with Purushottam as the waves to the sea, or the radiance to the sun. Nimbārka stresses that emancipation comes to the jivas only by dedicated devotion.

DVAITA. Madhvā, who was born in the year AD 1199 established the Dvaita school of absolute dualism, the opposite point of view of Shankara's Advaita. According to Madhvā, God, jiva, and Jagat are three eternal entities which remain fundamentally different from each other, although jiva and Jagat depend upon God. Madhvā regarded the distinction between jiva and Brahman as a real one which does not disappear even in the state of liberation. Jivas are infinite, and differ from one another according to the nature of their karmas in the cycle of births and deaths. The inanimate world is evolved out of prakriti and returns to it in the state of dissolution. Madhvā insisted upon the difference between God and the liberated souls, which were only dependent upon God. In this, he remained a firm believer in unqualified dualism, whereas Shankar extolled a pure monism.

All these five schools of Vedāntic philosophy based their interpretations upon the *Upanishads*, the *Gitā*, and the *Brahmasutras*, collectively known as the Prasthānatrayi, the three basic authorities on Vedānta. Although the interpretations differ radically from each other, there are many points in common. The differences reflect the individual approach of the protagonists and the degree of their realisation of God, the Ultimate Truth. Such differences exist in the absence of full realisation.

Shree Swāminārāyan accepted the basic doctrine of the Vishishtādvaita of Shree Rāmānuja, yet with subtle differences which indicate His own divinity. It was not necessary to follow the traditional pattern of polemical discussion to refute other philosophies, for in His own person Shree Swāminārāyan demonstrated the basic principle of His teaching that God manifests on earth either Himself or through His fully Brahmanised Saint. Divine power is also inherent in the temple images of God and His Saint. Such forms of God on earth should be meditated upon with devotion in order to attain redemption.

The Vachanāmritam of Shree Swāminārāyan is a treatise full of the quintessence of revealed scriptures. In one of His Vachanamritas, He praises Shankar for eulogising Vishnu, Shiva Ganapati, Surya, and other forms of God with attributes, thus exhibiting great tolerance for empirically minded people who are led to God through worship. However, Shree Swāminārāyan upheld the principle that either God manifesting on earth or in fully Brahmanised form should be chosen for meditation.

Philosophy claims the knowledge of Ultimate Reality, and religion the realisation of that Ultimate Reality. To attain knowledge of the Parā Swarup of Nārāyan (the highest form of God in man), one must seek a spiritual Guru. Shreemad Bhāgawat states :

> *Tasmād gurum prapadyeta*
> *Jijnāsuh shreyam uttamam*
> *Sābade pare cha nisnātam*
> *Brahmanyupashamāsrayam*
> (II-3-2I)

(The spiritual seeker must find proper instruction at the feet of a Guru who is well-versed in Vedas that lead to the knowledge of God.)

Shree Krishna says :   *Vedaishcha sarvairaham eva Vedhyo*[9] - 'It is I alone, the Divine, that the four Vedas seek to know; it is I who am the author of Vedānta and also the Knower of the Knower of the Vedas.' The Guru is one who has realised Parabrahman (The God) and remains in constant communion with Him, or conversely through whom Parabrahman reveals Himself. The Guru is therefore the body of Parabrahman through whom He reveals all His powers for the emancipation of the jivas. Purushottam or Parabrahman manifests through Akshar, the Divine abode. In the philosophy of Shree Swāminārāyan, Akshar has the unique place enjoyed by Shree or Lakshmi in the Shree Vaishnavism philosophy.

Shree Swāminārāyan did not only preach theological doctrines and ethical precepts, but in His own life and that of His spiritual successors demonstrated divinity by His inspiration and purification of all types of devotees.

According to Shree Swāminārāyan, Akshar and Purushottam are the primordial forms of upāsanā (devotion

---

[9] Bhagawada Gitā, XV-I5.

and worship), spiritually united yet also distinct. Like the dual form of Lakshmi-Nārāyan, or Sryah Pati of Shree Rāmānujāchārya, they appear as two separate entities but are 'one in two and two in one and their corporate identity is indispensable to the seeker after mukti.'[10]

The revival of this upāsanā of the eternal forms of Akshar and Purushottam, or Brahman-Parabrahman, brought about renaissance in the teaching of Vedic lore.

Lord Swāminrayan initiated this philosophy and upāsanā in the early part of the nineteenth century. Akshar was a forgotten chapter in the history of Indian Philosophy. Purushottam was interpreted only as residing in His Param dham (Akshar) served by Nitya Muktas (those eternally liberated in Vaikuntha). With the coming of Shree Swāminārāyan, the divine forms of Akshar and Purushottam manifested on earth in human form. Light dawned on earth with the revelation of the divine forms of Akshar and Purushottam which had so far remained unrevealed.

---

[10] Srinivasachari, P. N., The Philosophy of Vishishtādvaita, Adyar, 1943.

2 The Basic Philosophy of Shree Swaminarayan

The purpose of this work is to present the main features of the system of philosophy propounded by Shree Swaminarayan within the historical context of its development.

This is a complex philosophy with many subtle aspects. It must be remembered that a purely theoretical exposition cannot express the dimension of intense wisdom and devotion experienced in the presence of a Brahmanised Saint and his devotees. Much that may seem obscure from a purely intellectual point of view will acquire greater strength when viewed in the historical perspective of its enunciation by Shree Swaminarayan and His saints, as described in the later chapters.

Shree Swaminarayan has emphasised Akshar as the medium to attain Atmic bhav (divine feeling). The Vishishtadvaita of Shree Swaminarayan is therefore conspicuously based on the relationship between Akshar, Ishwar and the jivas, and finally on the relationship between Akshar and Purushottam.

Shree Swaminarayan rejects Shankara's doctrine of Kevala Advaita or absolute monism. Jiva, Ishwar, Maya, Brahman and Parabrahman, are eternal entities, but their relationship varies during different phases of cosmic evolution and devolution.

Jivas are many and monadic, i.e. basic units. They are sentient, and so pervade the body through the attribute of knowledge. They are bound by individual karmas (actions) performed with attachment, and thus move in the cycles of births and deaths.

Ishwar is the Cosmic God involved in the function of creation, sustenance and destruction of the universe, which He pervades as his body. He is also bound by ignorance, since he is attached to the activities of cosmic creation. Ishwars are many, but the whole category is described as 'Ishwar'.

Māyā is the divine power responsible for the evolution of the universe. She is characterised by the three gunas (qualities of matter): sattva, rajas, and tamas (purity, passion, and inertia). These gunas permeate the world of prakriti in which the jivas exist, and because of this, Māyā is difficult to overcome. Since she depends upon God for her action, she is also recognised as an adjunct of God.

Brahman (the Akshar) is the divine abode of God, serving Parabrahman (the Purushottam) in two ways. As the divine abode, Akshar supports Purushottam and the infinite number of released souls (jivas), and as His choicest devotee, Akshar serves Purushottam in revealing His infinite greatness and glory.

Akshar-Brahman plays an essential role in the scheme of redemption of jiva by removing the ignorance of Māyā. By his conduct he transforms the monadic form of subject-object which characterises the jiva, revealing the latent purity of a divine body. Just as ice, which is frozen water, resumes its form through heat, so through the spiritual alchemy of Akshar the jiva gains aprākrit, a divine body. Without this contact of Akshar, no seeker can be Brahmanised, and final redemption is not available to him.

God, the Purushottam, is the Ultimate Reality. He has a divine body and lives in His divine abode – Akshardhām. He manifests on earth merely by the exercise of His will, without leaving His divine abode. Many people do not recognise His divinity in such a manifestation because of the veil of Māyā, which is only removed by devotion and purity. Shree Swāminārāyan was recognised as God – Purushottam Himself – whose form is to be realised and whose bliss is to be enjoyed by all seekers. So too have His spiritual successors maintained divine manifestation for the benefit of devotees.

Purushottam is the material and efficient cause of cosmic evolution, but His activity is exercised through Akshar who is inspired by Him in this work, in turn inspiring Purush and Prakriti (Pure Spirit, and Primordial Nature) to commence cosmic creation (see Chart of Cosmic Evolution page 274). This work is not a Leela or divine sport, as proposed in the Shuddhādvaita of Shree Vallabha, but an act of divine compassion towards the jivas, to bring relief from their incessant movements in the cycle of births and deaths.

According to Shree Swāminārāyan, the jivas, Ishwars and Māyā constitute the Sharir (body) or Akshar, and Akshar is their Shariri (sustainer). And since Purushottam pervades Akshar by His all-sustaining power, as explained in the Shruti[1], 'Akshar is held to be the Sharir of Purushottam, and Purushottam is Akshar's Shariri.

In the state of final emancipation (Atyantik Kalyan), every released soul is held by God and enjoys His bliss. It is a state of identification with God, but not of assimilation, rather like the relationship between body and soul. In this state of release, which is also a state of ultimate knowledge (atyantik jnān pralaya), the differences of jiva, Ishwar and Māyā which exist in this empirical world are eliminated. Similarly Brahman or Akshar is held by Parabrahman or Purushottam, but in this state of total bliss, Brahman remains absolutely engulfed, losing all consciousness of separateness from Parabrahman. In

---

[1] Sa paryagac cukram akāyam avranam asnāviram shuddham apāviddham.
Ishāvāsya 8, Bhāsya by Gopālānand Swāmi, p. 11

the final state Parabrahman alone remains, with the qualified adjunct of Akshar. Thus, Shree Krishnavallabhācharya, an eminent scholar on the philosophy of Shree Swāminārāyan, terms this as 'vishishtadvaite api vishishtabrahmadvaitatvam', which means that Purushottam, the one and unparalleled (advaita), is qualified only by Akshar – an unexcelled doctrine, not only in the school of Vishishtadvaita but in the whole Vedāntic philosophy.

This learned author chites various Shrutis in support of his concept of Vishishtabrahmadvaitatvam.

Akshar has been held as the sustainer and all-supporter of the millions of macrocosms.[2] Again, Akshar is described as the Sharir or body of the various universes.[3] Further, one who knows this Param Dham (Supreme abode) enjoys the grace of Purushottam.[4] And again, one who has known Brahman, attains Brahmabhāv (Pure Consciousness, an attribute of Brahman) and earns the divine grace of Purushottam.[5] Akshar as the Ātman of all the ātmans (the soul of all souls) possesses unitive consciousness with Purushottam yet is still conscious of his dependence upon Purushottam.[6]

Shrutis specifically distinguish between Brahman and Parabrahman as separate. In Prashna Upanishad, Sukesha and Bhardvaj, even though they were Brahmanised, approached Pippalada to request the knowledge with which to attain

---

[2] Yad archimad yad anubhyo anu yasmin lokā nihitā lokinash cha tad etad aksharam brahma. – *Mundaka, 2.2.2.*

[3] Brahmaivedam vishvam idam varishtham. – *Mundaka, 2.2.II.*

[4] Sa vedaitat paramam brahmadhāma, and upāsate purusham ye.

– *Mundaka, 3.2.I.*

[5] Parātparam purusham upaiti divyam, and Brahmaved Brahmaiva bhavati.

– *Mundaka 3.2.8 & 9.*

[6] Ved vāham tam purusham sarvasyātmanah parāyanam.

– *Brihadāranyaka 3-9-10.*

Parabrahman.[7] Akshar, the Brahman, is separate from Parabrahman, the Purushottam.[8] And Akshar transcends the jivas, as Parabrahman transcends Akshar.[9]

Shree Swāminārāyan upheld Akshar (or Brahman) and Parabrahman as separate entities, and defined their relationships in His Vachanāmritam thus:

Brahman is always static and indivisible. When it is said that everything is Brahman, it implies the all-pervasiveness of Brahman. Again, Brahman is the cause of Prakriti and Purush and their sustainer; Brahman as such cannot be said to be separate from its causal effects, or conversely Brahman, by its power of concomitance or pervasiveness, is felt everywhere. However, Brahman does not degenerate and become jiva, which view is repugnant. Again, Parabrahman is distinct and separate from this Brahman and is its supporter, inspirer, and cause. With this knowledge of Brahman, the mumukshu (one desiring liberation) should identify himself with Brahman and worship Parabrahman as his Lord, upholding the ideal of Swāmi Sevak bhāv (service to spiritual master).[10]

The identity of the self is to be established with Akshar, the form of Sat-Chit-Ānand (the self of Being-Consciousness-Bliss), in order to imbibe the all redemptive attributes of Akshar. When the empirical self knows Akshar through wisdom, service and devotion, shedding the gross ego, there is identification with Akshar. This identification is the state of Ātmāvalokana, of jnān or full knowledge.[11] The mystical union

---

[7] Brahmaparā brahmanishthāhā param brahmānveshamānāhā. — Prashna. I.i.

[8] Etad vai Satyakāma param cha aparam cha brahma yad onkarah.
— Prashna, V.2.

[9] Sa sāmabhir unniyate brahmalokam sa stasmāt jivaghanāt parātparam purishayam purushām ikshate. -Prashna, V. 5.

[10] Vachanāmrit, Gadhadā Sec. II-3

[11] Eshātmanistha sudradaha jnānam ityupavarnitam.
– Satsangijivanam, IV-A, 67-8.

existing between Akshar and Purushottam is also enjoyed by the seeker who is identified with Akshar. Such God-intoxicated devotees enjoy the bliss of Paramātmā and live in the world to communicate this bliss to humanity.

In the course of His divine mission, Shree Swāminārāyan had to deal with many ignorant people who might have been misled by pseudo-religionists posing as great teachers. Sometimes He exposed the pretensions of impostors who played upon the credulity of simple people.

In spite of His own divinity, He cautioned against premature desires for divine visions of God, preaching that true awareness is achieved only when purity of thinking, purity of heart, and purity of intuition are perfected. He taught yoga methods of meditation, including visualisation of His own form at different centres in the body in a given order.

He emphasised the necessity of reconciling reason and intuition in order to attain knowledge of Ultimate Reality.

To the intellectuals, He recommended the study of scriptures and contact with His sādhus, from whose pure thinking developed higher intellectual modes. When heretics, sceptics, and dogmatic persons refused to believe Him or even campaigned against Him, He threw them into trances in which they saw vividly the hellish consequences of their folly.

To sincere devotees He sometimes showed visions of His own abode and divine form, surrounded by innumerable released souls. To devotees with separate affiliations towards Shree Krishna, Shiva, Ganpati, or other divine forms, He showed visions of the higher glories of such divinities. But above all, He stressed the need for constant pursuit of divine knowledge, since miraculous experiences were short-lived and did not always stimulate the seeker to the steadfast transformation of his life.

He taught that knowledge of God is a spiritual enquiry and necessitates spiritual endeavour, i.e. cultivating the six virtues – shām, dām, upārati, titikshā, samādhāna, shraddhā (mental tranquillity, control of senses, detachment from routines, endurance, concentration, and faith in God and scriptures).

He evolved a unique philosophy of universal appeal, which satisfied the needs of worship and devotion and could also meet the claims of reason. In spite of His own divinity, He honoured Veda Vyās as the highest authority, for Veda Vyās was also a partial manifestation of His own self. His discourses which have been compiled in the Vachanāmritam are sound in logic, subtle in depth, and true to the tenets of Vyās.

Most of all, in His own person, and in the succession of Brahmanised saints and teachers right up to the present day, Shree Swāminārāyan fulfilled the divine promise to manifest constantly on earth for the benefit of devotees and seekers. Shree Gunātitānand Swāmi who was the incarnation of Akshar, inspired his foremost disciple Shree Prāgji Bhakta, his spiritual symbol Jāgā Bhakta and many others such as Swāmi Balmukundāsji, Swāmi Yogeshwardāsji, Swāmi Tyāgvallabhdāsji and they attained eminence in Brahma Vidyā. Amongst other revered names Swāmi Shree Yagnapurushdāsji established full contact with his Guru Shree Prāgji Bhakta, and enjoyed the bliss of Paramātmā. In recent times, Swāmi Shree jnānjivandāsji brought divine knowledge to many different parts of the world, and His great work is now being carried on by Swāmi Shree Nārāyanswarupdāsji.

The divine message continues through the succession of saints, seers, and realised souls whose life and teaching are in absolute consonance with the spiritual, ethical, and theological precepts of our scriptures. In this system, the Absolute of Philosophy and the God of Religion are both combined, thus fulfilling the claims of logic as well as the needs of religious experience, opening the inner awareness of the seeker to spiritual realities.

By His radiant divinity Shree Swāminārāyan has not merely taught spiritual knowledge, but revealed it.

3 The Search for Gnostic Consciousness

During the latter part of the eighteenth century, India was ruptured and divided. The political, social and religious ties were loosened. The rise of perverse religion of the Vāma Mārga and the Shakta Cult led to deterioration in ethical and social values. Degeneration and decay undermined the morality of the country to such an extent that people in general became addicted to wine and meat. Adultery became rampant. The Vedas were misinterpreted so as to justify the performance of himsāmaya Yagnas (cruel sacrifices). People had abandoned every ethical code to indulge in the voluptuous pleasures arising from wine, women and wealth. Social and religious structure had largely crumbled. Internal warfare had disrupted society and lawlessness prevailed. Against this background, Swāmi Sahajānand or Lord Swāminārāyan took birth at Chhapaiya, near Ayodhyā in order to resuscitate the religious and ethical values. His father Dharmadev, a Sarvāriya brāhmin and a pundit of very high calibre, and his mother Bhaktidevi, an embodiment of love, were much delighted at the birth of this son. Suprasensible powers were evident in this child even as an infant. A learned brāhmin Mārkandeya once came to the house of Dharmadev. Dharmadev requested him to use his knowledge of astrology and foretell the future of this promising child. Mārkandeya beheld the unusual lustre of the boy. But withholding the supernormal aspect of the future which became visible to him, he said, 'In intelligence this child will be like Brihaspati and in tapas (austerities) like Kārtikeya Swāmi. There are various other unusual qualities in this child. He will redeem the miseries of thousands of people. Therefore he will be known as Hari (one who takes away the miseries of others). Further, as the child has a dark complexion, and as his features are attractive, he will be called Krishna or Ghanshyām. Thus both Hari and Krishna in one, the child will also be known in future as Harikrishna. But now you may call him by the name of Ghanshyām.' Dharmadev was delighted to hear all this. After some time the family migrated to Ayodhyā.

As he advanced in age, Ghanshyām began to study scriptures at the feet of his father Guru, Dharmadev. Ghanshyām underwent upanayana samskāras (sacred thread investiture) at the age of seven. Thereafter he studied the Vedas.

He used to wake up very early and go to the river Saryu for ablutions. He visited every temple in Ayodhyā, the choicest being Hanumān Gadhi, the famous temple of Hanumān. However, he never felt congenial at home and decided to leave as soon as a suitable opportunity was available.

During this period, several learned brāhmins of Benāres invited Dharmadev to be a mediator in a debate to be held between the Shankarites and the followers of Rāmānujāchārya. Ghanshyām requested his father to permit him to speak on behalf of the Rāmānuja creed. Ghanshyām's eloquent arguments based on Shruti Pramānas shattered the basis of Shankaravādins.[1] The brāhmin pundits were amazed to hear this young child expounding the Bhakti cult so eloquently, and bowed down at his feet. Dharmadev's delight knew no bounds as he could foresee the prediction of the learned brāhmin Mārkandeya being fulfilled in the person of his very dear child. After receiving a great ovation the father and son

---

[1] For details refer : Hari Digvijaya, Nityānand Swāmi, and Harililā Kalpataru,
                                                            – Br. Achintyānand.

returned to Ayodhyā.

Ghanshyām, however, felt that the mission of his life was to establish and spread the message of Bhāgawat Dharma. He was therefore planning to leave home. After Bhaktidevi and Dharmadev both passed away, Ghanashyām felt that the time was now approaching for renunciation.

The day of renunciation arrived. As usual, eleven year old Ghanshyām got ready in the early morning to go to the river Saryu. This time his belongings consisted of a small book (Gutika) containing extracts from Gitā, *Shrimad Bhāgawat, Upanishads* and *Brahmasutras*, Shāligram, the image of Vishnu, one Kamandalu (water vessel), one filter cloth, palasha dand (stick) and a waist-cloth. Emaciated by tapas (austerities), Ghanshyām looked brilliant. The matted hair on his head resembled a crown of glory. His wide forehead was besmeared with tilak and a round kumkum mark within. In the dim light of early morning Ghanshyām left home, left all attachment, and started for a greater mission to dispel the discord that had totally consumed the spiritual glory of Āryavarta. He reached the Saryu river, determined never to return. His mission for the spread of Bhāgawat Dharma (divine life) now commenced.

He became known as Nilkanth, since people who saw him noticed tapas, tyāg, dharma, jnān and yoga to be equalled only by Shiva, and so the beloved name of Nilkanth was given to him. His barefooted travels in the valleys of Himalayas, on the tops of Himalayas, in the jungles, and to all the holy places, sometimes without food and water, amply testified to his amazing yogic powers to sustain life. During these travels, he saw the great discrepancy in the life and preachings of many sādhus and the heads of various muths (monasteries); he saw avarice, he saw carnal desire, he saw lust for power and prestige. In fact he saw everything in such people that was incongruent with saintliness or preceptorship. Ignorance, superstitions, fear complex, false dogmas, bigotry, etc., amongst the people, helped to augment the number of these hypocrites.

Nilkanth saw a great danger to the spiritual heritage of India in the growth of these heretics. The sanctity of the pilgrim places was vitiated. Religion meant only visiting temples and feeding such 'flocks of naked bāwās.' Philosophy had lost the features of intrinsic knowledge. Nilkanth studied the problem. He could see the remedy for the eradication of these nomadic flocks only in the spread of Bhāgawat Dharma, i.e. jnān coupled with dharma and bhakti, which required an understanding of the concept of a real sādhu and also the cultivation of inherent taste for knowledge. They could only be achieved with the help of a band of spiritual workers dedicated to a life of renunciation, asceticism, and austerities. New band of sādhus of the calibre of Paramhansas should be raised. This process of churning went on in the mind of Nilkanth as he saw the same conditions prevailing in Jagannātha Puri, Rāmeshwaram, Madurai and all other holy places of worship. Wherever Nilkanth went, he won the grace of people and of kings by his saintliness, his love, his keen desire to uplift everyone from utter social and spiritual degeneration. Because of this, he sometimes faced the wrath of jealous nomads, sometimes at the peril of his life. However, Nilkanth conducted his mission in a very shrewd manner and these false sādhus quarrelled amongst themselves and ultimately left him alone.

Seven years of Nilkanth's journey from North to East, East to South and South to West made it abundantly clear to him that the religious life of the people was dwindling, philosophy was only in preaching or in dialectical warfare, morality was waning, and religious precepts being completely ignored. Every known major place of pilgrimage, every muth (monastery), whether it was in the jungle or in a remote place, known or unknown, was visited by Nilkanth, facing all difficulties. He travelled in incessant rains, under the scorching sun, in bitter cold. Sometimes he threw himself against the currents of flowing rivers, encountering great hardships. He did all this with a dedicated purpose, to find out the source of the spiritual light from which he could kindle the fire of spiritual regeneration.

To the head of muths or other preceptors, he used to ask five questions: What is jiva? What is Ishwar? What is Māyā? Describe Brahman. Describe Parabrahman. When they could not reply to these questions, it added fuel to the fire and only strengthened his determination. Nilkanth had the patience to endure all ordeals. He desired to find out whether there was any correct understanding of the traditional philosophical knowledge which might be enhanced so as to enlighten all. At first he was disappointed. He felt that gnostic consciousness was beyond the horizon.

4 The Happy Augury at Lojpur

The soil of Saurāshtra was touched by the footsteps of Shree Krishna some five thousand years ago. Thereafter the samkirtans (sacred singing) of Mirā, Narsinh, and other saints and bhaktas reverberated in this holy land, as if they were inviting Vibhutis (divine glories) to touch it and divinise it. The call was heard by Nilkanth who directed his steps towards this region.

In S.Y. 1856 on the sixth day of the dark half of Shrāvan, Nilkanth reached Lojpur, a village near Māngrol port. It was early morning, and he sat on the edge of a well in the outskirts of this village. Some women who came to fetch water saw this lustrous young sādhu with his eyes downwards and mind introverted. They refused to believe their eyes in as much as they could not for a moment imagine how a mother could have parted with such a charming and illustrious son. Though emaciated to the extent of skin and bones by tapas (austerities), the saintly features of Nilkanth made a great impression on the minds of the onlookers.

The news spread rapidly through the whole village. There was an āshram here of Swāmi Rāmānand; while he was away in Kutch the āshram was under the care of Swāmi Muktānand, the chief disciple of the Swāmi. Muktānand heard of this young saint and sent two sādhus to bring him to the āshram. These sādhus came near the well and saw the captivating personality of the young Nilkanth. They looked with widened eyes, wondering whether what they saw was a human being or a personified Tapas. With pots full of water on their heads, they stood nearly half an hour, waiting for the yogi to awaken from his deep meditation. Nilkanth became aware of the intense devotion of these two saints who were anxiously waiting to talk with him. So he opened his eyes. They slowly came near Nilkanth and with folded hands asked him, 'Young sādhu! Please tell us what is your name, who are your father and mother, and where do you come from?'

Awaking from meditation, Nilkanth was pleased to see the sādhus standing with folded hands, but immediately withdrew the feeling of affection because of his austerity. He replied resignedly, 'I have no relations, no father and no mother. One who delivers from the miseries of this samsār is a true relation, a true father and a true mother.'

With their heads bowed down the sādhus then said, 'That is true, Sir, but according to the customary practice of this Lok, we have just enquired. May it therefore please you to reply.' Nilkanth, beholding their modesty, related to them the story of his quest and asked them who they were. The sādhus told him, 'We are the inmates of the āshram of Swāmi Rāmānand, and Muktānand, the chief disciple of Swāmi Rāmānand, having heard about you, has sent us here to take you to our āshram'. Nilkanth said, 'I am much obliged to you for your invitation. But it is not proper for a sādhu to stay amongst people. I generally do not enter into villages or towns. You may, therefore, forgive me for declining your offer.' The sādhus, however, were inflexible. They said, 'If you will not come, our Muktānand Swāmi will come here to take you. And so we request you to come with us.' In the inner recesses of Nilkanth's heart, a sympathy was created for these sādhus and he agreed to go with them.

Coming to the āshram, Nilkanth saw Muktānand and Muktānand saw Nilkanth. Simultaneously they both felt that their hearts were meeting. They were known to each other. Nilkanth was delighted. Muktānand was moved with awe and respect and felt as if Swāmi Rāmānand himself had come here incognito. Muktānand, with a slim and attractive figure, eyes full of devotion, and heart exuberant with bhakti (religious emotion), was a saintly character and moved Nilkanth. But he was not to be swayed by his feelings. He wanted to ask the five questions which he had asked wherever he had gone. He wanted to test whether the knowledge the Swāmi possessed was in accordance with the true tenets of the scriptures. So he said, 'I would be much obliged if you will answer my five questions regarding the forms of jiva, Ishwar, Māyā, Brahman and Parabrahman.' Muktānand was very pleased to hear these subtle questions and felt that this varni (yogi) was an extraordinary personality.

With an unmoved calmness, meditating for a moment on the divine form of his Guru Rāmānand, Muktānand sat in a lotus-like posture opposite Nilkanth and bowing at his feet began to reply, 'Oh, most revered Varnirāj! I feel from the questions that you have asked that you have either realised God or are the Self of God. Our Guru Rāmānand has been teaching us to understand correctly these five entities, without the knowledge of which, he says, mukti (liberation) is not attainable.'

Whereupon Nilkanth said, 'Please tell me all about your Guru Rāmānand Swāmi.'

Pleased in his innermost heart to narrate the life of his Guru, Muktānand commenced:

'Rāmānand Swāmi was born at Ayodhyā in a brāhmin family in S.Y. 1795 on the eighth day of the dark half of Shrāvan. His father's name was Ajaydev and mother's name was Sumatidevi. As the child grew up he showed no signs of worldly awareness. He thus became a source of grief to his parents. After the Upānayan Samskārs, Rāmānand wished to leave home under the pretext of going to Dwārkā for yātra (pilgrimage). His father and mother tried to persuade him not to go alone, but he insisted and left home.

'He went to Vrindāvan and from there travelled to all the places of pilgrimage throughout Bhārat and came to Saurāshtra, where in the foothills of Girnār (Raivatāchal) he met Ātmānand Swāmi, the disciple of Gopāl Yogi of Gopnāth. At the feet of this Guru, he attained all the siddhis (powers) of yoga. But he felt that unless he had the darshan of Shree Krishna, these siddhis were of no use. [Darshan ('sight') implies communication of divine grace through proximity to saint or visions of forms of God.]

'So one day he said to his Guru, "I desire to have the darshan of Shree Krishna and you may grace me with that boon." The Guru thereupon said, "There is nothing beyond the light of Sat-Chit-Ānand that you are seeing." On hearing this he felt as if a thunderbolt had fallen upon him. He could not for his life believe that Shree Krishna was nothing but light. Realising that the Guru did not have perfect knowledge, he left him.

'Then he came to Shree Rangam in the south. He stayed there amongst the disciples of Shree Rāmānujāchārya and studied Gitā Bhāshya, Prapanchamrita, etc. This led him to believe that Rāmānujāchārya had Krishna sākshātkāra and perhaps he would also have it. One night after nearly two months, he concentrated upon Rāmānujāchārya in meditation and soon went to sleep. Rāmānujāchārya gave him his darshan, appearing in his dream, and knowing him to be a devotee in earnest quest, he initiated him in Vaishnavi Dikshā, giving him the twelve prints representing the armour of Vishnu on his body. When he woke up in the morning, he saw the prints on his body. He was rapt with delight as he realised the truthfulness of his dream. That same day he went into a trance and had the darshan of Shree Krishna with his consort

Lakshmi. He was greatly fulfilled. Then he left Shree Rangam, came here and established his āshram. By his grace, I have his immediate darshan in Pujā [i.e. his gracious appearance in worship].' So saying Muktānand paused.

Nilkanth was very pleased to hear this inspiring story of the life of Guru Rāmānand. Then he waited for Muktānand's reply to his questions regarding jiva, Ishwar, Māyā, Brahman and Parabrahman. These too Muktānand answered satisfactorily, whereupon Nilkanth said, 'Oh Muktānand! You have understood these forms as they are required to be understood by a true Sādhak.'

Hearing this, Muktānand with all the courtesy at his command said, 'Varniraj! I shall be much obliged if you will elaborate them for a clearer and more lucid understanding for all of us here.' Whereupon Nilkanth began the following eloquent narration.

5 Jiva, Ishwar, Māyā

'Jiva is described as imperceptible like a monad, an individual unit. He is as subtle as the thousandth part of the hundredth part of a hair. He is different from the three bodies, viz. the apparent or gross, the subtle, and the causal; he resides in the heart and pervades the whole organism by his chidrup shakti.[1] He is chidrupa, jnānswarup (of the form of consciousness and knowledge) and is also the knower (jnata) i.e. the shelter or ashray of knowledge.[2] This knowledge of jiva is inspired by the Sākshi - who resides in the jiva as Antaryāmi (the divine inner controller).[3] He is sanātan, i.e. not created at any time by anybody, and eternal. Weapons cannot cut him, fire cannot burn him, water cannot wet him and wind cannot

---

[1] Hrutstho anuha sukshmas chidrupo
Jnātā vyāpyākhilām tanum
Jnānshaktyā sthito jivo
Jneyo acchedyādilaksanahah
 - Shikshāpatri, 105

("Jiva, which is very subtle, resides in the heart. He is chidrupa and by his sentiency pervades the entire body. He is unpierceable, indivisible, and intangible.")

[2] Na kevalam jnānswarupaha
Kintu Jnānāshrayashchetyāhā
 - Shatānand Muni, Shikshāpatri Bhāshyam, p. 286.

[3] Hrudaye jivavajjive
Yo antaryāmitayā sthitaha
 - Shikshāpatri, 107.

("As Jiva resides in the heart Paramātmā resides in Jiva by His Antaryāmin Shakti.")

dry him. Since all these cannot change his nature, he is nitya, ultimate reality.

Jivas are innumerable.[4] They are bound by vāsanā (impression) according to their karmas (actions). For their ultimate release they have to perform actions as prescribed by the Vedas.[5] Jiva by nature is blissful. Shrutis describe him as *svatah sukhi*. As he feels, "I am smelling, I am seeing, I am hearing, etc.". . . it is inferred that one who smells, sees and hears, is different from the body and that is the jiva.

During the pralaya rest period, the jivas rest in Māyā, and at the time of creation they take birth according to their karma.[6] This metempsychosis of jivas comes to an end at the time when they are ultimately released from this bondage.'

Then Nilkanth began the description of Ishwar.

'Ishwar's body is composed of Panch Mahābhutas (five great elements) out of which the bodies of the jivas are evolved. The Panch Bhutas which compose the bodies of jivas are alpa, i.e. are not capable of further evolution. Jiva is alpagna, i.e. little-knowing, and Ishwar is sarvagna, i.e. omniscient.[7] Ishwar has three bodies, viz. Virāt, Sutrātmā and Avyākrut, is involved in the creation, sustenance and destruction of jagat, and is omniscient.[8] Brahmā, Vishnu, Mahesh, Hiranyagarbha, Bhumāpurush, Mahāvishnu, Rudra,

---

[4] Nityo Nityāyām chetanshchetanānām eko bahunām yo vidadhāti kaman
- Kathā, 2-5-13

Aparimitā Dhruva... - Shrimad Bhāgavata, 10-87-30

[5] Kartā vijnānatmā purushah. - Prashna, 4-9.

Kartā Shāstrārthavatvāt. - Brahmasutra, 2-3-33.

('He is the doer, the intelligent self, the purushaha.')

[6] Lord Swāminārāyan, Vachanāmrit, Vadtāl, 6.

[7] Ibid., Panchālā, 2.

[8] Dehatraye virādhādau vyāpyotpattisthitikshayān
Karoti jagatām yas tu sarvajno jneya ishwaraha
- Satsangijivanam 1-51-29.

Shankarshan, Aniruddha, Pradyumna, Pradhān Purush, Mahat Tattva are all called Ishwars."[9]

With Sattva guna (purity) predominating in them, they are ever blissful. Mahāvishnu rests in the womb of Mulamāyā known as Hiranmay kosh. Mulamāyā is nitya, unborn and of a single entity. At the time of creation, Parabrahman through Mahāpurush, who is Aksharātmak, conjoins with Māyā. (see Chart of Cosmic Evolution, page 274)[10.] Māyā then conceives Pradhān and Purush and through them Vairāj Purush is born. This Vairāj Purush is similar to jiva inasmuch as both are bound by Māyā. Jiva has three bodies. Vairāj Purush has also three bodies, viz. Virāt, Sutrātmā and Avyākrut, and, like jiva, is also encircled by eight spheres of Māyā. The body of Vairāj Purush is composed of twenty-four tattvas including the "mahattattva".[11]

Even though Purushottam is the inspirer (prakāshak) of Vairāj Purush, Vairāj Purush is bound by Māyā. If at the time of Prakrit Pralay, Vairāj Purush communes with Mahāpurush, he is freed from Māyā and is released. But so long as he is attached to Aniruddha, Pradyumna and Shankarshan, he remains involved in this activity of creation, sustenance and destruction of the "jagat". Millions of such macrocosms are created through such Vairāj Purushs who are as many in number as the macrocosms.[12]

All the Ishwars headed by Mahāvishnu ultimately rest in the womb of Mulamāyā known as Hiranmay Kosh.[13] Mulamāyā has the form of absolute darkness and is therefore known as "Mahattamā". Shruti describes it as *tam asit tamasā*

---

[9] Krishnavallabhāchārya, Vishishtādvaite-api-vishishta Brahmādvaitavam.

[10] Purushena ātmabhuten viryamādhatta viryavān.

- Shrimad Bhāgawata

[11] Lord Swāminārāyan, Vachanāmrit, Gadhadā Sec.II-31

[12] Ibid.,

[13] Krishnavallabhāchārya, Swāminārāyan Vedānta Sāra, p. 20.

gudham agre, i.e. "in the beginning there was absolute darkness."[14] Beyond this in Brahmalok there is no Māyā.

Mahāpurush is the cause of the evolution of Ishwar. Since he disturbs Māyā, he is the cause of Māyā also. But Mahāpurush, even though in contact with Māyā, has no desire for the enjoyment of pancha vishayas, as he derives the anand from the ever blissful form of Paramātmā.[15] He is therefore called "mukta", a released soul.'

So saying Nilkanth stopped.

Muktānand was amazed to hear such an eloquent exposition of jiva and Ishwar by Nilkanth, with Shruti Pramānas. He was anxious to hear further when Nilkanth started to describe Māyā.

Māyā is Prakriti, and the inspirer of Māyā into action is Maheshvana - *Mātān tu Prakritim vidyām nayinam tu maheshuaram*. She is the generator of evolutionary changes, is of the nature of ignorance (*avidyātmak*), unborn, holding eight forms and static, *vikarjanim ajnānmasta rupam ajām dhrivam*. She is *trigunātmik* (full of sattva, rajas and tamas gunas) and is non-sentient – *Prakritiryā māyākhyātā vyaktavyaktaswarupini* (Vishnu Purana). Inasmuch as she holds sentient and non-sentient elements within her womb, she is said to have manifest and unmanifest forms. She is the Kshetra of all the Mahat Tattvas as well as of jivas and is Parabrahman's shakti.

The Virāt Purush Lok, and above that the Shivalingajyoti Lok, above that Vishnu Lok, above that Mahāvishnu Lok and the Mahāvishnu of Mahāvishnu Lok, all rest in the womb of Mahāmāyā, which is called Hiranyamay Kosha. The influence of Māyā stops with this. Beyond this there is no Māyā.[16]

---

[14] Rigveda, Sutra 129 Mantra 10.

[15] Vachanāmrit, Gadhadā Sec. II-31

[16] Krishnavallabhāchārya, Swāminārāyan Vedānta Sāra, p. 20

Māyā is eternal, God-inspired and full of gunas. She is difficult to be transgressed. As the shakti of Paramātmā, she is responsible for the creation, sustenance and destruction of jagat.[17] She is the cause of identification of the jivas and Ishwar with their bodies and the relations thereof.'[18]

So saying, Nilkanth completed his narration and paused for a moment before expounding the form of Brahman – the Akshar.

---

[17] Swashaktyā māyayā yuktaha srujatyatti cha pāti cha.

- Shrimad Bhāgawata, 4-11-26

[18] Jivasya chāham mamatāhetur māyāvagamyatām - Shikshāpatri, 106

6 Brahman - The Akshar

Here follows the exposition by Nilkanth on Brahman – the Akshar with the addition of extra references.

'Brahman is the Divine abode of God. It is also known as Akshar. Though of a single entity it has two forms – one Nirākār in the form of an unfathomable homogenous mass of chaitanya (pure consciousness) which is called chidākāsh or Brahmamahol. The second, Sākār form of Akshar, is the nearest devotee and is in the constant service of Purushottam in His abode.[1] It is also described as Satyaswarup, jñānswarup, infinite, pure and devoid of evolutionary changes. It is also the inspirer of jivas, Ishwars and Māyā, and is their sustainer (sarvadhār).[2] Everything shines by its light - *tasya bhāsā sarvam idam vibhāti'*(Mundaka, II-2-10).

Endless and infinite macrocosms appear as atoms before the vast and immeasurable greatness of this Akshardhām. Just as an ant moving on the body of an elephant looks so insignificant, similarly before the greatness of the vast, immeasurable and all-pervading Akshardhām, the whole cosmos appears small. This divine abode – Akshardhām – has a divine form, but because of its infinite greatness and vastness it is beyond human visualisation.

Yad Aksharam vedavido vadanti[3] – the knowers of Vedas call it Akshar the *Pad* or Dhām of Paramātmā, wherein only the celibates can enter.

---

[1] Lord Swāminārāyan, Vachanāmrit, Gadhadā Sec. I-21

[2] Nishkulānand Swāmi, Bhaktachinatāmani, Ch. 39.

[3] Gitā, VIII - II.

It is the cause of all the causes. One which is greater than the other, is the cause of the other, and is subtler than that. Water is greater than earth and is the cause of earth and is subtler than earth. Similarly, fire is greater than water, air is greater than fire and space is greater than air. Again egoism, intelligence, Purush and Prakriti are progressively greater than one another. Above them is Akshar – the abode of Puruṣhottam – which is greater, subtler and the cause of the evolution or generation of all of them.[4]

Tad āhur Aksharam brahma, sarvakāranakāranam. (Shreemad Bhāgawat, III-11-41.) The greatness of this Akshardhām is described as *yasmin lok nihitā lokinash cha tad etad Aksharm brahma* – that in whom the Devas reside with their Loks. It is fully divine, devoid of all impurities of Māyā, *apahat pāpmā hysea brahmalokaha* (C. 8-4-1), and is the eternal light, *brahmajyotihi sanātanam.*

Akshar is described as one which is above Prakriti and Purush and is known as chidākāsh, is the abode of Purushottam and is also known as Brahman.[5] This Akshar is to be known or realised for attaining liberation. It is eternal and no one but Purushottam is higher. It is neither Sat nor Asat.[6] It has its limbs spread in all directions – *sarvatah pānipādam tat* and *sarvato akshishiro mukham.* (Gitā, XIII-13)

That Akshar Brahman, inspired by Purushottam sitting within it as antaryāmi, pervades the chit and achit form created by Prakriti. It is jnānam (knowledge), jneyam (deserves to be known) and is accessible only to those who are devoid of ego. Akshar, as such, is the highest eternal entity beyond which there is only Purushottam. It is the goal to be attained for deserving the Bhakti of Purushottam.[7] Akshar and

---

[4] Lord Swāminārāyan, Vachanāmrit, Gadhadā Sec. I-63

[5] Gitā VIII-3, Bhāshyam by Gopālānand Swāmi, p. 363

[6] Ibid., XIII-12, Bhāshyam by Gopālānand Swāmi, p. 541

[7] Gitā, XVIII-54.

Purushottam are two separate entities. Akshar is the sharira and Purushottam is its sharirin.

By the dhyān or meditation of Akshar, one attains Purushottam:

Ye tvaksharam anirdeshyam avyaktam paryupāsate...

Te prāpnuvanti mām eva...

(*Gitā*, XII 3-4)

(Those who adore the imperishable, indefinable, unmanifest... they too come to me...)

As the abode of Purushottam, it is described as unmanifest (avyakta), eternal (sanātan) and is the highest attainment, from which there is no return.[8] In this divine abode, Purushottam resides. It is, therefore, inferred that "after reaching Brahman (Akshar) one can by further development reach Purush (Purushottam) who is higher than Akshar-*Vāsudevaha Sarvam*".[9]

One which is beyond jivas or Kshar Purushs is "Akshar". Akshar beholds the Param Purush (Purushottam) residing in the hearts of all as Antaryāmi.[10] Immutable Akshar wherein dwell the self, the Indriyas, Prānas and Bhuta, is required to be known by the upāsak (seeker). This knowledge makes him omniscient and gains for him all the desired objects. That Akshar is Shubra, is devoid of gunas, sharir, blood, etc., and is required to be known for attaining Paramātmā.[11]

Akshar is related to Purushottam as Drishya-Drashta, sharir-shariri and niyāmya niyāmaka bhāv. "Paramātman pervades, controls and subdues Akshar and ātman."[12] The light emanating separately from jiva, Ishwar, Purush, Akshar

---

[8] Yad gatvā na nivartante tad dhāma paramam mama. - Gitā, XV-6.

[9] Modi, Dr P. M., Akshar - A Forgotten Chapter in the History of Indian Philosophy, Barodā, 1932.

[10] Prashna, V-5-7   [11] Prashna, IV-10-11.

[12] Lord Swāminārāyan, Vachanāmrit, Gadhadā Sec. I-64

and Purushottam apparently looks similar, but a great difference exists in its profundity. However, no one can visualise this difference unless God's grace is bestowed upon him. He can then see clearly that there is a great difference in the light emanating from jiva, Ishwar, Purush and Purushottam and can also see them separately as follows: "This is jiva, this is Ishwara, this is Purush and above all of them is Purushottam."[13] So jiva, Ishwar, Purush and Purushottam are all different entities.

"Akshar has two forms, Nirgun and Sagun. With its Sagun form, it upholds Purushottam and the Nitya Muktas (Shuddha Brahmasristi). Kāla, Māyā, Mahāvishnu; Virāt, Sutrātmā and Avyākrut the three bodies of Ishwars; sthul, sukshma and kāran – the three bodies of jiva, are all being sustained by Akshar with its Sagun Swarup. It is also the nearest devotee of Purushottam as His kinkara, and is constantly in His service. The immutable self of Akshar thus possesses the immeasurable, infinite, and unfathomable sustaining power for upholding the millions of universes. Akshar owes this greatness to Purushottam, as Akshar is controlled by Purushottam as its shariri. If Purushottam desires, He may absorb Akshar by His power (Aishwarya)."[14] As the power of Purushottam is fully assigned to Akshar, Akshar is also known as Purushottam.[15]

Akshar, as we have seen, is absolutely pure and has no relationship with the creative urge. Although pervading jiva, Ishwar and Māyā by its invariable concomitance (*anvayabhāv*), with them Akshar is separate and beyond them all, by its Vyatirek Swarup, which is Sat-Chit-Ānanda.[16] Further, Akshar

---

[13] Lord Swāminārāyan, Vachanāmrit, Loyā 15

[14] Gitā, XVIII-54.

[15] Aksharambaranta dhrute : and Sa cha prasasanāt.
— Brahmasutra, I. 3-9. 10

[16] Lord Swāminārāyan, Vachanāmrit, Gadhadā Sec. 1-7.

being all-pervasive, it is the inspirer of Prakriti, Purush, the Sun, the Moon and all the other demigods, but as a separate entity Akshar sustains no upādhi (vesture) of Purush and Prakriti and upholds only Purushottam as His sharir.[17] Therefore Akshar is described as fully divine and devoid of all impurities – *Apahatapāpmā hyesha brahmalokaha.*

The interpretation of Akshar as Prakriti is anomalous insomuch as Akshar is utterly divine and pure. For reconciling the Prakritibhāv in Akshar, Shrutis have assigned two natures to Akshar–Higher Brahman and Lower Brahman. Through Lower Brahman, described as Pradhān, the creative process has come into being.[18] Pradhān may be called Brahman because of the concomitance of Akshar within it. However, for meditational purposes, for attaining Purushottam, or reaching Brahmalok, the pure and untarnished eternal Akshar, the abode or the sharir of Purushottam, Akshar as an independent entity, entirely separate from Prakriti, is essentially required to be realised and known. "On account of the co-existence of Akshar (anvayabhāv) in Brahmā, Vishnu and Shiva, the forms of Brahmā, Vishnu and Shiva are not to be meditated upon."[19] "Because of the majority of texts (describing Akshar), that (i.e. Akshar) is more important as an object of meditation than Pradhān,"[20] Pradhān, therefore, even as Lower Brahman, is not fit to be meditated upon, as it is not pure Brahman.

Akshar, chidākāsh or Brahman is devoid of evolutionary changes and is sarvadhār, i.e. the support of all. Within this chidākāsh, Prakriti and Purush expand and contract.[21] Thus Prakriti and Purush expand and contract during the process of

---

[17] Ibid., Vachanāmrit, Sārangpur-5.

[18] Akshrarāt sambhavatiha visham - Mundak, I-I-7.

[19] Lord Swāminārāyan, Vedras, Nirmāni Prakaran, p. 177

[20] Modi, Dr P. M., Akshar - A Forgotten Chapter in the History of Indian Philosophy, Barodā, 1932.

[21] Lord Swāminārāyan, Vachanāmrit, Gadhadā Sec. I-46

creation and destruction, whereas Akshar is Kutastha,[22] i.e. static. So the interpretation of Akshar as Prakriti is not proper.

Akshar, when referred to as Prakriti or yoni,[23] is interpreted as kshetragna or the jivaghana shrishti. Since this is imperishable, the jivaghana shrishti is therefore described as Akshar. The individual jiva is absorbed in this jivaghana shrishti–Akshar–and this Akshar is absorbed in Māyā during the period of Pralaya or rest. So this Akshar cannot be taken as *Aksharam brahma paramam*. Akshar is higher than Prakriti and Purush is chidākāsh, is devoid of any trace of Prakriti, and is termed as Brahman, the abode of Purushottam.

This chidākāsh is extremely bright, is eternal and unborn. It is all-pervading. It contains sthul, sukshma and kāran absorbed jivas; millions of universes; Prakriti and Purush - the generators of the millions of universes. Akshar is within them all and still without as the support or sarvadhār. It is not absorbed any time, anywhere.[24]

Katha Upanishad refers to Akshar as the highest–*etadhye vāksharam param* – and prescribes it as the best refuge – *dhyānālam banesu shrestham*. It is only by resorting to Akshar or assuming Aksharbhāv that Param Purush can be meditated upon.[25]

Akshar is therefore intrinsically pure (shuddha Brahman) and is the highest abode of Purushottam. It is to be sought by the jivas, by rejecting their identity with the three bodies, and assuming that Akshar as one's own self or ātmā. This Akshar is beyond Māyā or Prakriti and is sāvayava, i.e. having a

---

[22] Kutastho akshara uchyate. - Gitā, XV - 16

[23] Mama yonir mahadbrahma tasmin garbham dadhāmyaham.

[24] Lord Swāminārāyan, Vachanāmrit, Gadhadā Sec. I-46

[25] Paramapurushadhyāne ālambanam iti jnātvā om ityanenaivāksarena Paramapurusham abhidhyayita itukta prakārena dhyānālambanam jnātvā.
Katha, 1-2-17, Bhāshya by Gopālānand Swāmi, p. 74

divine body, and is the nearest devotee of Purushottam. The jivas who know this Akshar or Brahman and identify themselves with this Brahman, will attain Parā Bhakti, i.e. they will then be accepted by Purushottam as his Kinkars [angelic souls].[26]

---

[26] Brahmabhutaha prasannātmā... madbhaktim labhate parām.

- Gitā, XVIII-54

7 Parabrahman — The Purushottam

Completely engrossed in the narration of the form of Brahman the Akshar, Nilkanth appeared to have been enjoying the bliss of Sat-Chit-Ānand. Muktānand could behold that light of knowledge emanating from his eye. He felt in his heart that Nilkanth was transcending all the conceptions that he had formed about him, and was rising to greater and greater heights. The disciples all around were spellbound. Nilkanth now began the narration of Parabrahman – the Purushottam, to which additional references have been added.

'This is the highest entity transcending even Brahman - the Akshar. Parabrahman is the shariri of Brahman. The desire[1] to know this form of Parabrahman is the chief characteristic of a mumukshu. He is the Ishwar of all Ishwars. He is the giver of the fruits of all karma, the support of all the supporters (*Sarvadhār*), the cause of the creation, sustenance, and destruction of the Jagat, is infinitely great, is the highest goal to be attained by the released souls, is the possessor of all the gunas,[2] leading to the ultimate salvation, and has the characteristics of infiniteness, controllership, sentiency (Chetanatva), etc. He transcends Kshar Purush and is the Uttam Purush called Paramātmā.

He is full of bliss and bliss embodied,[3] is subtler than jiva

---

[1] Athāto Brahmajijñāsā. - Brahmasutra 1-1-1

[2] Jnānādi ananta kalyānagunani.

[3] Ānandamayo abhyāsat. - Brahmasutra. 1-1-13
Ānandamātra karpātramukhodarādi.

and resides in the jiva as its controller.[4] He is Vibhu (all-pervasive) by His antaryāmi swarup. This swarup is the controller and giver of all the fruits of the karmas of jivas and is therefore considered as Sākār.[5] "Residing in His abode Akshardhām, He appears at various places simultaneously by His yogic powers. This simultaneous appearance in fullfledged Sākār form, is said to be the vibhutvam or His pervasiveness. But in no case does His pervasiveness imply the abstract form of space."[6] He is the goal for meditational worship for all, including Akshar Brahman. The other muktas, lshwars, etc. are not suitable to be worshipped or meditated upon independently.[7]

He is Param to all because He is the highest form for meditational worship. There is no higher entity than Him since nothing transcends Parabrahman. When Gārgi questioned Yāgnavalkya, "Where is the location of Prajāpati Lok?", Yāgnavalkya replied, "It is wrapped in the Brahmalok." And when she further questioned, "Where is Brahmalok?", then Yagnavalkya told her in an uncontrolled mood, "Don't ask me further questions. All Loks are wrapped in Akshar Brahman. In Akshar Brahman dwells Parabrahman which is pervaded by Him." Even though Yāgnavalkya knew this, he prevented Gārgi from further questioning since Parabrahman is not the subject of speech nor is He approachable by mind.[8] He is the object of experience only, by true knowledge. Brihadāranyaka Upanishad establishes that Parabrahman is beyond Akshar and is the highest entity, beyond which there is nothing else. He is Nārāyan, Parameshwar, Parabrahman and Purushottam,

---

4 Antaha pravistaha sāstā janānām sarvātmā brahma. - Brāhmi Smriti.

- Taittiriya Āranyaka, 3-II-2.

5 Lord Swāminārāyan, Vachanāmrit, Gadhadā Sec. 1-45

6 Ibid., II-64

7 Krishnavallabhāchārya, Shree Swāminārāyan Vedānta Sāra, p. 27

8 Yato vācho nivartante apprāpya manasā saha   - Taittiriya, 9.

is beyond Akshar and as such the Aishwarya abounds in Him in infinity.

He dwells as the witness in the jiva who is attached to the body and who enjoys the fruits of the samsār (the cycle of births and deaths). He is unattached and witnesses the karmas of jivas. "He is seated as Sākshi in the baddha jivas as well as in Mukta (released) jivas, and still He is aloof from that attachment of jivas and the non-attachment of the muktas. He is also the Sākshi of the Ishwars and also of Akshar and is still devoid of the upādhi attached to Ishwars. He is beyond them, viz. jiva, Ishwar and Akshar."[9]

In his divine abode Akshardhām, God and His blessed souls have a divine body (aprakrit vigraha). They are satyaswarup and are divinely lighted. They have a divine shape like a human being and are sat-chit-ānand swarup. He is served there by these blessed souls differently in different ways. That Parā swarup of Purushottam, having absolute mercy on the jivas for their ultimate redemption, has manifested on earth today, and is visible before you. He is the form of worship for you all and is receiving with grace all you offer. This visible form of Parā Swarup of Purushottam and the one which resides in Akshardhām, are one (swarupaikya). This Parā Swarup is, therefore, the controller of all jivas, Ishwars and all including Akshar, and is the Ishwar of all Ishwars, and the cause of all the causes, and is supreme, being the cause of all avatārs.[10] He is the form to be worshipped with single-minded devotion (ekantik bhāv). His previous avatārs also deserve to be prayed to and worshipped.[11]

He is the Ādi Nārāyan and is the material as well as the

---

[9] Lord Swāminārāyan, Vachanāmrit, Sārangpur-5.

[10] Sometimes the highest mode (para) is said to be Nārāyana or Brahman living in Vaikuntha, where God is said to exist in a body of pure Sattva. God in his infinite fullness transcends his own manifestations. Indian Philosophy, Part II-Theism of Rāmānuja, Dr Radhakrishnan, p. 689.

[11] Lord Swāminārāyan, Vachanāmrit, Gadhadā Sec. III-38

efficient cause of the Jagat. He transcends Akshar and is therefore the highest, *Uttam*. The Smritis describe Him as having a divine body, and not a body evolved out of Prakriti.[12] He is beyond Māyā and Mula Purush.[13] and is the Maheshwar of all Ishwars ranging from Virāt to Mul Purush.[14]

He is described as Nārāyan, Vāsudev, Vishnu, Parabrahman, Parameshwar, Param Purush or Bhagwān. One who realises Him and knows Him, is released. Without this realisation or knowledge of his descent in anthropomorphic form on earth in all His greatness, there is no other way of transgressing death.[15]

As Purushottam, He is unparalleled.[16] During the time of creation He becomes as many,[17] i.e. He enters by His antaryāmi swarup into the various yonis (jivas, lshwars, etc.) as their material and efficient cause, and according to the nature of the yonis, inspires them for the fulfilment and expansion of the creative urge. When the whole cosmos was in the state of rest (pralaya), He awakened it by His drishti and entered into it.[18] By *ekoham* it is not implied that excepting Him alone everything was void, but that it was in the state of rest (pralaya) from which He awakens jivas for their release.

Since He initiated this creative urge through Purush – one of the released souls (Nitya Mukta) of Akshardhām – the progeny of Purush knew only Purush from whom they were evolved. This Purush is the controller of Prakriti, and is still different in nature from Prakriti, is indivisible (akhand),

---

[12] Na tasya prākruta murtihi. Varāha, A. 75-44.

[13] Ādityavarnam tamasaha parastāt. – Taittiriya, 3-13

[14] Tam ishvaranām paramam maheshvaram - Shvetashvatar, 6-7

[15] Rute jnānān na muktihi. Tam eva viditvā ati mrutyum eti nānyaha panthāhā vidayte anyanāya.

[16] Ekamevādvitāyam brahma - Chhāndogya, VI-2-1

[17] Eko aham bahu syama prajāyeya. - Chhāndogya, VI-2-3

[18] Tad shrustvā tad-anuprāvishte. - Taittiriya, 6.

eternal (anādi – because of being Nitya Mukta), infinite (anant), sat (self-illuminated), omniscient (sarvagna) and possessing a divine body (divya vigraha), is the cause of evolution and is kshetragna.[19] Scriptures have therefore described this Purush as Purushottam.[20] Akshar and Purushottam had remained unmanifested so far, and since the knowledge and contact of Purush was perceptible, Purush only was acclaimed as Purushottam. The ultimate Purushottam in His abode Akshardhām was beyond knowledge, beyond approach, and beyond realisation. Therefore Purush in the form of Purushottam had become the goal for meditational worship, knowledge, etc. The venue above was unknown. This Parā Swarup of Purushottam was therefore not so far cognised for upāsanā, for meditational worship or for final realisation, as He had so far never manifested (in His fully-fledged form) on earth.

A question would therefore arise as to what is the difference between Purush – the Scriptural Purushottam – and the Parā Swarup of Purushottam? The difference certainly exists. "Just as there is a difference between jiva and Ishwar and between Ishwar (Mahāvishnu) and Purush, similarly there is a great difference between Purush and Purushottam (Vāsudev Bhagwān). Purushottam Vāsudev is the Lord (Swāmi) of all. Purushs, in the form of Akshar Muktas, are many and they all worship the lotus feet of Purushottam Vāsudev."[21]

With the status of Purush so described, a doubt would arise as to the Sākshi Swarup residing in jivas and Ishwars, whether the Sākshi is Purush, Akshar or Purushottam? However, Purushottam is the ultimate Sākshi, even though Purush may

---

[19] Lord Swāminārāyan, Vachanāmrit, Gadhadā Sec. 1-12

[20] Ete parabrahmādyanvitabhāvena tat tad rupatyā varnyante.
   -Shri Krishnavallabhāchārya, Shikshāpatri Kirnāvali Bhāshya, p. 110

[21] Lord Swāminārāyan, Vachanāmrit, Gadhadā Sec. II-31

have been described as the form of Purushottam in the spiritual texts.[22]

Purush – the Akshar Mukta – is described as Purushottam[23] by all scriptures because of the concomitance of Purushottam within it. But for ultimate release, the knowledge and meditational worship or realisation of the Parā Swarup of Purushottm is entirely indispensable. That Purushottam is independent, Isha of all and should be known in His true form.[24]

This therefore is the description of Parabrahman – the Purushottam. The description in Shrimad Bhāgawat as "Jyotiswarup, jñanaswarup, Tattva, Sākshi, Niranjan, Kshetragna, Sarvakāran, Parabrahman, Purushottam, Vāsudev, Vishnu, Nārāyan, Nirgun," etc., refers to this Parā Swarup of Vāsudev only and to none else."[25]

So saying, Nilkanth paused for a while then said, with a significant smile on his face, 'Muktānand! The light emanating from that Parā Swarup is here before us. We all have to realise Him.' Muktānand and the sādhus of the āshram could not quite follow this allegorical aphorism.

However, his eloquence, learning, etc., had a very great impact on Muktānand and the other inmates of the āshram.

Muktānand prayed Nilkanth to stay there until Rāmānand returned, and Nilkanth accepted the request with grace.

---

[22] Ibid., Loyā, 15

[23] Purusham evedam mahāntam. - Purusha Sukta

[24] Jneyah svatantra Isho asau sarvakarmaphalapradaha.—Shikshāpatri, 107.

[25] Lord Swāminārayan, Vachanāmrit, Gadhadā Sec. II-39.

8 Nilakanth - Head of the Fellowship

Even though Nilkanth agreed to stay, his deep detachment, his renunciation, his sense of duty, and his extreme devotion were all so profound that he changed the atmosphere of the āshram to a mode of living more suitable for celibate sādhus.

He saw that there was a hole in the common wall of the āshram from which the sādhus used to take fire from the women folk of the neighbouring house. He believed that the sādhus who have to observe eightfold celibacy should avoid all contact with women in every respect.[1] He therefore filled up the hole. Further, he observed that women were freely partaking in the discourses of Muktānand Swāmi held every night, and were mixing with sādhus. This practice also transgressed the strict rules for observance of celibacy. He therefore arranged separate meetings for males and females.

These innovations and the insistence on rigorous observance of the sādhu dharma by Nilkanth led Muktānand to believe that there was a composition of strong fibre behind this apparent weakling. He was glad, since he believed that the observance of eightfold celibacy by sādhus was absolutely essential for attaining Brāhmic consciousness.[2] Muktānand

---

[1] Samkalpo nischayash chāpi na kartavyas tadaptaye
Sparshas tu kartavyo daravyā api yoshitaha

- Dharmāmruta, 230

[2] Yad ichachhto brahmacharyam charanti
Tat te padam sangrahena pravakshye – Gitā, VIII - 11

very much wished that Nilkanth should stay here at least until Rāmānand returned, and therefore allowed free play to Nilkanth to introduce reforms for the good of the āshramites.

Nilkanth was now known as Sarjudās since he came from the lands of the Saryu river. He engaged himself in service of the inmates of this āshram. He went out for bhikshā (begging food), he cooked for them, he collected dung for fuel, he washed their loin-cloths. In short, he did everything here to promote the ideal of service. During his leisure hours he also taught them yoga. Muktānand was amazed as he saw this emaciated sādhu moving like a whirlwind.

The immense flow of compassion, love, vairāgya, bhakti, etc., which surged out from the person of this young sādhu, drew Muktānand closer to him. At times when Nilkanth talked, the āshramites felt that no realms were unknown to him and no heights had remained beyond his reach. By his amazing yogic powers he could see the restless minds of these sādhus when they were in meditation. The revelation of this power before the sādhus and the proper guidance given by Nilkanth to enable them to attain perfection in dhyān, led Muktānand to believe that Nilkanth's powers and spiritual status were beyond any measure.

When Nilkanth expressed his desire to go to Bhuj for Rāmānand's darshan, Muktānand dissuaded him as he did not want him to leave the āshram. He therefore wrote a letter to Swāmi Rāmānand in Bhuj wherein he tried to describe Nilkanth thus:

'A young yogi, Nilkanth by name, from Koshaldesh has come here. His body is reduced to bones and skin. Even though of a dark complexion, his charm has attracted us. We have all paled into insignificance before his immeasurable virtues. If our minds are diverted to other objects whilst in meditation, he catches them and tells us all about it. We therefore sometimes feel that perhaps you have come here incognito to test our devotion. Even though wedded to the great yogic siddhis, he is deeply detached, and he has still been serving us all with great devotion. He has only one desire – to have your darshan. May it therefore please you to guide us whether we should send him to you or will you be coming here soon.'

He then requested Nilkanth to write to Rāmānand. Nilkanth wrote, expressing his deep desire to have his darshan.

Both these letters were sent to Rāmānand in Bhuj through Shree Mayārām Bhatt, one of the disciples of Shree Rāmānand. Mayārām returned after some time with Rāmānand's reply, which informed them that he would soon be coming to Saurāshtra and would then call upon them for darshan. Nilkanth therefore decided to stay at the āshram until Rāmānand arrived in the district.

After some time Rāmānand came to Piplānā, a village near Mãngrol port, and sent Kurji Dave to Lojpur with a message that Muktānand and all the āshramites should come to Piplānā with Nilkanth. They were all very much delighted at the news, and each of them gave some present to Kurji Dave for bringing such auspicious tidings. Nilkanth was perplexed, as he had nothing to give him. But after some time he said, 'Kurji! I have nothing now to give you, but later on I shall give you my Akshardhãm – the highest abode.' The significant words of Nilkanth were not noticed by anyone else, and since Kurji did not receive any tangible gift, he looked at Nilkanth in a bewildered manner. Nilkanth simply smiled at him.

At early dawn they all started for Piplānā. Nilkanth was too weak to keep pace with the sādhus, who were moving fast for their guru's darshan. He fell down two or three times. Then Muktānand said to him, 'How shall we get there in time if you show this physical weakness? I know that you can move like the wind with your yogic powers.' Nilkanth then stood up, tightened his girdles, and with the speed of the arrow released from Rama's bow, he shot ahead. The river Ojasvati was in full spate. The sādhus stopped but to their amazement they saw Nilkanth walking over the water. Afterwards they crossed the river and then they all went to Narsinh Mehtā's house, where Rāmānand was waiting for them.

It was not to be a meeting, but a happy union of souls who longed to become as one. They knew only one thing, that they were going to have their guru's darshan. Their mind and heart were centred on Rāmānand. Rāmānand equally was awaiting them anxiously. When they arrived they rejoiced at the darshan of the guru. Muktānand introduced Nilkanth to Rāmānand.

Nilkanth prostrated before Rāmānand. Rāmānand immediately got up and embraced Nilkanth. Muktānand stood at a distance and watched. He was bewildered and mentally divided as he saw Nilkanth ascending to greater spiritual heights. He knew the height of glory attained by his guru Rāmānand who realising Nilkanth in true form, adopted a passive submission before this young sādhu. Muktānand's vision was sharp. He could realise the greatness of Nilkanth, but his allegiance to his guru was dominant. The subconscious awareness of the divinity of Nilkanth was submerged. Devotion to his guru came first.

On Rāmānand's enquiry, Nilkanth told him the names of his father and mother, his native place, caste, etc. Rāmānand recalled that Nilkanth's father and mother were his disciples and they had met him at Vrindāvan. He was pleased to see this relationship renewed with Nilkanth. However, with his great yogic powers, he could perceive that Nilkanth was not merely the son of Dharmadev and Bhaktidevi. He was much more than that. But he did not desire to disclose this fact now. He wanted his disciples to discover this through the work that Nilkanth was destined to perform. Rāmānand therefore only hinted to his disciples, saying, 'I was merely a conch-blower. But the actual player (Natrāj) is this Nilkanth.'

At this, Lālji, one of the disciples of Rāmānand, impatiently asked Rāmānand, 'Is Nilkanth like Muktānand or is he like you?'

Then Rāmānand replied enigmatically, 'He is beyond description.' Lālji looked blank, as to him there was nothing beyond Rāmānand. Thereafter the ceremonies of the first meeting were completed.

Rāmānand knew that the personality he was awaiting had emerged to take up the newly spun thread and weave it into a fine muslin. He therefore accepted Nilkanth as his disciple. Later on he gave him Vaishnavi dikshā (initiation) and baptised him as Swāmi Sahajānand.

Thereafter Rāmānand asked all his disciples to assemble at Jetpur. Here he told them, that he would install Sahajānand in his place and then retire. Many of the disciples did not like this decision as it meant superseding the right of Muktānand, who was the foremost disciple of Rāmānand. Besides, Sahajānand was only a boy of twenty. How could he bear the brunt of so high a position, which deserved to be inherited only by Muktānand? However, Rāmānand's decision was irrevocable. He was repudiating the right of Muktānand as some believed, but for the performance of a greater task – the establishment and the spread of Bhāgawat Dharma – Sahajānand was the only possible means. Muktānand was not at all perturbed. He had already partly realised the greatness of Sahajānand and dimly sensed the role that he had to play. Besides, he believed in implicitly obeying the Guru. He was therefore anxious that Ramanand's orders should be implemented in full.

Sahajānand Swāmi was installed by Rāmānand as Āchārya (preceptor). Wide powers were vested in Him so that He might be able to conduct the fellowship, initiate new saints, issue injunctions, preach without restrictions (i.e. talk and preach to women), wear valuable clothes and ornaments, ride on horses or travel by chariot, cart or other vehicles. True Bhāgawat Dharma or natural theology was to be inculcated in the minds of people who were indulging in theological sophistry.

Accustomed to the ascetic life, Swāmi Sahajānand was very reluctant to accept this position which offered many attractions. But Rāmānand knew that Swāmi Sahajānand would never be drawn to any attachment. His personality, His demeanour, and His preaching would, on the contrary, eradicate the desire of others for worldly attachment and render them pure. Rāmānand insisted that Sahajānand should accept this position for the good of the many, and Sahajānand submitted.

Sahajānand's heart was full of piety, compassion and love to bear the sufferings of other people, even though He had Himself undergone severe privations during His travels, and had denied Himself all comforts. So He requested Rāmānand to protect the members of the fellowship now under His care, from any miseries, or if such be their lot, to inflict them many times over upon Him instead; but in no case allow others to suffer. Further, if the members of the fellowship under His care were destined to suffer from want of food and clothing, that such lot should fall upon Him rather than that they face such scarcity.

Rāmānand felt that Sahajānand had asked for these two boons with a far-sighted vision. He willingly said, 'May your desire be fulfilled.' Swāmi Sahajānand believed that an empty stomach would never relish the problems of theology. So the necessities of life should be met first and then only could the spiritual needs be catered for. Rāmānand believed that Swāmi Sahajānand was capable enough of removing these miseries, but the traditional relationship between the preceptor and the disciple demanded this procedural behaviour and Sahajānand respected this law accordingly.

Thereafter the whole fellowship moved to Faneni, a centre for spiritual learning established by Rāmānand. Rāmānand now desired to obscure himself in order to permit a wider latitude to Sahajānand, so he withdrew to the oblivion of the jungle at Faneni.

9 Achievements

Young Sahajānand realised that Saurāshtra was politically disintegrating as a result of the small feudal chiefs fighting amongst themselves. Besides, the kāthi looters also made life unsteady and unsettled. All customs, conventions and traditions were discarded, all scruples neglected, and proper social life had come to an end. The mood of the people was to grab anything that they came across, since food and clothing had become scarce. In short, the social and political atmosphere was not congenial for spiritual preaching.

To add to this grave problem, some of the disciples of Rāmānand now rose against this young spiritual master. Raghunāthdās, Meghjeet, Harbāi, Vālbāi, and many others refused to recognise His authority. But Sahajānand, even though young, had the requisite tenacity, and dealt with all of them, requesting them either to accept His authority or to leave. Ultimately some of them surrendered and some of them left the fellowship. Raghunāthadās went to Ahmedābād. Meghjeet surrendered, and Harbāi and Vālbāi, being too proud of their position in the fellowship of Rāmānand and feeling insulated by the separation of male and female meetings, also left. Sahajānand wanted to weed out such unworthy elements and purify the whole fellowship in order to avoid impediments to His great mission. Within a short time the authority of Shree Sahajānand was realised and firmly established.

In order to ameliorate the social conditions of the people, He began to distribute free food and establish centres. Service of humanity, particularly the poor and the needy, was the first principle that He inculcated in the minds of the sādhus around Him. He planned that these sādhus should be engaged in such services as would satisfy the needs of the people for food and water. The sādhus went out for bhikshā, cooked food and distributed it to the needy and the poor. They dug wells and ponds, and made water available where it was scarce owing to the continuous failure of the monsoon. Sahajānand believed that humanity should be humanely treated and its problems should be thoroughly solved. The charm which was part of His personality, the heart full of love, the eyes flowing with compassion, the penetrating speech and the various other virtues, gave a suprahuman aura to His personality. As a result, people began to throng around Him.

The growth of superstition through illiteracy, belief in polytheism, dread of petty gods and goddesses, engendered despair and discontent in the lives of the people. It appeared as if intellect, wisdom, and scruples were all at a low ebb. This situation was soon to be changed, with all the force of an avalanche.

Young Sahajānand with a small physique had unimaginable potential powers within Him. He was not daunted by the gravity of any problem. He never wanted to wield the great yogic powers He possessed inasmuch as He believed that the inherent knowledge in people would best work to ameliorate their lives. He explained to them that there is only one God, who is the Almighty, and who can do and undo all things. As such there was no cause to harbour any fear of petty gods who were not all-powerful. This Almighty God should be propitiated by good deeds. He is the symbol of love, truth, compassion, etc. and should therefore be approached with love only and not with fear. Petty gods and goddesses have no authority to give the fruits of good or bad deeds. So they should be entirely ignored. Indulgence in superstitions is ignorance, and should be shed entirely. Religion does not only mean rituals or ceremonies, but love towards God and the cultivation of a pious, truthful and scrupulous life. Pseudo-religionists should be shunned. Customs should be observed if they uplift social and moral life; otherwise they should be boldly discarded.

The impact of these sermons was very great on the masses. Shree Sahajānand Swāmi started a socio-religious movement on a mass scale. He stressed that everyday living should be co-ordinated with religious precepts which would enhance the values of life as well as the status of society. But He insisted that the preachers themselves should implement religion in their lives which really called for a harmonious synchronisation of practice and precept. The assimilation of religion into life is entirely indispensable. He taught that life becomes worth living only if religious virtues are developed; otherwise preaching is mere breathing like a pair of bellows.

Shree Sahajānand sent His sādhu disciples in groups to various villages, instructing them only to preach but not to demand anything from the villagers. They should live a life of mendicancy and should fast if nothing was made available to them voluntarily. No malice or ill-feelings should be harboured towards anybody, even if they do not listen to preaching or make offerings to the sādhus. They should leave any place where they entertained or eulogised. Love – sheer love – as much towards people as towards God, should be the guiding principle for a true sādhu or a Paramhansa.

The injunctions issued by Shree Sahajānand Swāmi at various times were difficult to observe unless one discarded attachment to physical comforts. The strictures and austerities imposed by Him were rigorous and firm. But these sādhus enjoyed observing these injunctions, as they could behold in their Master something which surpassed a great yogi or a great sādhu. As they served Him they loved Him, and as they loved

Him their hearts were purified, and they could behold a great divinity emerging from His person. They were amply satisfied as now they felt that Ramanand's selection had been fully justified. These sādhus knew the zeal of their Master and mustered courage to follow His word even if it should cost their lives. They knew they were serving a noble cause.

This spiritual band of sādhus, daily being reinforced by valuable additions, worked day and night. Observance of Brahmacharya (celibacy) by avoiding the eightfold contact of women in all respects, and discarding wealth (even the touch of coins) were the main morals observed apart from many other virtues developed by these sādhus. Wherever they went, they were respected and heard patiently.

This stimulated fury amongst the dishonest sādhus who had so far deluded the masses, and had not disclosed before them the attributes that a true sādhu should possess. They had so far retained a wider latitude to behave in their own way. But now the mode of living of the sādhus of Sahajānand, their character, their virtues, the development in them of inherent saintliness, all so apparent to the people, exposed other sādhus as impostors. They then feared that their cult which preached free indulgence in wine and women, would be annihilated. They therefore took up arms against the sādhus of Sahajānand to preserve their own power. Persecutions began.

First they attacked the almshouses established by Shree Sahajānand Swāmi. They looted the grain and beat the sādhus. Since this activity of giving free food to the poor and needy enhanced the popularity of Sahajānand, they wanted to destroy it. They attacked the sādhus, cut off their sacred threads, their double-stringed tulsi necklaces, and the hair plumes over their heads; they mutilated their images of worship and snatched away their belongings. They brought debauched women and pushed them before the sādhus in order to pollute their celibacy. They threw meat or onions into their food and made it uneatable. But these sādhus did not lose courage. They thought that their Master Sahajānand was testing their strength. They proved invincible.

However, the nomadic bāwās tried hard either to uproot them or to convert them to their own debased creed. But these sādhus had great forbearance and did not harbour any malice towards them. On the contrary, they believed that their Master had contrived such an acid test. For days together they had to live upon either scant food, on vegetable leaves, or even on dried earth from ponds, or ultimately to fast. Their Master had often narrated various stories from the *Upanishads* which had amply revealed the need for implicit obedience by disciples to the orders of the teacher or Guru. The quest of the disciple for inner realisation should be so intense that he can never be distracted by hardships of the worst order.

He once told them the story of a teacher who was living upon a pound of rice daily. One day a disciple came and requested the teacher to accept him, whereupon the teacher said, 'I have nothing to offer you, as I live only on a pound of rice.' The disciple immediately said, 'Master! I shall be satisfied with the remnants of rice grains which may have stuck to the vessel after you are fully served.' The teacher was thereupon pleased and accepted him. After some time a second disciple came and requested the teacher to accept him and the teacher told him of the shortage of food. The disciple then willingly said, 'Sir, the water with which you wash the rice before cooking, will be enough for me for my sustenance.' The teacher gladly accepted him. After some time, a third disciple came, and on being informed of the difficulty of food, offered, 'Sir, the water with which you wash the vessel of cooked rice will be sufficient for me.' He too was accepted. Then ultimately a fourth disciple came. He was prepared to live on the water with which the teacher's dish was washed. All these four disciples had an inner quest and zeal for attaining knowledge and even at the cost of all comforts they were anxious to be accepted by the teacher who taught Brahma Vidyhā. The Master then said, 'Here I am to transfuse that same God consciousness within you provided that you have such an indomitable faith in My work.' These sādhus had that faith, that craving, and deep attachment and love for the Master, and as such they willingly underwent all hardships. The sonorous words of their Master rang continuously in their ears and kept awakening their consciousness to continue the mission entrusted to them.

Sahajānand's influence on these sādhus and on the masses was gradually increasing. As their love towards Him deepened, their intuitive knowledge of Ultimate Reality widened, their consciousness developed, and they would realise that the Ultimate Reality which is God was manifested in the person of this young Sahajānand. Knowledge of this Reality is not a sense-perception or a mind-perception but is an experience of the self - Ātmasattā or Ātmānubhav – through the mind and sense-organs. Those who were enlightened with this knowledge of the self of Sahajānand were delighted, and talked about this to the people. Some wise people with confidence in the truthfulness of these sādhus believed them and became followers. Others laughed at their credulity and resisted the movement. However, their influence began to spread and the fellowship expanded.

As the veneration of people towards Sahajānand grew more intense, their hearts were filled with devotion for Him. Constant thinking of or meditating upon His form, either physically or mentally, led to their Prānas, manas and indriyas (subtle vitality, mind, and senses) being merged in Him. People lost their physical consciousness, and enjoyed the bliss of the Brāhmic consciousness – samādhi – in which they saw the divine form of Swāmi Sahajānand in Brahmadhām. This samādhi, which had no trace of the usual eightfold yoga but was initiated only by the krupā (grace) of Shree Sahajānand Swāmi, became the order of the day. Swāmi Sahajānand led an infinite number of jivas into this samādhi by drawing their Prānavrutti (modes of vitality) into the Brahmaswarupātmā. Consequently the influence of the divine powers of Shree Sahajānand began to be experienced by many who chanted the 'Swāminārāyan' Mantra.

The great impact of this samādhi was widely felt on the masses throughout India. Swāmi Sahajānand now came to be known as jivanmukta. The chanting of the very name of jivanmukta by known or unknown individuals filled people with a bliss never before experienced. Because of this, sādhus and sannyāsins from all over India, wanted to have the darshan of this jivanmukta by going to Dwārkā. Their first meeting with Him impelled many of them by an overwhelming inner force to join this jivanmukta Panth (group). Thus a band of spiritual workers gave further impetus to this movement.

The news of this samādhi reached Muktānand Swāmi who was travelling in Kutch. He was greatly amazed, as he believed that without the perfection of the usual Sadhanas – Yam, Niyam, Āsan, Pratyāhār, Dhyān, Dhāranā (moral injunctions and prohibitions, withdrawal of senses, concentration, meditation) – the attainment of the state of samādhi was inconceivable. He therefore thought at first that Sahajānand's indulgence in such feats amounted to displaying cheap miracles. The greatness of his own position as the foremost disciple of Shree Rāmānand Swāmi asserted itself in him, and forgetting the knowledge which he had of Nilkanth's all-transcending condition, he immediately hastened to Meghpur to meet Sahajānand. He then rebuked him, saying, 'Please don't be an impostor in Satsang, as the samādhi state, which is difficult to be attained even by great yogis, is not so easily attainable to ordinary people.' Sahajānand Swāmi simply smiled and said, 'All these sādhus and satsangis gather here and worship Rāmānand. In doing so, some get the samādhi.' But Muktānand still did not believe this.

Santdās, one of the disciples of Rāmānand Swāmi, who was sitting nearby was told to sit in meditation. Immediately his Prānas (vital currents) were drawn into his heart and he saw an immense light in which Sahajānand was seated on a high dais and Rāmānand was standing before Him with folded hands. Innumerable Nitya Muktas were sitting around. During this state of samādhi, Sahajānand asked Muktānand to examine the pulse of Santdās and to lift his head. Muktānand felt the pulse which he realised had stopped beating. He then tried to lift the head and could not do so, as it had become very heavy. Muktānand realised that these were unusual signs. Then he was asked to awaken Santadās, which he could not do. Then Sahajānand, with a slight touch awakened Santdās and told him to tell Muktānand what he had experienced. Santdās told him everything that he had seen in samādhi. However, Muktānand was still not convinced. His own disciples Mādhavdās and Jethābhāi expostulated with Muktānand in order to convince him, but he was unmoved. With a confused mind and in a melancholy mood he went to Kālwāni with Sahajānand and other disciples.

Here the people had been given the unique experience of samādhi by Sahajānand previously and so they all thronged to meet Him again. They were extremely joyful as they felt that they would now have darshan in samādhi of their Upāsya deities. Sahajānand fulfilled their wishes and all of them were sent into samādhi. They had darshan of Rāma, Krishna , Shiva, Vishnu, Dattātreya, Ganapati and various gods and goddesses according to their mode of upāsanā or worship. The Jains had darshan of Tirthānkaras and Māhāvira, and the Muslims of their paigambers. All these devotees lay motionless, enjoying the darshan of their deities, and when Sahajānand desired, they all awoke. Then He said, 'Even if millions of people say that this state of samādhi, which is attained by sheer grace, is spurious, the truth will be revealed ultimately.' Muktānand was then completely humbled. He recalled how he had seen the divine personality in the young Sahajānand when he was with Him as Nilkanth in Loj. He recollected the words of Rāmānand to Lālji in Piplānā in an open assembly, that Nilkanth's greatness was beyond description. He bowed down humbly to Sahajānand and said, 'Oh Lord! I believe you are God incarnate.'

Sahajānand smiled at the realisation which Muktānand had achieved and said, 'The state of samādhi is attained by grace only and was realised by the Gopas by the grace of Krishna when they were shown the Golok Dhām. Since you have ascertained and known the truth, I bestow that grace upon you. People whom you desire to do so will go in samādhi.' Muktānand was delighted at this grace bestowed upon him, and felt greatly fulfilled.

Samādhi became a common word in those days, inasmuch as the chanting of the name of Sahajānand, hearing His voice, having His darshan or mere touch carried people into this state, in which they were seeing what they desired and enjoying the innermost bliss. The influence of Sahajānand so much elevated the life of the commonest, the most downtrodden and neglected persons, that even the priests of the highest order were amazed at the great achievements that this Godlike young sādhu attained during such a very short span of time.

Sahajānand's contentions were correct. He claimed that a society submerged in illiteracy, rotting in hunger, indulging in false beliefs and superstitions could not be uplifted unless one assimilated with the people, loved them, taught them by one's own character and mode of living, and educated them into helping themselves to eradicate the false beliefs, customs, conventions, and polytheistic worship. He alone could successfully carry out all these reforms and improve the lot of the kāthis, the looters, the plunderers, and the dacoits. He did not rest there. He taught them philosophy and religion, and

He made them live a life of utmost devotion which impressed many great men. Through these great achievements, His influence on the Christian leaders of those days was so great that Henry G. Briggs, in his *Cities of Gurjarashtra*, Bombay, 1849, wrote, 'A natural aptitude for learning soon led this young Sahajānand to form an intimate acquaintance with the shastras, while the morality which imbibed his breast prompted him to regard with disgust the anomalous character of the priesthood whose lives were at variance with the precepts they inculcated.' The famous Bishop Heber described the system of Swāmi Sahajānand as 'a strange mixture of theism and Hinduism and of a sound and discreet morality.' Even though Swāminārāyan was a contemporary of Rājā Rāma Mohan Rai, Bishop Heber said, 'While Rājā Rāma Mohan Rai's name is about being forgotten, Sahajānand's will wax brighter by that waning influence.'

Modern thinkers like Dr. K. M. Munshi refer to Sahajānand as a great conciliator between the conflicts of casteism and Dharma.

He removed irregularities from society and propagated the true precepts of knowledge and morality; He stopped adultery and suffering, which were both rampant in those days. Through His efforts, the demoralised classes of Gujarāt were uplifted. Being a brāhmin, a versatile Pandit, a staunch Vaishnava and an ideal sannyāsin, this sādhu-cum-reformer added a great enlightenment to the culture of Gujarāt by His life and living. A representative of a lost religious era was reappearing on the threshold of the nineteenth century.[1]

---

[1] Munshi, Dr K. M., Gujarātni Asmitā, Mumbai, 1939

10 Paramhansas

At an assembly of five hundred of His saints at Kālwāni Shree Sahajānand heard their stories of the sufferings inflicted upon them by ignorant and dishonest nomads. He was grieved at the great miseries inflicted upon His saints, but He was, however, very satisfied by the great virtue of forgiveness cultivated by these sādhus, as it added to the loftiness of their saintly character. But to test them still further, He suggested, 'Oh! great saints. You have suffered enough. Even though the virtue of forgiveness is so great and retaliation is not the dharma of sādhus, a spirit of retaliation may be displayed to prevent further harassment.'

The saints, realising the test to which they were being put, at once replied, 'Oh Lord! Please do not say that. We are Your sādhus and to hail Your name we shall still undergo any sufferings but will never think of retaliating.'

The Lord was very gratified and felt that the attributes of saintliness in Janak, Jadbharat and Kadraj, were being manifested by these sādhus. He said to them, 'May you attain still greater heights of saintliness. Your forbearance will destroy the evil forces. Your virtues are your weapons which will in the end eradicate the force of these demons.' So saying, He again addressed them, 'Oh, upholders of Dharma! You may now discard the sacred thread, the plume of hair on the head, the double stringed tulsimālā (Kanthi or necklace), and the worship of images, and move freely with an introverted meditational worship. The damage to these outward signs by the asuras (demons) cannot then disturb you in your worship.

I bestow upon you the Paramhansa Dikshā[1] and release you from all bondage of performing rituals and ceremonies'. This order of their Master elevated them to the highest status of a sannyāsin. However, their belief in tradition made them hesitate in discarding all outward signs. This being so, it was no mean achievement of the young Sahajānand to eventually prevail upon these sādhus, great stalwarts in their own spheres to discard all outward signs and accept this Paramhansa Dikshā.

Shree Sahajānand Swāmi believed that these Paramhansas, who have to mould the life of the people and to elevate them morally and culturally, and bring about a renaissance in the field of philosophy and religion, should be true philosophers and religionists themselves.[2] He therefore asserted the strict observance of five Vrats (the Panch Vrats), viz. freedom from egoism, passions, covetousness, taste and affection. A Paramhansa should not neglect any of these five Vrats and the failure to observe any of these would deprive him of attaining the highest mukti – ātyantik moksha.

According to Shree Sahajānand Swāmi observance of these Panch Vrats, undergoing strictures, suffering, bearing insults, are not the only component virtues of a true sādhu. When He told this assembly of sādhus that He was going to impose more strictures upon them, they readily said, 'Oh Lord! There

---

[1] Amongst the four types of Sannyasins, viz. Kutichak, Bahudak, Hansa, and Paramhansa – the last is the highest amongst all the four. One who can distinguish between Sat and Asat, and who knows and realises Ātmā and Paramātmā as two separate entities, is Hansa. The culmination of this knowledge and realisation in One – is a Paramhansa. He is above all rituals and ceremonies as he is fully engrossed in the self, is above all dualities and is equipoised and attached only to God. The vidhi and nishedh (do's and don't's) prescribed by the scriptures do not apply to a Paramhansa as he has no actions to be performed.

[2] A true philosopher accepts the truths of religious faith, experiments with them and experiences them. The differential of philosophy is the venture of the mumukshu to know reality, and that of religion is the realisation of reality as Brahman. - Srinivasachari, P. N., The Philosophy of Vishishtādvaita, p. 18, Adyar, 1943

is nothing that You desire that we cannot observe. If You desire we will not allow our eyes to blink, we will not take food, we will discard even the protecting cloths, will dwell in icy cold places, will stop drinking water, will observe utter silence or will sit in any posture disregarding any physical pain that it may entail. We hold that courage and believe that nothing is unattainable which is desired by You.'

Extremely pleased at the pragmatic wisdom of these Paramhansas in desiring to gain His grace, Sahajānand Swāmi knew that it was not physical suffering only which would raise them to the status of Brāhmic consciousness. He wanted to transfigure them by awakening that inner consciousness which belongs to Ātman, and so He told them 'Oh Paramhansas! I know that you are capable of behaving in this way. However, I want you to develop and live in that consciousness which belongs to the Ātman, by shedding physical attachment."[3]

It was a new experience, a new revelation of awakened Brāhmic consciousness which the Lord wanted to infuse in them, which should be lived and which should be personified. This implied realising Brahman - the Akshar. The Lord was serene, so eloquent, so earnest, that the hearts of these Paramhansas were filled with unbounded bhakti for Him. They readily accepted this teaching. A new pattern of living, purified by the ceaseless and steadfast thought of believing in and behaving as Brahman only - a consecrated life at the feet of the Lord - should be lived for gaining His ultimate grace.

'One who discards attachment towards his body and all connected with the body, who identifies his ātman with Brahman, who is devoid of all vāsanā (desires), who acts according to the dharma prescribed for him, and who is dedicated to God, is a sādhu.'[4] By saying this Swāmi Sahajānand desired to

---

[3] Nishkulānand Swāmi, Bhaktachintāmani, Gadhadā, 1881

[4] Lord Swāminārāyan, Vachanāmrit, Gadhadā Sec. I-44.

remodel the institution of the Paramhansas to a divine pattern. He told the assembly in a dignified tone, 'Even though this beauteous and blissful state of permanent God-consciousness in a sādhu is difficult to be attained, I desire that you should reach this sublime height.' The Paramhansas realised that the Master had decided to bestow upon them that highest grace enjoyed only by Brahman - the Akshar. They desired that such overflowing grace should be showered on them.

The number of sādhus and disciples gradually began to increase. They came from different parts of India. Some of them were great pundits, some of them were heads of muths with a great following, and some were simple seekers in quest of God. They had heard the name of Sahajānand Swāmi from others returning from Dwārkā. They were thus drawn to Him. Many of them decided to stay. His very name created a great furore and many were converted to the doctrine of His philosophy. Thus this movement gathered a great momentum.

It would not be out of place to give here short life sketches of some of the most outstanding Paramhansas who did vital fundamental work in the establishment and spread of Bhāgawat Dharma under the guidance and inspiration of Shree Sahajānand Swāmi. Even though they believed that their collaboration in this task only amounted to bhakti, future generations should remember their activities in creating this movement - a great transformation of human life which we can study today, the development of Bhāgawat or Ekāntik Dharma.

Nitytānand Swāmi

Born in a brāhmin family at Datiyā in Lucknow District, Dinmani Sharmā had no trace of worldly attachment from

earliest childhood. His father Vishnu Sharmā and mother Virājadevi were greatly delighted at the birth of this child. After the Upānayana Samskārs, Dinmani received inspiration from the Gāyatri Mantra to observe celibacy and to seek God.

He left home at a very early age and went to Varanasi to study the Vedas, Upanishads, Darshan Shāstras and other scriptures. Completing these studies, he began a pilgrimage, hoping that God would meet him somewhere in holy places. After visiting Badrikāshram, Jagannāth Puri and Rāmeshwar, he decided to go to Dwārkā. Coming to Gujarāt, he heard at Visnagar that Shree Sahajānand Swāmi known as Swāminārāyan was God incarnate and that He was travelling with His Paramhansas and devotees. With this news his heart was filled with joy. He went to Dwārkā, enquiring at every place about Swāminārāyan and ultimately came to Unjā, where he had the darshan of Swāminārāyan in a big congregation. At this long awaited darshan of Swāminārāyan Dinmani was overjoyed, and felt greatly fulfilled. He requested Him to accept him as His disciple. He was duly accepted and at Meghpur in Saurāshtra he was given the Vaishnavi Dikshā and renamed Nityānand.

Nityānand had an incomparable scholastic genius, and as a first rank pundit he contributed literary works in Sanskrit on the life and philosophy of Shree Swāminārāyan.[5]

Gopālānand Swāmi

Born at Todlā, in Idar State, in a brāhmin family, Gopālānand Swāmi displayed amazing yogic powers from childhood. This child, named Khushal Bhatt, knew by his yogic powers that he was destined to meet Swāminārāyan and work for the spread of Ekāntik Dharma. Sarveshvārānand Swāmi, one of the Paramhansas of Shree Swāminārāyan, who was travelling in this district to spread the message of Bhāgawat Dharma of Shree Swāminārāyan, met young Khushal Bhatt at Nabhoi. Khushal Bhatt was much impressed by the talk of this Paramhansa on the life and work of Shree

---

[5] Literary works by Nitytānand Swāmi: (a) Haridigvijaya - A work in Sanskrit on the life and philosophy of Shree Swāminārāyan, (b) Commentary on Veda Stuti, (c) Commentary on Bhakti Sutras of Shree Shāndilya Muni.

Swāminārāyan. He became impatient to meet Swāminārāyan. One day he left home and came to Dabhān, near Ahmedābād. Here he had the darshan of Shree Swāminārāyan and was extremely exhilarated by the bliss radiating from His person. He was lost in a mood of utter ecstasy. Suddenly Shree Swāminārāyan told him to go back home as the time had not yet matured for union and He would send for him later on. Khushal Bhatt, disappointed but still pleased in his heart, returned home.

After some time he again set out with a brāhmin who was going to Gujarāt. This brāhmin looked after him very affection-ately during the journey and when they reached Jetalpur, the brāhmin told him that Swāminārāyan was in this village. Khushal Bhatt entered the village and came to Swāminārāyan who was pleased to see him. Khushal said that he was brought here by a brāhmin, who served him on the way, and who only parted from him here. But later on Khushal Bhatt learnt that the brāhmin was none other than Shree Swāminārāyan him-self! Thereafter at Gadhpur, Khushal Bhatt was given Vaishnavi Dikshā and was named Gopālānand Swāmi. He played a major part in the spread of this mission. As a literary genius, his contribution to the literature of the fold was vast and intense in divine feeling.[6] His deep devotion, service and untiring work for the spiritual upliftment of the masses reoriented the values of life and infused the spiritual con-sciousness of the people of his time, transforming their lives.

Gunātitānand Swāmi

Gunātitānand Swāmi was born at Bhādra, near Jāmnagar, in a brāhmin family, and is considered the incarnation of Akshar Brahman - the highest abode of Parabrahman. His original name was Mulji Sharmā. When he was four years old, Mulji

---

[6] (a) Bhaktamanoranjani Bhāshya on Shrimad Bhāgawata, (b) Bhāshya on Upanishads, (c) Bhāshya on Gitā, (d) Bhāshya on Brahmasutras and (e) on Veda Stuti — all in Sanskrit.

once told his mother that he would like to renounce the world and become a sādhu. Pregnant with wisdom, these words of Mulji were not palatable to his mother. Thereafter Mulji often talked to his mother about religion, saying that Parabrahman had descended on earth in human form, had left home after the Upānayana Samskāras, and that within a few years He would be coming here. The mother recalled the words of her Guru, Ātmānand Swāmi, that 'Akshar Brahman will be born in your child.' Mulji's precocious wisdom filled his mother with great rapture. When Mulji went to Piplānā for Ramanand's darshan, he saw Sahajānand there as Nilkanth. When Rāmānand introduced Mulji to Nilkanth, the latter smiled and said, 'This Mulji is the incarnation of Akshar Brahman, my abode, and will in future profusely display by his talk and discourses, the greatness of my form.' These prophetic words of Nilkanth had then fallen on deaf ears.

After the retirement of Rāmānand Swāmi, Sahajānand travelled in Sorath and Halar Pradesh, and came to Bhādra, where he stayed for one month. One day He was invited by Mulji to take dinner with him. Here Sahajānand disclosed before those present that the unsophisticated and rustic looking Mulji was the incarnation of His Divine abode. Then He explained that Akshar Brahman was infinite and eternal, possessing powers of granting ultimate redemption. The whole assembly was surprised to hear of the greatness of Mulji. They were greatly pleased as they had many times experienced the strange force of Mulji, but owing to his youth and family setting had not understood the divine powers that he possessed, and took him to be only a simple brāhmin.

One day Mulji had the darshan of Shree Swāminārāyan when he was working in field. He was mildly rebuked for his lethargy in being slow to take up the mission for which his birth here had been ordained. Immediately Mulji left the field and went directly to Gadhpur for the Lord's darshan. The Lord was pleased with him, and after some time performed a

2. Aksharbrahman Gunātitānand Swāmi

3. Swãmi Shree Yagnapurushdãsji

great yagna (religious ceremony) at Dabhān to initiate Mulji in Vaishnavi dikshā. Thousands of devotees took part in this yagna and witnessed the dikshā of Mulji Sharmā, performed with impressive ceremonial rites. Mulji was named Gunātitānand Swāmi.

The role which Gunātitānand Swāmi played in this mission amply demonstrated the need for the realisation of Akshar Brahman and the majesty of Parabrahman. As a devotee, as a preceptor, as the head of the organisation, Gunātitānand Swāmi displayed that wisdom which belonged only to Swāminārāyan. The absolute love which flowed from his heart for his Master, sometimes perplexed devotees as they saw him totally merged in the Master and the Master revealed completely - speaking, touching, seeing - through him. The relation between Shree and Nārāyan was evident in the dual form of Swāmi and Nārāyan.

As the pontifical head of the Swāminārāyan Temple at Junāgadh, Gunātitānand Swāmi played a great part in teaching Brahma Vidyā and in raising many of these disciples to the Brāhmic status. The impact of his very forceful and subtle discourses on the masses was so great that the precincts of the temple were thronged by thousands of disciples daily from distant places. He explichitly explained to the masses that Sahajānand Swāmi was the Purushottam, Bhagwān, Parā Swarup, the highest manifestation from whom emanate the various avatārs. The people accepted this conviction with indomitable faith since they saw the intrinsic devotion for his Lord in the heart of this other-worldly saint.

Shatānand Muni

Son of Vishnudata, a learned brāhmin of Mithilā Puri, Shatānand displayed from his childhood detachment from all sense-objects and was attached to Paramātmā only. He believed that ultimate realisation was not possible without having the Sākshātkār of Paramātmā. He therefore left home and went to Badrikāshram. Here he started meditation and lived on roots and fruits. By his severe austerities he had the darshan of Nārāyan. He prayed to Nārāyan to remain always before his eyes, whereupon Nārāyan said 'It is not possible. But as I have taken birth to protect the path of Dharma, you may enter my service.' Pleased at the command of Nārāyan, Shatānand left Badrikāshram and, travelling throughout India, came to Gujarāt. Here he heard that several Vaishnavas were performing Vishnu Yagna at Dabhān. He went to Dabhān and saw Sahajānand Swāmi before the yagna vedi surrounded by various Paramhansas. He immediately recalled the form of Nārāyan who had given him darshan at Badrikāshram. He was greatly exhilarated to behold Nārāyan before him in mundane form, yet still beyond all empiric knowledge and ever-transcendent.

Thereafter he was accepted by the Lord and taken to Gadhpur. He was given Bhāgawati Dikshā. He was inspired to write various works in Sanskrit[7] eulogising the Lord and His work.

Vyāpakānand, Swarupānand, Swayamprakāshānand, Ānandānand, Kripānand and a host of others who ranked as the heads of various muths, temples or institutions, were not only attracted but charmed by the personality of Shree Sahajānand Swāmi. They therefore accepted Him as their Master, to teach them Brahma Vidyā. It is really inconceivable that so many religious leaders, the veterans and the stalwarts in knowledge, tapas, vairāgya and in many other branches of a saintly life, should have come to accept the authority of Shree Sahajānand Swāmi, the God of the Paramhansas, but the attributes of sheer divinity shining from His person were either seen or experienced by them all. They came not just in ones or twos, but in hundreds. They were as if bewitched by the other-

---

[7] (a) Anvaya Dipikā Bhāshya on Shikshāpatri, (b) Nārayana Charitam (c) Harivākya Sudhāsindhu (a Sanskrit rendering of Vachanāmrits spoken by the Lord), (d) Uddhav Siddhānta and many others.

worldly personality of this young Master. They came to realise
the Ultimate Reality. Gradually, by the grace of the Lord,
wisdom dawned on them and they realised that the Ultimate
Reality was now before them. They were enraptured with this
knowledge. Each one of them proved a co-ordinating link in
the spread of a great mission, unparalleled in the history of
religious movements.

These Paramhansas, the true altruists, inspired the people,
not by mere preaching but by living a life in consonance with
the scriptural precepts. Such, therefore, was the potential
power and the dignified loftiness of these Paramhansas - an
embodiment of spiritual force released for the moral and spiritual elevation of the masses.

11 The Reform of Sacrifices

The ignorance of the masses had been exploited by the perverted pundits who, with their malignant preaching, had put many impediments in the path of Shree Sahajānand Swāmi in His task of establishing spiritual regeneration. He saw that those who were brāhmins, to satisfy their own ends, were misleading the people by encouraging them to perform sacrifices which involved the killing of beasts. They gave the authority of the Vedas to sanctify such killings. Thus the brāhmins, the custodians of all that was religious, debased religious usages. Eating meat, drinking wine, and practising adultery became rampant among them. Once a class of high preceptors, who from the pedestal of their authority had moulded the fabric of the society, they had now completely fallen into degeneration. Sahajānand Swāmi thought that when the preceptors had stooped so low, society was bound to fall into the same black pit. He decided to end this practice of killing beasts in the name of religion, and to teach people to perform ahimsak or sāttvic sacrifices, which did not involve cruelty.

When Sahajānand Swāmi was in Bhuj, He learnt that Jagjivanrām, the Diwān of Kutch, an arrogant brāhmin and an outright Shakta, was to perform a sacrifice. His brother Kuberjit invited Sahajānand Swāmi to attend this sacrifice as He knew that He was a learned pundit and therefore His very presence would add to the glory of the festival. Sahajānand Swāmi decided to attend the function whereupon some of His disciples tried to dissuade Him from going, as they knew that Jagjivan's vanity would be roused if the Master reproached him for killing beasts in the sacrifices. But Sahajānand Swāmi said, 'It is a religious tradition that on such occasions one should attend the festival even if not invited. Therefore, I would be breaking that tradition if I did not attend the sacrifice even after invitation.' The disciples did not argue further. They realised that every act of the Master was a crusade against the evil practices and that there was a meaningful purpose behind the Master's decision to attend the function.

Accordingly Sahajānand Swāmi came to the place of the sacrifice with His retinue of saints and devotees. He saw the goats and other beasts which were being kept ready to be killed for offerings to the sacrificial fire. He could not bear the sight, and trembled with pity at the plight of the innocent beasts. Such sacrifices had no authority in the Vedas and as such they were not acts of sanctity. He therefore told Kuberjit, 'The wise brāhmins should not perform such sacrifices wherein animals are killed and offered to the sacrificial fire. Every sane man would condemn such acts which do not have any sanction of the scriptures. The objects to be offered into the sacrificial fire as prescribed by the Vedas are rice, curd and ghee. You should therefore release these creatures and break off this vile tradition which has been fostered and supported only by selfish brāhmins to satisfy their own desires.'

These words of Shree Sahajānand Swāmi were like rubbing salt into a wound. The irritated brāhmins provoked Jagjivanrām to defy the authority of the new guide Sahajānand, who they thought had taken it upon Himself to be the preserver and the custodian of the scriptural traditions.

Before Kuberjit replied, Jagjivan immediately retorted, 'You are not the only wise brāhmin in this land. There are thousands of learned brāhmins here much wiser than Yourself, who have so far performed many such sacrifices, knowing full well that the Vedas have prescribed such offerings. You are invited here to witness this sacrifice and not to advise.' With these words, Jagjivan heaved like a pair of bellows and full of anger, stared at Sahajānand Swāmi venomously.

Sahajānand Swāmi replied calmly, 'I have come here to witness this function. But when I find that the Law of Dharma is violated, it is My duty to explain to you the truth. If I did not do that, I would be failing in My duty to uphold the Vedic traditions.' He then cited many Vedic verses in support of His contention, but Jagjivan was in no mood to hear. He was provoked to the extent of almost openly defying Sahajānand, but this he could not do, as inwardly he was afraid of opposing this towering personality. However, he ordered Sahajānand to quit the place.

Smiling at the ignorance of this petulant brāhmin, Sahajānand Swāmi again stressed that he should refrain from such acts and respect the Vedic traditions, otherwise the Law of Dharma would not spare him. With this warning, He left the place with His disciples.

The words of Swāmi Sahajānand were prophetic. Jagjivan found himself in trouble on the third day after this encounter. The king of Kutch summoned him and reprimanded him for insulting Sahajānand Swāmi, who was acclaimed as a great divine personality. In utter disregard of the king's caution, Jagjivan and his brothers Ramachandra and Kuberjit revolted, and as a result they were all ordered to be executed by the king. Thus they met their fate for disregarding the Law of Dharma.

Ahimsā is the greatest Dharma. Under this precept the qualities of mercy, forgiveness, charity, tapas, and truthfulness are developed. Sahajānand Swāmi therefore started performing ahimsak yagnas like Vishnu Yāg, wherein 'Ajā' which was interpreted as goat by the deceitful brāhmins, but which really meant rice, was offered to the sacrificial fire. Many brāhmins took part in such sacrifices and discarded their previous erroneous beliefs. They could now behold the truth in the preachings of Swāmi Sahajānand, and realised that the scriptures have specifically pronounced Ahimsā (non-violence) as one of the greatest features of Dharma, the observance of which will restore the status of Brāhmanatva to the brāhmins.[1]

However, it was not an easy task to eliminate completely this deep-rooted tradition established by the Vāma and Shakta brāhmins. They saw Swāmi Sahajānand as a great opponent of their hereditary practices. They thought His work of reformation, the restoration of the Vedic Dharma of Ahimsā and Brahmacharya was a great danger to their power over the masses and to their established practices of adultery, wine drinking, and meat eating. They opposed this movement of Swāmi Sahajānand with fanatical ferocity. Vithobā, the Subā of the Peshwās, residing at Ahmedābād, was provoked and instigated to capture Sahajānand either alive or dead.

This Subā's father had died suddenly and the reason assigned by the brāhmins for this calamity which had fallen on the Subā, was the performance with impunity of the ahimsak yagnas by Sahajānand Swāmi in his kingdom. According to them, the Goddess Kāli was thereby enraged, and had gulped the Subā's father as a sacrificial offering. Wisdom does not prevail with people who are saturated with power and fanatical notions. The Subā was again warned that the mighty power of Sahajānand might some day also depose him. The Subā's anger was roused to a wicked flame.

He conspired to kill Sahajānand Swāmi and invited Him to his palace for this purpose. He fixed a seat for Him over a deep tank which was full of oil. The magnificently decorated hall of the Subā and the gorgeous gādi for Sahajānand Swāmi gave the impression of great respect for his honoured guest.

---

[1] Ahimsānirato nityam juvhāno ātavedasam Sādāra nirato dātā sarve brāhmana uchyate. - Yamasmriti.

But the Subā had failed to realise that this spiritual genius had the power of understanding all secret thoughts. As soon as Sahajānand Swāmi came to the entrance of the hall, the Subā stopped His retinue from following Him inside. Swāmi Devānand who was by the side of his Master, sensed some evil in the Subā's motive. However, he followed the Master and entered the hall. The Subā stood with all honour and respect, welcoming Sahajānand Swāmi and offered Him the special seat prepared for Him. With a smiling gesture, Sahajānand Swāmi replied, 'I am a sannyāsi and therefore it does not become a sannyāsi to sit on this gādi which deserves to be occupied either by the king or his Subā. So this honour rightly falls upon you as a representative of the great Peshwās.' The Subā was greatly perplexed by this remark but gained courage and again requested the Master to occupy the gādi. With a roar of laughter, Sahajānand Swāmi pushed the gādi with His stick and immediately the gādi fell into the tank. The evil plot of the Subā was thus revealed and he stood aghast. Devānand in a mood of great anger tried to utter a curse, but the Master silenced him. The Subā and the whole audience stood as if petrified.

After a while, the Subā regained control of himself. He could not bear the sight of Sahajānand Swāmi standing before him. He ordered Him to go to the outskirts of Ahmedābād and never again enter the city. Thereupon Sahajānand Swāmi said, 'I am prepared to obey your orders and not come to this city. But I shall appreciate it if you will indicate the period of time during which I am prohibited from visiting this city.'

'While the Peshwās rule this city You are forbidden to enter,' was the curt reply of the Subā.

Sahajānand Swāmi immediately left the city with his disciples. Within a year, the Peshwās fell to the British and the prohibitory order was automatically annulled.

Sahajānand Swāmi's influence was becoming stronger day

by day, and the British rulers realised His greatness as His love, preaching and righteousness, converted bandits into law abiding citizens, and looters into devotees. It was difficult, even with the help of a modern army, to subdue the obdurate kāthis of Saurāshtra. But Sahajānand Swāmi did this with the help of His rosary alone. In fact, the history of Gujarāt and Saurāshtra during this century was created by Sahajānand Swāmi and His sādhus, as they fought against resurgent evil forces with the weapons of ahimsā, love, and the spirit of sacrifice. Their devotion for the cause of spiritual development was so deep and intense that no sacrifice, insult, or malice could deter them. As a result, the evil social elements were completely eliminated from the soil of Gujarāt and Saurāshtra. The historians have taken special note of this.

Thus the mission of Bhāgawat   Dharma became widespread, social vices uprooted, and society awakened to a greater enlightenment. The Vishnu Yāg in Dabhān, where hundreds of thousands of people assembled, was an eloquent testimony to the ability of Sahajānand Swāmi to raise people to a higher understanding of knowledge. It also amply exhibited the strength of His following and the love of the people for Him and His cause.

Similarly at Jetalpur and other places, He performed ahimsak yagnas which many thousands of people attended. Simultaneously Vāma Mārgi brāhmins also mustered courage and attended these functions to create disturbances, which were however ably averted by the Kshatriya followers of Sahajānand Swāmi. Evil priests rose again and again like the demonic army of Ahirāvana, only to be crushed to the ground every time.

Ultimately Lolangar, the head of the band of nomadic sādhus who kept weapons, was provoked to oppose Sahajānand Swāmi. This Lolangar used to tie an iron chain round his waist to exhibit his strength and his eyes were red like fire. Sometimes he spent the whole day completely drunk. His unsubdued arrogance used to terrify people. He tried to belittle Sahajānand and attempted to capture Him. However, he met the fate which others of his kind had met previously, and fled, his power broken.

Thus all opposition was gradually curbed. Sanity prevailed amongst the decadent brāhmins and they realised that nonviolence, truthfulness, abstinence from the evils of adultery, wine drinking, meat eating or theft elevate life and help man to fulfil his destiny. They came to understand that the activities of Swāmi Sahajānand and His sādhus were for the promotion of the social and ethical standards of the people.

He had never for a moment craved popularity or believed that such a great following raised His status, as to Him the merging of the self into God was the highest goal. He wanted the people to enjoy this ultimate bliss, and the fulfilment of this mission was in His work for the spread of Bhāgawat Dharma.

His path, strewn with difficulties, was now being cleared. The gnostic consciousness amongst people was now rising higher and higher above the horizon.

12 Molecules turned into Mountains

The fight against evil was not yet complete, although the stronghold of the Shaktas had been shaken. The Shaktas, who were determined to spread their own supremacy as preceptors, could not tolerate any interference in their sphere. Their sacrilegious activities had received a great blow from the preachings of Shree Sahajānand Swāmi, aimed at the establishment and spread of Bhāgawat Dharma.

Pibek, a great fetishist of Bengāl, was put to great ignominy by Sahajānand Swāmi, who, as Nilkanth was then travelling on foot among the various pilgrim places. When He came to Sirpur (Bengāl), He had occasion to meet this arrogant brāhmin, a worshipper of Goddess Kāli. Pibek never observed the rules for pure devotion. He had killed many innocent men and animals to propitiate the Goddess. Influenced by these perverted ethics, he developed hedonistic tendencies. Life to him meant fulfilling carnal desires.

During the time Nilkanth was passing through Bengāl, His esoteric powers were revealed to many, and this tantalised Pibek. He thought that his sphere, which had so far remained unassailed, had now been encroached upon by an upstart yogi only in His teens. He therefore aimed to curb the growing influence of this yogi.

It happened that Nilkanth had come to the place where Pibek had set up his camp. In the course of His worship, Nilkanth was meditating when Pibek came there with his followers. His eyes were red with rage. He was heavily drunk and had tied human skulls and bones round his neck and waist. Smeared red with sindur, and carrying a trishul (ceremonial trident) in one hand, he came before Nilkanth with the intention of offering Him to the Goddess Kāli. He roared loudly, shattering the nerves of the people there. The whole atmosphere froze to a dead silence. Nilkanth slowly woke up from meditation and looked around. The people around Him immediately warned Him about the powers of this siddha. They beseeched Him not to challenge him lest He might lose His life. Nilkanth quietly smiled and said, 'Do not worry about Me. Let him release all his powers on Me!'

Pibek heard this and immediately threw some grains energised with a mantra (spell) on a tree, and in a moment the tree shed all its leaves and dried out. Seeing this, the people around him trembled in fear. Seeing the result of this ghastly experiment on a tree, they thought that this power would prove fatal to the life of Nilkanth. They again requested this young yogi not to defy Pibek. But Nilkanth had no fear. He was quite unmoved.

Wild with rage Pibek assumed an expression of unbounded fierceness and began to chant mantras for invoking demons. But to his surprise, none of the demons dared approach Nilkanth. This furiously enraged Pibek. The people were also surprised that all his fetishist powers had failed and he found this yogi really invincible. He was baffled. Up till now the gods and goddesses invoked by him had fulfilled his mission, but this yogi remained immune from their influence. Pibek therefore felt that this young yogi was not just a mundane individual but manifested divine power. His ego melted. His sense of being a brāhmin of high origin reawakened. He ran in front of this yogi and prostrated before His feet with tears in his eyes. Nilkanth affectionately patted him on his back. He told him to discard the activities which were abhorrent and sinful. He advised him to adopt Bhāgawat Dharma, read Gitā and Bhāgawat. Pibek eagerly drank all the words of Nilkanth like nectar. He realised that he had degraded himself. He shed all his garments immediately and accepted the Vaishnavi Dikshā from Nilkanth. The discarded knowledge of Brahma returned to Pibek.

Since Pibek had deserted his disciples, they left his company and went to other parts of the country. Here, among the bands of similar tāntriks, they spoke wildly about Nilkanth and told them of the ignominy that He had inflicted upon Pibek. Even though they had seen the powers of Nilkanth they did not fully realise His divinity, as they were infatuated with fury and rage. When some of them came to Gujarāt and Saurāshtra, they recognised in Swāmi Sahajānand their old foe Nilkanth. They watched for an opportunity to kill Him. In the meantime, they incited the brāhmins of the Kaula and Shakta sect to stop the influence of this protagonist of Vaishnavism.

During this time, Magnirām, originally a devotee of Shāradā Devi but converted to the Shakta sect by the influence of the brāhmins of Bengāl, came to Gujarāt. This great pagan who was the same type as Pibek, extracted huge amounts of money from small feudal chiefs and other rich people as a gesture of worship towards him. Either they paid the amount demanded, or they were assailed by his tāntrik powers. His name spelt terror among the people. The followers of Pibek joined him and told him about the ever growing influence of Swāmi Sahajānand over the people. Magnirām was furious, and planned vengeance.

He came to Māngrol port in Saurāshtra. Here he demanded a huge amount from the feudal chief, who immediately retorted, 'You have an equal match in Swāmi Sahajānand. If you can extract this amount from Him, I shall give you twice the amount demanded by you.

Magnirām laughed. He said cunningly, 'When the

mountain moves, atoms are powdered. I will take twice the amount from you. It is your stake.'

Magnirām was a giant amongst men, very wild and depraved. When angered, it was as if he became a terrible demon. The matted hair on his head hung loosened. He smeared his eyes with black ointment, made sindur marks on his forehead and other parts of the body, and held a long dagger in one hand. Thus he came to Swāmi Sahajānand, who was holding spiritual discourses with His sādhus and other disciples. With a fearful roar he shouted, 'Oh, Sahajānand! I have come here to demand my dues. You pay and propitiate me or else face the consequences. So saying he stretched his dagger towards Swāmi Sahajānand with one hand on his waist, and awaited his reply.

The disciples seated around Shree Sahajānand Swāmi were startled. They immediately rose up to capture Magnirām, but the Master deterred them with a smile. Magnirām became wild with rage at the cool and unperturbed attitude of this young Swāmi. He again roared, 'Pay heed to my demand or else the demonic goddesses at my command will devour You.'

Still passive and seated in the same posture, Sahajānand Swāmi advised him, 'Your goddesses can do no harm to Me. Those who devour are not great – only those who deliver are really great. Your mantras will recoil upon you like the roars of lions before the mountains.'

Magnirām was taken aback. These words struck a ray of fear that penetrated into his heart. He replied, 'I am Magnirām, the propitiator of Devi, a different calibre to be dealt with. However, I am giving You some time and shall come tomorrow to collect my dues. Be therefore prepared.' So saying he left. His disciples were surprised at the crestfallen attitude of their master whom they had believed invulnerable. However, they hoped for more startling results the next day.

The same night Magnirām, by a relentless sādhanā,

invoked his gods and goddesses of the demon cult. But they refused to attack or even approach Swāmi Sahajānand since they knew that their powers were futile before this divine personality. Magnirām was shocked at this as they were his only invincible weapons and at the last moment they had failed to assist him. He began to rebuke them saying, 'I have wasted all these years, for now I understand that your powers are useless before the mighty strength of that yogi.'

The Goddess Kāli then replied, 'Oh Magnirām! Wisdom should dawn upon you. Sahajānand is not merely a yogi but the Supreme Lord, manifested on earth for the redemption of jivas and for the spread of Bhāgawat Dharma. You should therefore shed your ego and approach him. He will purge you from your sinful life.'

Magnirām was stunned, then felt a great desire to humbly shed his evil life. After a while he saw before him a vision of Sahajānand's slim and beautiful figure. Magnirām felt a great void within himself, then slowly became revitalised with the virtues of a true brāhmin. He immediately got up, took a bath, and sat with a rosary in his hand before the image of Vishnu. But he saw Sahajānand in Vishnu. He was overjoyed. The light had dawned in his heart. He prepared to go to Swāmi Sahajānand, but it was still dark. He became incredibly impatient for darshan of the yogi. It was not the sun of the previous day which dawned for him. It was a new sun – a new light which inspired him to shed all attachment to the Shakta sect. Wearing a dhoti, he besmeared tilak and a kumkum mark on his forehead, and with a rosary in one hand he went to Swāmi Sahajānand chanting loudly 'Swāminārāyan', 'Swāminārāyan'. He saw the very same slim figure as in his vision, now seated in the midst of the sādhus and other devotees. He ran to Him and immediately prostrated, with tears in his eyes, praying to Him to forgive all his sins. Sahajānand Swāmi threw a merciful glance at him and blessed him. It was a glance impregnated with divinity and it rejuvenated his life. He knelt down before all the sādhus and disciples and took the dust of their feet which he put on his head.

He again prostrated before Sahajānand Swāmi and requested initiation in the Bhāgwati Dikshā. But first Sahajānand Swāmi wanted to test him still further. He said, 'I am still not convinced that you are completely released from the Shakta sect. Your ego as a tāntrik might still deflect you.'

Magnirām had lost all words for justifying his sincerity. He therefore said, 'Lord! I am prepared to do whatever you will order me to do.' With these words, he rolled down at the feet of the Lord.

Unmoved by all these emotional exhortations, Sahajānand Swāmi told him, 'Your head and face should be clean shaved. Your hair should be scattered on the road so that people may tread on it. Magnirām immediately agreed. To him the hair which was once the proud treasure of his dignity, had lost all significance. He felt that the path for ultimate realisation was not only prepared for him but was completely hallowed by the Lord. It was only the final ascent that was now to be attained. He was prepared for the effort. He therefore completely surrendered himself to the will of the Lord for a consecrated life. Soon after he was initiated in the Bhāgawati Dikshā. Magnirām was reborn as Advaitānand.

Such characters appeared before Sahajānand in the course of His work for the spread of Bhāgawat Dharma. But they all ultimately came to learn wisdom. Sahajānand Swāmi had nothing but love and grace to shower on them. He was amiable towards all. He knew no foes, and helped His disciples to fight against their foes of avarice, passion, anger, and egoism, and released them from their bondage. He turned molecules into mountains.

13 The Rosary replaces the Sword

With the waning influence of the Shakta and Vāma sects, people were awakened to the necessity of living in consonance with the code of morality. However, many of them were still in the grip of dire ignorance and illiteracy, and it was not easy to move them from their inertia. The brāhmins had opposed this new movement for fear of losing their livelihood as priests. They therefore condemned this movement as non Vedic with their sacerdotal authority. Even though they had inwardly realised the truth and the sanctity of this movement, they preferred to remain engrossed in performing familiar rituals and ceremonial activities. This, according to them, was the only Vedic cult and it was their monopoly. They argued that according to *Gitā* this movement of Sahajānand Swāmi was a new departure and to follow it was fraught with danger *para dharmo bhayāvahah*.

The other opponents of Sahajānand Swāmi called themselves Vaishnavas and followed only their own āchāryas, whose profligate living was at variance with the status of their religious leadership. These Vaishnavas, because of their stark ignorance of religious precepts, developed a sort of quietism and meekly submitted to the antinomic behaviour of their āchāryas. They believed that they would deliver them from the bonds of Māyā. Their imbecility helped to augment malpractices. Credulity and the fear of the wrath of God deterred these Vaishnavas from breaking out of this vicious circle.

But other individuals who had polytheistic beliefs, decided to add one more to the list of demi-gods to whom they owed allegiance, and approached Sahajānand Swāmi. They were prepared to receive what He would give them. And they received from Him buddhi yoga – light, as a result of which they discarded their polytheistic worship. They shed all fear and vices and began to live a pious life. The preaching of Shree Sahajānand Swāmi and His sādhus in simple colloquial language appealed to them more than any other teaching. A change began to develop in their ways of living. Thus deliverance was made available to a community, formerly completely devoid of proper understanding. Even criminals were affected.

Joban Pagi of Vadtāl, an adept in tracking down thieves and dacoits, was a great dacoit himself. His name was a great terror to everyone. The very news that Joban was near the outskirts of a town frightened people, who closed their doors and hid inside.

Joban learnt that Sahajānand Swāmi had a fine mare Mānki, which raced like the wind. He decided to steal this valuable animal, and with his accomplices went to Dabhān where Sahajānand Swāmi was performing a big yagna. At midnight they all went to the place where Mānki and the various other horses belonging to the feudal chiefs were kept. The horses were all tied to separate trees and some watchmen were keeping guard over them. The watchmen were all asleep when Joban moved from one horse to another to discover Mānki. But to his surprise, he found Sahajānand near every horse, either patting the horse or cleaning it or feeding it with fodder. He was disappointed. He therefore slipped away, deciding to come the next night.

The next night too he saw the same surprising figure of Sahajānand Swāmi near every horse, and moreover found himself charmed by His personality. However, he stifled this emotion which he believed was cowardice. He decided to come again the third night.

The third night too, the same slim and beautiful figure of Swāmi Sahajānand was seen by him, patting and caressing every horse. He was exasperated. He decided to snatch away Mānki in open daylight from Sahajānand. However, when his accomplices told him that Sahajānand Swāmi was not to be underestimated he paused to think for a while. He then told his accomplices, 'Tomorrow morning when we go to Him in His assembly, if He calls me by my name, tells me the purpose of our visit here, and gives me a rose garland, I will believe that He is the divine Godhead.'

The next morning they all went to the assembly of the great Master. Sahajānand Swāmi was seated here on a high dais and thousands of people were sitting before Him, listening to His spiritual talks. It was difficult to find a way into this assembly. But Sahajānand Swāmi saw them, and instructed the patrolling guards to bring Joban and his accomplices before Him. Immediately the assembly was divided into two divisions and a small passage was formed. Joban and his party were brought before the Master. Joban saw the same slim figure which he had seen successively on the three previous nights. He found himself delighted, even drawn into a vortex of happy thoughts which the association with this divine Master had brought to him.

But suddenly the silence was broken. Sahajānand Swāmi, with a smile welcomed Joban, extending His gracious hands and said in a sonorous voice, 'Oh! You have done us a great favour by visiting our function. But may I ask you whether you succeeded in your plan to steal Mānki?' The assembly was startled as the people recognised this great dacoit. The kāthi devotees put their hands on their swords and tightened up their girdles. But Sahajānand Swāmi told them, 'This is not an occasion for drawing swords. Joban has not come here to commit any robbery. He desires to change his life.' So saying, He gave him the rose garland which was on His neck. The obdurate Joban had fallen before the captivating influence of the Lord. All his three conditions were fulfilled. He immediately prostrated before the Lord. With tears for all his sinful life, he begged for atonement. The Lord accepted him and expiated him from all sin by His blessings. Joban felt a new life beginning as he took a rosary from the Lord.

The rulers of the various states and other chieftains heaved a sigh of relief at the happy conversion of this mighty dacoit. The ruler of Barodā State arranged to pay a pension to him for life.

Once Joban went to Petlād to collect his pension from the State Treasury. The officer-in-charge glanced at him and asked him to wait. Joban had a rosary in his hand and was chanting the Swāminārāyan Mantra. Nearly two hours passed before the officer deigned to look at him again. Then with a cunning smile, he winked his eye and asked, 'Well Joban! I hear that Swāminārāyan converts an ass into a cow. Is it a fact?'

Joban could feel the sarcasm in his words and immediately felt angry. But regaining his awareness as a dedicated devotee, he replied mildly, 'I think you have no commonsense as you miss seeing the obvious fact. I was an ass but I am now converted into a meek cow. If I were my former self, you would not dare to sit here counting coins and keep me waiting for so long.' The officer realised the situation and immediately paid him his pension amount. Joban's life thereafter was completely dedicated, and all his possessions in Vadtāl were put at the disposal of the Lord. If Vadtāl has now become the main centre of the diocese of the Swāminārāyan sect it was because of Joban's deep devotion for the Lord. Afterwards the Lord erected a big temple at Vadtāl.

Innumerable characters of the type of Joban were subdued and their course of action and belief changed. People now witnessed them living a totally dedicated life. The sādhus moving in groups through various villages, towns and remote parts at the command of the Lord, preached the need to live an elevated life, a life bereft of hedonistic pleasures, but still not puritanical, a life of devotion, a life of singing the praises of the Lord, and dancing at His will, merging in the ecstasy of bliss emanating from His self. People were charmed. They were impressed by the sustained efforts of these sādhus for a cause so dear to them, a cause which did not bring them physical comfort, yet spiritually fulfilled them to the utmost in respecting the commands of the Lord. Self-purification is the only course of self-perfection. Sahajānand Swāmi therefore expediently introduced such injunctions as would gradually eliminate nebulous notions.

Even though the kāthi disciples followed Him with utter respect and faith, it was difficult at first for them to change their confirmed mode of living. They tried sincerely to follow the prescribed injunctions of the Lord, but their fickle minds sometimes gave way to suppressed notions, and they violated His orders, albeit unknowingly.

It was a custom amongst the kāthis that if a female child was born, she should be immediately killed by drowning her in a milk-pot. This was because they had to spend huge amounts on dowries at the time of the marriage of the girls. Since they could not afford to raise such amounts, and did not have the courage to discard such customs, they adopted such abhorrently sinful methods of dealing with the problem. However, in doing so, they never had the slightest notion that they were committing a sin. Sahajānand Swāmi told them to stop this sinful practice. But they could not resist the temptation. The Lord implored them again and again. He told them that if they did not discontinue this practice they would be compelled to do so by law, which would be shortly enacted by the new rulers coming from the West. This advice was eventually heeded and the practice ultimately abandoned.

The Lord with inborn mercy could not tolerate the slightest injury or misery inflicted either on human beings, animals or small forms of life. In contrast, the kāthis, having a pugnacious spirit, never hesitated to kill anyone at the slightest provocation. Stealing other people's property had also become a common practice for them. But, when the Lord reprimanded them, they bent their heads in shame and repentance. Even though they wanted to observe all the rules of a divine life, they often could not resist the temptation to derive benefits from improper actions if opportunities were offered.

Surā Khāchar, a staunch and foremost disciple of the Lord and the feudal chief of Loyā in Saurāshtra, once came late to a meeting. The Lord asked him why he was late. He replied, 'Mahārāj! My two oxen were stolen yesterday.'

Immediately the Lord said, 'Then the ploughing must have stopped,' and felt grieved at the loss the devotee had suffered.

But Surā, intervening, said, 'No Mahārāj, the ploughing and drawing water from the well are going on. I have taken four oxen from others!'

The Lord was startled at this act of gross violation of the simple rule of non-stealing and said, 'Surā, you have infringed the rule of non-stealing.'

The utterly credulous devotee replied, 'My Lord! The violation was from the other side first.' The whole assembly burst into laughter at Surā's unconventional attitude.

This illustrates what type of tough characters the Lord had to handle. However, behind this insensitivity, he could perceive a sheer transparency of heart. This was enough to awaken their inner consciousness. Thus Surā, Māmaiyā, Allaiyā, Matrā, Rāthod Dhādhal, Vastā, Jivā and various other kāthi warriors, even a whole tribe of unscrupulous chieftains, played a great part in consolidating Bhāgawat Dharma. It was the mortification of their desires, will, avarice, anger that the

Lord had started. They had drunk the nectar for transfiguration into sublime God-consciousness. Explaining the conditions under which this kind of transformation is possible, the modern writer Aldous Huxley said, 'The complete transformation of consciousness, which is "enlightenment", "deliverance", "salvation", comes only when God is thought of as a Perennial Philosophy affirms Him to be – immanent as well as transcendent, suprapersonal as well as personal – and when religious practices are adopted to this conception.'[1] To these devotees Sahajānand was God, personal and still suprapersonal, immanent and still transcendent.

Sahajānand Swāmi wanted to revive true Vaishnavism which had fallen into disrepute. The stronghold on which He based Bhāgawat Dharma, were mainly Dharma and Bhakti (duty and divine love). Bhakti coupled with Dharma – mainly Ahimsā and Brahmacharya (non-violence and celibacy) would bring ultimate deliverance. Describing this Movement as modern Vaishnavism, and Shree Sahajānand Swāmi's love for Dharma, Sir Monier Williams said, 'This sect is worthy of notice, both because it affords a good example of the best aspect of modern Vaishnavism and because the efforts of its founder to deliver the system of Vallabhācharya from the corrupting influences of the profligate Mahārājās, is worthy of praise.'[2]

---

[1] Huxley, Aldous, The Perennial Philosophy, London, 1946.

[2] Williams, Sir Monier, Religious Thought and Life in India, London, 1883.

14 Dedicated Servants of God

Sahajānand Swāmi's spiritual power had fallen on those heretics who were indulging in blasphemous activities. His band of devoted workers was growing to the size of an army. Five hundred Paramhansas lived a life consecrated to a spiritual renaissance that had been instituted by the unceasing efforts of their Master. His commands for observance of the eightfold celibacy, and total abstinence from possessions or wealth, enhanced their spiritual status. This spiritual force was raised to dispel the ethical discord which had permeated the soil of India. The unflinching fidelity of the devotees towards their Master gave them such strength that their every nerve pulsated with the vigour of this new morality. Wherever they went they sang the splendour and praise of their Master. The influence of the Vāma sect waned. People began to realise that pseudo-religionists and sceptics had held them in their grip. Their innate virtues now developed by the contact of these new Paramhansas. Thus Sahajānand Swāmi touched their inner life so that they hungered for a higher realisation. He organised the whole fellowship in such a way that it developed the ethical and moral life of people. With the mortifications of worldly desires, bhakti - intense love - began to develop, and a feeling of dedication for a divine cause arose in the hearts of the people.

One day Sahajānand Swāmi sent a circular letter from Bhādra, a village in Halar district, near Jāmnagar, and ordered that Mānchā, Surā, Somlā, Allaiyā, Mulu, Nānjā, Matrā,

Māmaiyā, Ajā, Jivā, Veerdās, Lādhā, Kālā, Kamalshi, etc. etc., should, on reading this letter, immediately leave home, go to Jetalpur and take initiation into Bhāgawati Dikshā at the hands of Anand Swāmi, and then come to Bhuj. The letter was sent through a personal messenger, who went to every village where these disciples were residing. The solemn order of the Master was immediately executed. The sanctity of the order was so respected that after reading the letter these disciples felt that they had forfeited their right to enter their houses, if they were in the fields or out of the village. Each of them was a small ruler or a feudal chief. But they had now cast off these notions as superfluous to their spiritual development. Their pugnacity was transformed into passivity by the influence of their Master. In short, their mundane frame was slowly being transfigured into a Brāhmic structure.

As this band of dedicated servants of God was passing through the village of Rāmgiri (Saurāshtra), a young disciple Ajā Patel heard of them. His marriage ceremony was being performed. But he could not resist the temptation of the darshan of this holy band of Paramhansas. He immediately broke the matrimonial knot and ran to meet them. He enquired why all had taken to renunciation, whereupon they showed him the letter of the Master. On reading the letter, he immediately cast off the bridegroom's dress and joined this band. They attempted to dissuade him, telling him that his name was not mentioned in the letter. He quietly replied, 'It is the wish of the Master. Otherwise He would not write "etc." after your name. I am in that "etc." category.' All were stunned at the poignancy of his love towards the Master which impelled him, just on the threshold of enjoying a happy wedding, to reject the matrimonial ties.

This band of eighteen new Paramhansas went to Bhuj to meet the Master. When Sahajānand Swāmi heard that His disciples, in obedience to His order had renounced the world and were coming to Him for His darshan, He was overjoyed –

not because His order was respected, but because He felt that they had reached His lofty ideal. They deserved not only the praise of the Master but His respect. The Master went to receive them Himself – not walking, but prostrating at every pace. The disciples saw from a distance their Master coming to them prostrating. They ran to hold Him, and they were all caught up in His divine love. An ocean of love enveloped them. Tears of joy fell from their eyes.

'No realms have remained unconquered by you. You have fulfilled today My desire that you should hold the beacon light to lead people to the realms of spiritual wisdom.' So saying the Master once again embraced them all.

After some days, the Master ordered them to go back home and revert to their original position as householders. On hearing this they were dumbfounded, as if a thunderbolt had struck them. But the Master infused in them words of wisdom and said, 'There is not the slightest trace of worldly attachment in you. You are the embodiments of purity and perfection and as such I desire to spread this Bhāgawat Dharma through you. You have fulfilled My mission.' They then returned home. Ajā Patel, the stubborn youth, did not desire to change the mode of his position in life. He beseeched the Master to absorb him in the Paramhansa fold. And the Master granted his request. Since his was an unparalleled renunciation in throwing away the delights of matrimony, he was named Adbhutānand Swāmi – one who had performed a wonderful act.

Thinkers, philosophers, religionists and reformists became aware that the masses, totally apathetic to theological questions were now infused with the spiritual vision of Sahajānand Swāmi. Their polytheistic beliefs were curbed. Allegiance to the supreme God was now firmly founded, since God Himself was before them. Sahajānand Swāmi did not simply establish this miracle by mesmerism for, as Sir Monier Williams describes, "Some attribute his influence to a power of mesmerising his followers but he probably owed his success to a remarkable fascination of manner combined with consistency of moral character, and other qualities which singled him out as a leader."[1] He wanted to make them after His own image.

And the attributes of Dharma, Jnāna, Vairāgya and Bhakti, all in profundity in Him, were reflected in a great measure in His disciples. This amply testified to the great influence of His character upon them. He never for a moment allowed them to deviate from the path of Dharma. He taught them to shed their ego of the physical self, ever maintain and perfect the four attributes of Dharma, Jnāna, Vairāgya and Bhakti, the ingredients of the perennial philosophy, which would take them to the heights of the divine realm. In conformity with His desire, they had broken the shackles of worldly bonds just as a snake discards its skin.

Dosābhāi of Bandhiā, a town near Gondal (Saurāshtra), was a man who had a very lucrative business. He used to remain at his shop all day. Cartloads of gur (raw sugar) were being unloaded in his warehouse throughout the day. Even though he was one of the outstanding disciples of Shree Sahajānand Swāmi, members of his community laughed at him for his unceasing business activities. Unmindful of them, he always attended his business. Once some of the members of his community had occasion to pass through Gadhpur, where Sahajānand Swāmi was residing. Here they all went to Him for His darshan. Sahajānand Swāmi received them very lovingly and enquired about His beloved Dosābhāi. With a gesture and caustic smile, they retorted, 'Dosābhāi is absorbed in business and has no time even to chant Your name.'

Hearing this, Sahajānand Swāmi smiled and asked, 'Would you join this fellowship if Dosābhāi renounces everything and becomes a sādhu?'

---

[1] Williams, Sir Monier, Religious Thought and Life in India, London, 1883.

They were surprised at this question and said, 'It is impossible.' The Master laughed, and advised them to come again soon.

Then Sahajānand Swāmi sent two of His pārshads with a letter asking Dosābhāi to take up sannyās and reach Gadhpur within a couple of days. He also sent with them the alfi - the Paramhansa garment. When these servants reached Bandhiā, they saw Dosābhāi collecting cartloads of gur and weighing them. Dosābhāi met them and immediately prostrated before them. The pārshads then gave him the Master's letter. Dosābhāi read the letter and immediately called the barber and got his head and face shaved. He then took his bath and put on the Paramhansa garment sent by the Master. Thus he prepared himself for being escorted before the Master as a dedicated servant. The pārshads told him to wait for a day if he wished to entrust the affairs of his business or house to his sons. But he said, 'The Master has made these arrangements and has called me. I have nothing to do now. We must go to Gadhpur immediately.' The pārshads were surprised at the total unattachedness of Dosābhāi towards the world, and realised that this was due to his profound devotion towards the Master. They then left Bandhiā and reached Gadhpur within a couple of days. The Master was pleased to see Dosābhāi in the attire of a Paramhansa. When the members of his community returned to Gadhpur, they were amazed to see Dosābhāi in saffron robes. They realised that the influence of Sahajānand Swāmi was unbounded, and that Dosābhāi's conversion was due to his total dedication at the feet of the Master. His outward activities did not touch his inner self.

It was evident from the history of this Satsang (fellowship) as recorded by contemporary Paramhansas, that the Master's teachings, His influence, His love, His ideal of service, His very keen interest in the life of every disciple, even though they numbered hundreds of thousands, transformed their lives. They were closely interwoven like one vast family. In their outright dedication all obstacles were overcome whether from their family members or anybody dear to them.

The disciples of Shree Sahajānand Swāmi from amongst the sādhu or the laity groups numbered many hundreds of thousands. The history of the life of each Paramhansa inspired followers to tread in their footsteps and implicitly obey the Master. We have mentioned only striking illustrations and omitted many others for fear of being thought extravagant. But the wonder of this spiritual renaissance could not be exaggerated. The spontaneous flow of the infinite divine attributes emanating from His Divine Self spread throughout the whole of Bhārat, and this new sect of jivanmukta was being watched by everybody with a keen interest. The name of jivanmukta by which Sahajānand Swāmi was known at that time, was heard in every corner of the land. The congregations held by Sahajānand Swāmi began to be attended by enormous throngs of people of every caste, creed and colour, and news of these congregations spread everywhere like wild fire. The liberation started on an unprecedented scale was such as never before witnessed in the spiritual history of India. He desired to bestow grace on every one. It was a gift offered to all, even to the ungrateful ones. He meant to redeem them of their avidyhā (ignorance) as that was His solemn pledge. It was fulfilled in abundant measure.

15 Gadhpur - The Holy City

The Swāminārāyan fellowship had been centred at Gadhpur, the seat of Shree Sahajānand Swāmi for nearly thirty years. Why should Sahajānand Swāmi, who had an inveterate desire for habitation in jungles and mountains, and who had the nature akin to that of Bharat, Shukdev, Dattātreya and Rishabhdev for living in a secluded life, prefer to stay in a town and mix with the people? The extreme austerities that He had willingly undergone during His travels amply exhibited His capacity for tapas (austerity). However, all the extravagance in dress and ornaments was accepted by Him. And not only the comforts, but the luxuries offered to Him by His devotees, were enjoyed by Him. Why the paradoxes in His way of living?

It must be remembered that in His divinity He was totally without attachment to material affairs, and lived for the benefit of His devotees.

He said His determination to stay in Gadhpur was because of the unflinching love of the feudal king of Gadhpur, Shree Dādā Khāchar, and his sisters, who lived a life of abstinence, austerities, and absolute celibacy. The observance of eightfold celibacy by the sādhus and of sevenfold celibacy by the householders, is an absolute necessity for attaining the Brāhmic state. Sahajānand Swāmi imposed the strictest observance of this Vrat. He says, 'I have stayed here because I find that nishkām dharma, the tenet of celibacy, is being strictly observed here by Dādā Khāchar and his family members.'

The life of Shree Sahajānand Swāmi and the history of the Swāminārāyan Fellowship would be incomplete without mention of the life of Shree Dādā Khāchar and his family, whose single-minded devotion brought to rest the protracted wanderings of this unique spiritual Master and tied Him here with the fetters of love.

The political scene of those days had been one of continuous warfare. Small feudal chiefs fought amongst themselves for aggrandizement. Looting and murdering had become the rule of Law. Religion had become obsolete and malpractices in the name of religion had flourished. King Abhay, Dādā's father, and his family, who were living a pious life and observing all the tenets of ethical religion, felt unhappy at the corrosion which had set into the spiritual and moral life of the people. They used to read *Shrimad Bhāgawat* and *Bhagawad Gitā* throughout the day and chant Krishna mantra. They felt in their hearts that Shree Krishna must descend on earth to protect the sādhus and regenerate the obliterated dharma. Often in a mood of hope, they saw good omens and expected better tidings.

One day, Mānchā Khāchar, one of their relatives and the feudal chief of Kāriyāni, a town nearby, came unexpectedly to Gadhpur. It was raining heavily then. The whole family was delighted to see him and received him with great cordiality. They enquired of him the reason for his sudden visit in such heavy rain, whereupon Mānchā told them, 'I have brought you the news that the unseen form which you have been worshipping for so long has become manifest and He will be coming to Kāriyāni within a short time.' Thereafter, to quench their appetite of great inquisitiveness, he narrated in detail the life and work of Shree Sahajānand Swāmi, whose darshan he had at Māngrol. His unique personality, charm, eloquence, love, and compassion were all described in detail, hearing which the whole family was merged in great rapture. Their longing for a divine union was to be fulfilled. They believed that Vishnu had descended on earth and they all would now be redeemed.

After some time, Shree Sahajānand Swāmi came to Kāriyāni at Mānchā's invitation, to celebrate the Vasant Mahotsav, a spring festival. King Abhay came with his son Uttam Kumar (or) Dādā Khāchar and two daughters, Jayā and Lalitā, for His darshan. They were all attracted to the divinity flowing from the person of this great incarnation. Their hearts flowed with extreme love which expressed itself in the form of tears. When Mānchā introduced them to Sahajānand Swāmi, He said smilingly, 'I know of their pre-natal relationship with Me. They will now be strengthened, as I am going to stay with them.' Everybody heard His sonorous voice. They were all greatly delighted that the day of deliverance had come. Abhay, with folded hands, requested Sahajānand Swāmi to come to Gadhpur. And He said, with great compassion, 'Your town and your family are woven in my heart. I am going to stay there and nowhere else.' Greatly fulfilled by this solemn promise, King Abhay stayed at Kāriyāni with his family and handed over the administration of his kingdom to his son-in-law Nāgmal, until he returned to Gadhpur.

When Sahajānand Swāmi came to Gadhpur, He was overpowered by the unalloyed love and pure devotion of Lalitā, Jayā, and Dādā Khāchar, the prince. But still at times He tested their patience and love for Him and made demands which were impossible to fulfil. But the realisation which they all had, that Nārāyan was now manifesting as Sahajānand Swāmi, replenished their inner strength and they rejoiced at the great fortune which was their lot.

Jayā and Lalitā both had to marry as part of their duty. But they still lived a life of absolute piousness and celibacy. They never even allowed the shadow of a male to fall across them within a reasonable distance. They lived a life of utter austerity and rejected extravagance in food, clothing, and ornamentation. The unceasing devotion that they offered, coupled with the dignity that they felt in serving the Paramhansas and the other devotees of their Master who were coming for His darshan, consolidated their position in the innermost heart of their Lord. The exuberance of their devotion towards Him tied Him with strong fetters of love.

Once Sahajānand Swāmi had to go to Vadtāl to attend the annual congregation (samaiya). He ordered all the Paramhansas and the kāthi devotees to be ready. He mounted Mānki, His mare. However, Mānki did not move an inch. He flogged the reins, patted her and goaded her but Mānki remained motionless. He was very surprised, since Mānki always used to respond as soon as He mounted her. Soon He realised that He had not taken permission from Jayā and Lalitā. The force of their devotion did not permit Mānki to move an inch. He immediately came to Jayā and with great apology requested her permission to go to Vadtāl. Jayā was grieved at the separation but said, 'Lord! You should return here immediately.' With this promise given, Sahajānand came to Mānki. He mounted on her, and the mare galloped with the speed of an arrow of Shree Rāma. Premānand Swāmi, the poet devotee and a singer of great reputation, has narrated this incident in one of his poems.

Antagonism against King Abhay developed after the grace of Shree Sahajānand Swāmi made him immune from all border troubles. Evil-minded people contrived to spread scandal about his two daughters Jayā and Lalitā for intimacy with Shree Sahajānand Swāmi. Abhay was a Kshatriya of hot blood. He loved Jayā and Lalitā, not as his daughters but as the dedicated disciples of Shree Sahajānand Swāmi. But on hearing such loose talk, his mind became overcome and the innate tenderness, love and devotion for his daughters was momentarily obscured. He rushed into the apartment of Jayā with a drawn sword. Jayā was merged in singing a devotional prayer requesting her Lord to drink milk. Abhay stood still and saw Jayā shedding tears before the small image of Harikrishna – Shree Swāminārāyan. Furious at the absorption of Jayā, he shouted her name in a loud voice. Jayā awoke from the divine slumber in which she was enjoying the embrace of her divine consort. She saw Abhay in a mood of utter discord and cried, 'Bapu!' But the pugnacity in Abhay had flared up. For the moment he was caught in a vortex of fury. He cried, 'Jayā! Your Swāminārāyan should drink this milk here and now before me, or else your head will fall on the ground.'

Stunned at the attitude of her father, Jayā mildly said, 'Bāpu, the Lord is ever present here and He accepts everything that I offer. If it is your wish, He will drink milk from this jar.'

'No cajoling, Jayā. My word is final.' Jayā's vision was pure, untarnished. She could see her Lord standing before her, smiling. The Lord also felt the infatuation in the mind of King Abhay, which had cast a lurid shadow on the unalloyed life of His beloved devotee. He drank the milk from the jar and Abhay saw this. He did not believe his eyes, but it was a fact. He bowed down at the feet of Jayā and apologised for his suspicious attitude. The veil of ignorance that had covered his knowledge was removed. He saw Jayā engulfed in the divinity of her Lord.

Lalitā, too, exhibited an equally untarnished love for her Lord. Even though she did not want to marry, she had accepted her duty and become the wife of Khodā Dhādal, a feudal chief of Botåd. Sahajānand Swāmi had expressed His desire that she should stay at her husband's home and not come to Gadhpur, even for His darshan. Once she went to Gadhpur with an alluring desire to have the darshan of her Lord, but Sahajānand Swāmi forbade her to come even near Dādā Khāchar's darbār. In implicit obedience to her Lord's order, she did not wait an instant, but immediately returned to her husband's house.

She observed all the rules of piety and celibacy at her husband's house. Special facilities were provided for her by her husband so that she could live a life of complete purity and devotion. They all realised the absolute love that she had for Sahajānand Swāmi, and did not force her into sexual life. She enjoyed rapport with the Lord so much that once when she was invited to play *rās* (religious dance), her presence illumined the atmosphere and every woman playing the *rās* had the darshan of Sahajānand Swāmi. In intensity of devotion and love, there was no comparison between Jayā and Lalitā, and as Sahajānand Swāmi often used to say, Jayā symbolised Lalitā and Lalitā symbolised Jayā.

Every word of Shree Sahajānand Swāmi was a Rule of Law for them. They believed that every order that He issued was for enhancing their moral and spiritual status. Once Sahajānand Swāmi called Dādā Khāchar and told him, 'Dādā, you should give away your kingdom to your two sisters, since you do not stand to gain anything by enjoying it.'

Immediately Dādā Khāchar, with folded hands, replied, 'May it please you, Lord.'

The next day, by a deed of assignment, he transferred the kingdom in favour of his sisters. After some time Sahajānand Swāmi called the two sisters to Him and said, 'You do not need Dādā's kingdom since you live a life of absolute austerity. You should therefore transfer it to his name.' The order was carried out immediately. By such orders, which may seem strange and difficult, Sahajānand Swāmi indicated that His devotees should not bear the slightest attachment towards any of their belongings or should not become elevated by the possession of worldly riches. They should be able to shed such things without a moment's regret.

Dādā Khāchar had proved his spiritual longing for

liberation. His every nerve pulsated with the desire to propitiate his Lord and His Paramhansas. Once, at midnight during the rainy season, Gunātitānand Swāmi came from Junāgadh. He was resting under a neem tree which dripped rain water. Suddenly Dādā's wife woke up and opened the door. She saw the great saint chanting Swāminārāyan Mantra, even though being showered by rain water. She immediately woke up her husband who realised that they had not provided proper accommodation for the saints. They instantly decided to take a vow of celibacy and remain separate, Dādā with the saints, and his wife with the other female devotees, and put their own apartment at the disposal of the saints. The apartment was then immediately vacated and handed over to the saints.

Dādā Khāchar's life exhibited his divine love. He himself lived with great restraint, but lavishly surrendered all that he possessed for the comforts and enjoyment of his Lord, His saints and devotees. The living in love, knowledge and religion that he exhibited was an achievement made possible by the proximity of his Lord. The high pedestal of dedication on which Dādā stood afforded a great inspiration to the whole fellowship. The pangs of devotion are suffered because the joy of ultimate bliss is enjoyed therein.

His intense devotion culminated in offering his everything at the feet of the Lord. The temple of Gopinath in Gadhpur is a living monument to the total sacrifice of this king and his two sisters, whose every action was in perfect harmony with the wish of Shree Sahajānand Swāmi. Such exuberant love, flowing with absolute spontaneity, expressed superbly the attachment Dādā and his two sisters had towards the Master whose mere glance thrilled all their nerves. Gadhpur was therefore not merely a town but a pantheon, here Sahajānand Swāmi lived permanently with all His divinity and divine souls. Dada's shining example generated that divine spark of devotion in the hearts of those who remembered him and his family.

16 The Divine Life

A life thoroughly detached from worldly desires and possessions, and elevated by a glorified love and devotion, is both a philosophical and religious life. Sahajānand Swāmi lived a life which symbolised His preaching. He never separated religion from philosophy but wanted both to flourish together. He accepted with great equanimity the luxuries in ornaments, dress and food offered to Him by His disciples, and also simultaneously bore the insults flung upon Him at many places by the ignorant. He said, 'When I visit great cities like Surat, Vadtāl, Barodā and Ahmedābād, My disciples offer Me a sumptuous reception, offer Me gold and ornaments, rich food, dress and other luxurious articles, but when I meditate inwardly, I enjoy the bliss of Myself so intensely that the riches of this world look insignificant before it.'[1] He wanted His disciples to adopt this way of living wherein worldly riches could be easily discarded for the enjoyment of a glorious life in the proximity of the Lord.

Gordhanbhāi, a rich merchant of Māngrol (Saurāshtra) was the disciple of Shree Rāmānand Swāmi. When Sahajānand Swāmi, then Nilkanth, came to Māngrol during the first part of His sojourn from various pilgrim places, He was offered some rich food by Gordhanbhāi. He then asked him, 'How was this food prepared so quickly?'

Gordhanbhāi said hesitantly, with his eyes cast down, 'We are performing today the shrāddh (funeral rites) of my aunt,

---

[1] Vachanāmrit, Gadhadā Sec. III-39

and the food was therefore prepared.'

Nilkanth then smilingly said, 'Your aunt is now roaring in hell because she had wrongfully kept the gold deposited with her by your Guru Rāmānand Swāmi.' Gordhanbhāi was astonished to hear this secret from the mouth of a stranger who did not even know the language of the soil.

Thereafter Rāmānand Swāmi told his disciples that Nārāyan was manifesting in the form of Nilkanth. Gordhanbhāi realised the truth of this statement on many later occasions when Nilkanth, as Sahajānand Swāmi, displayed the attributes of His Lordship (aishwarya), touching the inner life of his soul. His business had suffered a reverse of fortune. He transacted all business in the name of Shree Swāminārāyan. His account books showed the debit and credit to Swāminārāyan only. After some time he became penniless. So Muktānand told Shree Sahajānand Swāmi, 'Gordhanbhāi has lost everything.'

Shree Sahajānand Swāmi smilingly said, 'He has risen to that equanimity where heaps of gold and earth equally have no distinction for him.' Gordhanbhāi used to remain so much engrossed in the divine form of Shree Sahajānand Swāmi that all his sensory organs lost external cognition of taste, touch, hearing, etc. His was a life of embodied devotion. Although a householder, his actions were in entire consonance with the wishes of his Master, who had become the living soul of his life.

Again, Parvatbhāi, a poor farmer of Agatrai, but a mystic soul, lived a life in complete harmony with the wish of the Lord Shree Sahajānand Swāmi. He experienced the absolute proximity of his Lord in waking, dream and deep sleep states. Once while he was ploughing his field, he was offering some food to Swāminārāyan in his mental worship. The bullocks stopped pulling his plough. But he remained in the state of meditation. His brother, who was just behind him with his plough, not realising Parvatbhāi to be so deeply engrossed in mental worship, goaded him with a stick and he saw food falling from his hands. He was surprised. He asked him, 'What were you doing?'

Parvatbhāi said, 'I was offering food to our Master Shree Swāminārāyan!' Thereafter Parvatbhāi was asked to retire from all everyday activities.

Once in Gadhpur Parvatbhāi remained without food for eight days; Mulji Brahmachāri, the personal attendant of Shree Sahajānand Swāmi, thought he must be dining with Dādā Khāchar. Dādā Khāchar thought he must be dining with Shree Sahajānand Swāmi. After eight days, when Sahajānand Swāmi inquired, 'Where do you dine?', he said with folded hands, 'I have been enjoying the brahmarās of your divine form and so I do not need any food.' Food is required to sustain prānas (vital currents), but when prānas are engrossed in Paramātmā, they are sustained by the All-Sustainer. A poor farmer, not having the knowledge of even the rudiments of yoga, moved prānas by the force of intense devotion and sustained life on the nectar flowing from the divine form of his Lord!

The divinity emanated so intensely from the person of Shree Sahajānand Swāmi that His devotees could not resist the temptation of immersing themselves in His grace. The fellowship conducted by Shree Sahajānand Swāmi was to thrive only on strictures, austerities and denials. Food and physical comforts were totally denied. Unceasing travels for preaching, even in the biting cold, scorching heat, or incessant rains, were the order of the day. During these travels, they were fortunate if they were not molested. But this they accepted as their lot.

The temptation of His divine presence was so great that one day Mulji and Krishnaji of Mānkuvā in Kutch, returned to Gadhpur. Sahajānand Swāmi, on seeing them, scolded them severely and asked them to go away. They left, but returned again after a year with some bags of money. Sahajānand Swāmi asked them, 'Where did you get this money?'

They said, 'Lord we served one farmer and received this as remuneration.'

'But why? I told you to return to your village.' He assumed a mood of anger. 'You are both married and you do not enjoy the marital life. I have received a complaint from your family.' They realised that this was not a command of the Master to enjoy the matrimonial life, but a rebuke for having undertaken the matrimonial ties. The family members had desired them to fulfil matrimonial obligations. But that amounted to reversing the inner core of their lives. They immediately decided to shun marriage. Touching the dust of the feet of the Master, they retired.

After some time they both came to Gadhpur again and requested an audience with the Master. Still testing them severely, the Master refused to see them and asked His attendant to dismiss them immediately. They were beaten and sent to the opposite bank of the river Unmatta Gangā. In the dead of night, they started singing songs praising the Lord. The songs, sung devoutly and in perfect harmony, requested the Master to accept them. The Master had known their potentialities, but to test them fully became stern and called His attendants, 'Look, I am being disturbed in my sleep by the songs of Mulji and Krishnaji, so drive them outside the outskirts of this town.'

The attendants went to them and told them of the Master's order. They said, 'We will abide by His order. But we know that He will accept us. Please therefore let us know His wish.' So saying they both bowed to the attendants and smeared the dust of their feet on their heads. The attendants went back to the Master and placed before Him their request which had been made so ungrudgingly.

The Master was moved. He got up and told them, 'Bring

them before Me. My every limb craves to embrace them. They have suffered the insult of a dog.' Immediately both the brothers were brought before the Master. He took them to His breast with overflowing love as if the happy union was never to end. They were then both given Vaishnavi Dikshā and accepted in the Paramhansa fold. One of them, named Aksharānand, was immediately appointed as the head of the Vadtāl temple. On being questioned about the propriety of the new Paramhansa being installed in such a high position so as to become the pontificial head of the Vadtāl temple, Sahajānand Swāmi said, 'I know what they have done for Me. It is beyond your conception.'[2]

The divine willpower expressed by Shree Sahajānand Swāmi in conducting the fellowship, helped Him to gather personalities of great genius. Although He demanded strict discipline in observing the rules of conduct, the splendour, amiability, magnificence and the majestic calm of His personality attracted everyone. Lālji Suthār, a disciple of Shree Rāmānand Swāmi had taken a solemn vow that no allegiance should be offered to anybody except Rāmānand Swāmi. But Shree Rāmānand Swāmi knew Nilkanth as Nārāyan, and when He appeared on the scene at the proper time he asked all his disciples to transfer their allegiance to Nilkanth, who was the deliverer. This had a unique effect on Lālji. Again, his intimacy with Mulji Sharmā of Bhādra helped him to know Nilkanth as possessed of infinite attributes. Since then Lālji nourished the desire to work as an anchorite with Shree Sahajānand Swāmi.

Once Sahajānand Swāmi desired to go to Kutch. He told Lālji to give Him a capable guide like himself. Lālji was very shrewd. He thought that since his own capacity was restricted to himself, the Master desired his company. He immediately made preparations.

---

[2] In order that their wives might not enjoy any conjugal relations with them, they had both castrated themselves.

He took some money, food, and a jug of water so that the Master might not have to undergo the hardship of a dry journey, for the route passed through a desert. But Sahajānand Swāmi wanted him to realise that His comforts did not depend upon the scant possessions of Lālji. However, He did not say anything immediately. The journey began. Just as they were about to enter the desert, they came across some thieves. They were both halted, and the thieves took away the food and water from Lālji. They searched his pockets to find money but could not locate any. In despair they had to be satisfied with what they got and left. But Sahajānand Swāmi called them back. He said, 'You do not possess the skill of your occupation. This Lālji has money, although you could not find it.' So saying, He suggested that they search his shoes. The thieves took away the money from the shoes of Lālji and felt greatly gratified at the kind gesture of the Master. They bowed down to Him and went away.

Lālji felt humiliated in being looted in the presence of the Master. He was stunned, as he could not think what he would now offer to the Master in the dry desert. And soon the Master demanded water. Lālji became speechless. Then smilingly Sahajānand Swāmi said, 'There is an oasis here and you will get sweet water.' And He pointed to a spot for Lālji to dig with his hands. Lālji knew from experience that there should be no oasis anywhere in this part of the desert, but with great remorse at having failed to serve the Master, he began to dig this spot in utter despair. Within seconds, he found water oozing out. He tasted the water and found to his surprise that it was very sweet. He immediately filtered the water and brought it before the Master, who drank it and thanked Lālji. Then they started to move on but Lālji lagged behind and again tasted the water. It was saltish. He knew then that the grace of the Master had worked a miracle.

During the journey they reached Adhoi, a small village. Here the Master sat under a tree to rest. Lālji began to examine the feet of the Master, which had been pierced by thorns. Suddenly the Master said, 'Lālji! Bring Me some food. I am very hungry.' Lālji said, 'Sir, we have no money to get food.'

'Go for bhikshā and beg the food,' replied the Master.

Lālji hesitated and said a little bashfully, 'Sir, I cannot go begging in this village as it happens to be my father-in-law's place.'

Hearing this the Master laughed and in great humour said, 'Look Lālji! Now we shall get the most sumptuous food, because your wife lives here. If, however, you are ashamed to approach her in this dress, I shall change your figure.' And immediately Lalji's head and face were clean-shaven. He was given the robes of a sādhu with the name of Nishkulānand. As Nishkulānand, Lālji shone with the lustre of personified vairāgya. Then Sahajānand Swāmi ordered him to go for bhikshā nowhere else but to his mother-in-law's house.

'Pray give bhikshā,' the so-called Nishkulānand Swāmi muttered in a sonorous voice, 'Nārāyan Hare Sachidānand Prabho!' His voice created a thrilling atmosphere.

The old lady come out, and seeing her son-in-law in the attire of an anchorite, immediately went indoors, called her daughter and said, 'Lālji has become a sādhu. You have to bring him back to his original state of a householder. So dress well and go before him with these two children.' The daughter followed the order and appeared before Lālji in an attractive attire with her two children.

Lālji looked down. He said in a low voice, 'No seduction is going to help you now. If you desire to have redemption from the clutches of births and deaths, then seek the refuge of my Master. I have come here for bhikshā to offer Him food.' These words of wisdom prevailed and the lady immediately retired. After a while, she returned with sweet food and offered it to Lālji. Lālji, still with head downcast accepted the bhikshā in his bowl and went away quietly.

When Nishkulānand came to his Master with bhikshā, the Master showered praise on him, since another person might have made a shameful retreat in such a situation. Nishkulānand proved the worth with which his Master regarded him. It was a bold transfiguration. The Master kept him there and then left for Kutch.

The pre-natal memories of Nishkulānand Swāmi began to return in his poems, which were full of vairāgya. In one of these poems he says, 'I am the eternal soul but was wrapped in Māyā. By the grace of my Master, I am released from the bondage of Māyā and have realised that all worldly relations are a myth. I am Brahman – the untainted; this realisation has dawned on me. One should not therefore unnecessarily quarrel with mythical relations. Man is made out of a drop of semen and becomes the creature of conjugal merriment. With the grace of my Master, my true goal is achieved. I had an unmanifested desire when I was performing tapas in my previous births. My Master knew this and gave me this birth for the fulfilment of that desire which has now been achieved, as I have known my Master in His present manifestation.'

He composed poems impregnated with deep vairāgya and sang them in Adhoi. These poems of deep devotion and renunciation inflamed the feelings of the people for total vairāgya. They then requested him to stop singing, or else the folk of the whole village might be converted to this creed, and all useful activities come to a standstill. His poems contained the quintessence of *Shrimad Bhāgawat, Bhagawad Gitā*, and *Upanishads*, and mostly expressed deep love for the Lord.

17 The Power of Redemption

Shree Sahajānand Swāmi did not recognise the grades of worldly status. The love radiating from His heart embraced all who longed to receive it. All those who approached Him, He knew only as Ātman or Brahman – their original self-without recognising the distinctions of caste, creed, rich, poor, successful or fallen.

Sagrām, a devotee from a very low caste, secretly nourished a desire to be graced by a visit of His Master to his small hut near Limli. He was afraid to disclose his wish before the other devotees as it seemed beyond all limits to expect such a divine Master to grace the hut of an insignificant low-caste devotee. The decorum of the upper class would not allow such thoughts. But his unswerving love for the Master assured him that his desire might some day be fulfilled.

After some time, it so happened that Sahajānand Swāmi prepared to leave for Limdi with His sādhus headed by Brahmānand Swāmi and other devotees including Surā Khāchar, the head of the Loyā group, who possessed a joyful wit. They almost reached Limli just before sunset. They halted there a while and were about to proceed when Sahajānand Swāmi suddenly said, 'We shall halt here for the night.'

'But it is still some time before sunset and we shall reach Limdi within an hour,' Surā argued. They were at a small village consisting of a few huts belonging to low class vāgharis.[1] The disciples therefore thought that proper amenities could not be provided for the Master in such a place. Surā, therefore wished them to reach Limli soon. But the Master had decided otherwise. He said , 'Nature in her naked form is so lavishly exhibiting her grandeur here. It is an aspect of the Almighty's divine phase which can be enjoyed here only and not in township. I therefore do not desire to move an inch.' His followers could not contradict Him. They managed to bring a tattered cot and some bedding for the Master. But it created a feeling of remorse in them, since they did not wish the Master to rest on such a poor and maimed bed. However, the Master did not relish physical comforts, inasmuch as the enjoyment of the integral bliss of His Own Self far outstripped the profundity of all riches, even of other worlds, that could be offered to Him. Neither had He really stayed there to enjoy the magnificence of nature. He only wished to respond to the innate desire so affectionately cherished by His devotee Sagrām. However, He did not say anything and rested after the usual nightly Sankirtan and singing of the Leelā, which were characteristic features of the Master's daily routine, and the description of His all-absorbing personality.

At midnight Sahajānand Swāmi woke up. He placed a puppet figure of cotton blankets on the bed, wrapped with a covering in such a way that the bed would not look empty. He then quietly slipped past the guard of His personal attendants, who were wrapped in deep sleep. He reached Sagrām's hut and called in a low tone, 'Sagrām'.

Sagrām immediately woke up and recognised the familiar voice of His Master. However, he enquired meticulously, 'Who is that?' But in the meantime, he heard the jingling of the Master's foot bracelets. He opened the door and peeped out. To his unbounded joy he saw his Master. He could hardly

[1] A class of nomads who generally roamed into jungles, looted people and indulged in hunting.

believe his eyes and rubbed them to clear his vision. But in the meantime, the Master entered. Before Sagrām could prostrate before Him, He locked him in His embrace saying only, 'Sagrām'. Sagrām was overwhelmed. He could not utter a word. Tears of joy rushed from his eyes, which were beaming with light. He had sought God, and now found him.

In a mood of thrilling joy flowing freely, Sagrām suddenly realised that he did not know what to offer to the Master. The Master laughed at his bewilderment and bent down to take up an earthenware jar with fresh curd and some corn flakes mixed in it. He began to devour this eagerly, leaving aside the usual decorum. Sagrām's inner vision saw the great commiserator, not simply rescinding social decorum but doing so by suppressing His infinite divinity in human form, mixing with a band of outcasts to redeem them from their plight. Sahajānand came out with his hands and mouth besmeared with curd, just as Brahmānand and Surā Khāchar arrived, and they saw their Master caught red-handed in this plight![2] They returned to their resting place, overwhelmed by His love for all.

Once Sahajānand Swāmi was performing a very great yagna at Jetalpur, near Ahmedābād. People had gathered there in many thousands. Kings, chieftains and the rich, all assembled to shower their opulence at the feet of this great Master. The Master held meetings every day on the bank of a great pond which had a historical fort around it. He used to sit on a beautifully decorated seat on a high pedestal erected specially on one of the platforms provided in the fort, so that the assembled masses could have distinct vision of Him. The conduct of the meeting was so disciplined that no one could intrude or approach the Master without the special permission of the kāthi guards.

---

[2] Brahmānand never spared an opportunity to celebrate such inspiring incidents in the life of the Master by composing poems full of the ravishing love of the Lord.

A very poor farmer entertained a desire to serve food to his Master. But it was difficult to pierce through the crowd and approach Him with a poor dish of food. As the days passed, the yagna was approaching its conclusion. All the farmer's hopes were dissipated and each day food was prepared for the Master but was only consumed by his family. The final day arrived. The poor devotee mustered all his courage and started out with the loaf of pulse and with vegetables prepared out of leaves, both lacking any palatable taste.

The morning's meeting started. It was just time for the sun to light the sky. Sahajānand Swāmi was seated, wearing a dress · richly decorated in silver and golden embroidery, profusely ornamented with gold and pearl ornaments, and wearing a garland of scented flowers around His neck. His forehead was besmeared with sandal paste mixed with saffron and perfume. The turban on His head, prepared from fine gold threads and woven with rich silk fabrics, reflected the sun's rays falling on it. For all the eyes questing for His darshan He had become the focus of vision. The meeting was packed and everyone was lost in a delicious languor. All of a sudden, people saw the Master waving His two hands ordering people to make way. They all looked from the Master to the back of the crowd. To their great wonder, they saw a poor farmer, holding in his hand a mutilated utensil covered with dirty rags. But it was the order of the Master that he be allowed to pass through and approach Him. The Master sent His attendants to help the poor devotee. Wrapped in torn linen, the poor devotee was replenished with strength by the extended welcome offered by the Master. Every eye was focused upon him. The saints and devotees were all anxious to know the mystery of the contents of the dish. As the farmer approached nearer, the Master got up from His seat and with a tender hand patted the devotee, and warmly took the dish from his hands. He began to eat the pulse loaf, unripe and raw, but still full of the flavour of love, flowing from the heart of a true devotee.

Brahmānand Swāmi and Surā Khāchar soon saw that the Master would consume the whole dish and the raw contents might create an ailment to His bowels. So they each approached Him for prasād – the graced offering – and the Master gave each of them small bits. The rest of the loaf and vegetables were consumed as prasād by the saints and devotees sitting nearby. The recounting of this remarkable incident in the scriptural texts[3] by learned saints, amply demonstrated how instinctive love pouring from the heart of a devotee was lavishly rewarded by the Master in His traditional way.

Innumerable incidents of this kind showed the deep compassion of the Master bringing out prominently the significance behind the manner in which every individual devotee was esteemed by the Master, and rewarded for devotion.

In a small village near Vadtāl, a poor boy with a heart full of tender love for the Master, was staying with his father. He was maintaining a fruit orchard. The boy tended the orchard with infinite care to save it from the vagaries of the season. He had decided to offer fruits to the Master from the first crop, and then sell the rest.

When the crop was gathered, he took some fruit in a basket and started for Vadtāl which was four miles away. But on the way he started thinking, 'The Master is too great a dignitary to be offered such fruits by me. I should therefore eat them here.' So thinking, he sat under a tree and took out his knife. But then he thought, 'Oh, it is a sin to eat these fruits as I have taken a vow to offer them to the Master.' So he pocketed his knife and continued his journey. After going a short distance, his mind again resisted but he started arguing with himself

---

[3] Snātam chandan charchitam. . . .

and his wavering mind rejected all. Eventually he reached Vadtāl.

Sahajānand Swāmi was sitting in a meeting of the saints and devotees who were patiently listening to His talks as if closely woven together. Apart from the resonant voice of the Master, absolute silence prevailed. The boy entered the precincts of the temple and was first greeted by the Master. The audience looked at the boy, surprised at this significant greeting. The Master called him close to Him and, extending His hands to bless him, accepted the basket of fruits. He then asked for a knife and immediately cut the fruit and ate it with great relish. The boy was completely gratified at the Master accepting his fruit so cordially and eating it before him. He was then about to leave, when the Master asked one of the sādhus to give the boy about ten seers (pounds, in weight) of sugar-cane. The boy took them gratefully and left.

The following day one of the baniās (merchants) who had been in the meeting the previous day, brought some fruits expecting that he would also get a similar quantity of sugar. The Master simply smiled at the offering and rejected it. He said, 'I gave sugar to the boy yesterday, not because he had brought the fruits, but because he had successfully resisted the temptations raised by his mind. But you have brought fruits with the expectation of receiving sugar. I am not to be tampered with so easily.' The baniā, with his head cast down in shame left the meeting, his covetousness exposed.

The Master could not be propitiated by any earthly riches but only by the instinct of pure devotion. When the construction of the Gadhpur temple was complete, Sahajānand Swāmi held a meeting of the devotees. He informed them that each should contribute towards the cost of construction of the temple. The devotees seated in front who were mostly the feudal chiefs or businessmen, contributed in thousands according to their means. The figure went on mounting.

All of a sudden, an old man wearing linen and a turban of rags slowly came forward. The kāthi chiefs in their usual humorous way laughed and murmured, 'How many thousands are you offering, old man?' The old man trembled as he came forward. Suddenly Sahajānand Swāmi cried a halt to further contributions. Then He came near the old man and extended His hand for his contribution.

The old man took off the ragged turban and loosening the many knots, took out thirteen coins (equivalent to thirteen paise in present currency) and handed it over to Shree Sahajānand Swāmi. The Master said to him, 'Bhattji! Better buy a new turban with these coins.'

But Dubli Bhatt swiftly replied, 'Lord! This turban would work for the short span of life now left to me. But I would lose a great opportunity of offering my humble contribution at this function.' So saying, Bhattji put the turban on his head and went away.

Shree Sahajānand Swāmi told the audience, 'No more contributions are needed now. The full cost of the temple will be met from the contribution received from this Bhattji.'

Surā Khāchar's sarcasm flared up. In a bantering tone he asked, 'How can Bhattji's little contribution fully meet the cost of construction?'

Sahajānand Swāmi smilingly said, 'Surā! Bhattji has given his all and has not spared the smallest coin for his needs. His dedicated devotion has elevated his donation. You all have spared something to depend upon and have forgotten that I am the sole sustainer.'

Surā became quiet. He realised the demand for total devotion. It is a feature that comes spontaneously from the heart of the devotee, without even being aware that he makes a sacrifice. He makes no demand, has no desire for return except the absolute grace of God which enlivens his life.

The symbolic perfection of infinite divine attributes which were embodied in Shree Sahajānand Swāmi, brought out the fullness of His divinity and His redeeming will. Any act of devotion, however materially insignificant, would have the significance of a mountain to Him.

Jivā Khāchar, the uncle of Dādā Khāchar, had an unflinching love for Sahajānand Swāmi. But gradually he began to feel annoyance and his respect for Him dwindled. This was because Dādā's dedication knew no bounds. He lived for Sahajānand Swāmi only. Sahajānand Swāmi was the virtual owner of all his estates. His affinity towards Dādā had grown out of all proportion. This had an adverse effect on Jivā Khāchar's allegiance towards Him, and the inborn fire of jealousy began to burn. He started campaigns against Sahajānand Swāmi which were not in consonance with the devotion he had towards Him in the initial stages. He even plotted to do away with the Master.

Eventually his jealousy knew no bounds, and expressed itself in hatred. One night, Sahajānand Swāmi asked His attendant Bhaguji to put the lamp into the latrine, before He went there to relieve Himself. Bhaguji was surprised at this unusual order, but he obeyed and took the lamp. As soon as he opened the latrine to put the lamp inside, he saw a man hiding there with a drawn sword in his hand. Bhaguji realised the significance of the order and immediately caught the man and brought him before the Master. The swordsman, Rāma Khāchar, a local kāthi, trembled as he saw the kāthis sitting around the Master drawing their swords against him. The Master quietened them all and said, 'Rāma Khāchar is not at fault. Do not harm him.'

Quietly prostrating before the feet of the Master, Rāma Khāchar took the dust of the Master's feet and smeared it on his head. Then he said trembling, 'Sir, Jivā had hired me to perform this heinous act. He offered me a pair of bullocks and a piece of land. Kindly forgive me.' So saying, tears rushed from his eyes, 'I am the wickedest man on earth.' And he clutched the feet of the Master. The Master threw a glance of compassion at him and said, 'Rāma, you are not at all at fault. The impulse of hatred so furiously burning in the heart of Jivā Khāchar has engineered this plot. But again, Jivā is also helpless against the propelling forces of vice which have seized him. I want to outroot them and purify Jivā.' The assembly heard with rapt silence the most noble words of the Master whose magnanimity knew no bounds. They realised the unfailing attributes the Master exhibited, irrespective of the feelings towards Him.

Some time after this, Jivā's sister Amlā came to Shree Sahajānand Swāmi and begged pity for Jivā's sins, as he was now on his death bed. With eyes beaming with great compassion, Sahajānand Swāmi said, in a low tone, 'Amlā, Jivā's acts of deep reverence towards me in the initial stage cannot be forgotten. I have never become displeased. Jivā is redeemed.' With the sense of relief from the grief that had seized her on account of her brother's behaviour towards the Master, Amlā's heart overflowed with great veneration towards the Master.

18 The Teaching of the Master

One had to walk on a razor edge to live according to the preaching of Shree Sahajānand Swāmi. The quest to establish harmony with the Ultimate Reality was to be fulfilled in this life. And to achieve this task these Paramhansas had to mould their lives so that they would not become susceptible to the vitiating influences of worldly pleasures.

Muktānand Swāmi and Brahmānand Swāmi, together with other sādhus, were going from village to village preaching. The sādhus affiliated to spurious cults had created an antagonism against these Swāminārāyan sādhus. Their austere living according to the tenets of moral conduct lowered the prestige of these false sādhus who had flouted all moral codes. They were afraid that they would be ultimately exposed and lowered in the eyes of the people. They therefore aroused the feelings of credulous people against these true sādhus. Widespread agitation was started to do away with the Swāminārāyan sādhus wherever they were found. Muktānand and Brahmānand fell into the sacrilegious hands of these heretics. They were arrested and taken to a secluded place. Here they were tightly bound by a rope to a tree and threatened with disfigurement by cutting off their nose and ears.

Brahmānand and Muktānand, who had entirely dedicated their lives to the wish of their Master, had no grief. They believed that the disfigurement of the face does not disfigure the Ātmā which is offered to God. They were specialists in spiritual teaching and their lives and thought were blended in the service of God only. Death was not a handicap in their sādhanā. The absolute passivity with which they introverted their senses in harmony with God, left them in no peril. They silently chanted the Swāminārāyan mantra.

In the meantime the heretics were sharpening the knives to finish their job quickly. All of a sudden the head of their band came there. He saw the heretics sharpening the knives and enquired, 'What are you doing here? Why are these sādhus tightly fastened?'

'These are the sādhus of Swāminārāyan. They are to be punished today.'

'You fiends!' With these words in a guttural voice, he jumped over them and snatched away their knives. He then went to the sādhus and released them from their bonds. With folded hands he said, 'Please excuse the heinous crime of these hirelings. Now do not bear any fear. I shall take you to a safe place.' So saying he escorted them up to a place where there was no danger to them and then allowed them to go.

Muktānand said to Brahmānand in a soft voice, 'The Lord's compassion is all-pervasive. It invoked the feelings of this man and removed our danger.' And then they started off to meet their other fellowmen.

Swāminārāyan never believed in exhibiting supernatural powers to give relief to His disciples from the worldly miseries. He believed that the fruits of our actions should be borne by us with complete equanimity. Prayers or other means should not be adopted to seek relief from miseries; the sādhanā is to seek God through Ātmā, and the comforts of the physical body are a handicap in the attainment of Ātmic consciousness.

Vyāpakānand Swāmi was passing through Botad, a town in

Saurāshtra, to reach Kāriyāni for the darshan of His Master. In Botād he met the kāthi disciples, who were all absorbed in grief. He was surprised, as these disciples had known no grief and always used to enjoy with exuberance the sight of a Paramhansa. He therefore asked, 'You, the best of disciples, to my great surprise are found absorbed in grief! Why has the divine joy of the Master so suddenly disappeared from your faces?'

The kāthis could not restrain the sorrow which had overtaken them. One of them, coming up to Swāmiji whispered, 'The best of our horses has died today. It is difficult to bear the loss.'

Vyāpakānand, as if nothing serious had happened, said in a bantering tone, 'But the heavens have not fallen. Where is the horse lying?' He was taken near the dead body of the horse, and immediately started chanting the Swāminārāyan mantra, then sprinkled some water on the dead body. To the great surprise of all, the horse was revived. Then Vyapakānand left for Kāriyāni in a natural mood of great rejoicing.

Sahajānand Swāmi received Vyapakānand with fervent love. He immediately said to His attendant, 'Look, the Lord has come. Bring him the most sumptuous dinner, as he has performed a feat unnatural for a common being.'

Vyāpakānand was amazed at this speech of the Lord, which sounded sarcastic. With folded hands and with head lowered, he said, 'Lord! I am merely your servant. Through inborn compassion I have revived the dead horse of our kāthi disciples.'

The Master replied, 'If that were our mission here on this earth, nobody would die. But the natural law is that death is imminent to all. We have not come here to remove death but to teach people to overcome death by knowledge. Supernatural powers create hallucinations in the minds of illiterate and ignorant people and through great credulity they form a spurious conception of God.' He paused for a moment and then said, 'You have succumbed to momentary compassion, but that has done great harm to their spiritual development. The worldly belongings are ultimately perishable, so why create an affinity for them in the hearts of our disciples who have to dissociate themselves from the body and bodily relations and attain the Brāhmic state?'

Vyāpakānand was stunned. Even though he had been preaching and living a life for attaining Brāhmic consciousness, he had not resisted the temptation, due to inborn weakness, to uphold the uncanonic law of physical survival. He prostrated before the Lord with tears in his eyes, and said, with folded hands, 'Lord! Please forgive me. I did not realise that the exhibition of real compassion rests in uplifting the soul to its ultimate Brāhmic state for which mundane happiness is to be totally disregarded.' With these words he again fell at the feet of the Master. The Master patted him for his candid expression and again exalted him to the high pedestal of spiritual consciousness, from which he had fallen in an unguarded moment.

Sahajānand Swāmi inspired all His Paramhansas and other disciples to maintain an unceasing contact with Him. Any relaxation or detraction in preserving this divine contact, from the assumption that one had already attained the Brāhmic state, would deter the disciple from the path of sublime divinity, since the real Brāhmic consciousness is aware of Parabrahman only in His fullest form.

Swarupānand Swāmi, one of the closest Paramhansas of the Master, with an awakened spiritual consciousness, had firmly established his chittavrutti (mental awareness) in the divine form of his Master. He enjoyed his position and used to relax in a secluded place drinking the nectar emanating from the absolute divinity of the Master. He had the notion that this was the Brāhmic state beyond which there was now nothing else to attain. However, assuming one's own self as Brahman manifesting in person (the form of the Guru) dissolves the ego of the self, and permits repose in God. This is the pure Brāhmic state or nirvikalpa samādhi.

The Master knew that Swarupānand Swāmi had not grasped this subtle principle. In order that he might realise this truth, the Master inflicted severe pain upon him. His chittavrutti was deflected and the agony of pain amply brought out his physical attachments. He came to the Master and complained, 'Lord! I am lost in an ocean of grief due to unbearable pain. Please relieve me of my misery.'

The Lord smiled and said, 'So long as the physical body is sustained, pain is felt; but the same is to be borne with equanimity. You have, however, a delusion that you have realised yourself. But unless you maintain constant contact with My esoteric and exoteric form, you will never attain the Brāhmic state. The Brahman only knows Parabrahman. Discard your physical consciousness and act as Brahman. Dedicate yourself to Me, think of Me and repose in Me, otherwise the ocean between the temporal here and chidākāsh beyond will not be bridged.'

Swarupānand Swāmi realised the folly of his staying away from the Master under the illusion that he had realised Brahman. It had worked as a detriment to his spiritual progress. The physical consciousness persists so long as the body is sustained. But when the chitta (mind stuff) is merged in the absorbing personality of God, Prāna is controlled. Jiva is then relieved from the vitiating influences that affect it through Prāna. Constant attachment is necessary, therefore, with the personal God or Brahman who may be manifesting on earth and assuming the form of Brahman, with an awakened consciousness to stop the vitiating influences penetrating within, as the only sādhanā for attaining the Brāhmic state. However, merely sitting in seclusion and thinking of or meditating upon God or Brahman leads one only to quietism or passivity. Generally, but erroneously, this state is taken as self-realisation, but it deters the spiritual ascent. The consciousness which is necessary to be kept awakened is stilled or attenuated in this state of quietism which gives the bliss of laya but not the bliss of Sat-Chit-Ānand which is of Brahman. Swarupānand Swāmi bowed down at the feet of the Master and accepted His advice to maintain physically and mentally His contact during the three states of waking, dream and deep sleep.

Sahajānand Swāmi's teachings were simple but subtle and penetrating. His whole life was devoted to establishing and promoting Bhāgawat Dharma, the observance of which in this life is a prerequisite for spiritual progress. He did not waste time simply talking or preaching but insisted upon living up to the tenets of Bhāgawat Dharma. He wanted to educate His disciples to insight in knowledge which did not mean just knowing facts but removing falsity or ignorance and proceeding further and further on the path towards the Ultimate Reality.

His amiable personality continued to attract people towards Him. He examined them thoroughly, understood them and tackled their worldly disposition for a spiritual transformation. All His disciples willingly submitted to Him and harmonised their living according to the teaching of their Master. It became clear to all that people who were previously discarded as downtrodden now lived a life rich in piety, and in consonance with all the ethical codes. They realised the importance of outward as well as inward purity, which pleased their Master. This religious and ethical grandeur reached its pinnacle and the Swāminārāyan code became the order of the day. Gradually it became a rule in many of the States, that in those towns and villages where there was a Swāminārāyan temple or small shrine, the need for a police force was waived, as the prevalent Swāminārāyan code of behaviour inhibited all activities contrary to the rule of Law. The British Officers of the period were absolutely amazed when the pugnacious kāthi tribe was ennobled by Lord Swāminārāyan with the power of the rosary. This movement, under the leadership of Shree Sahajānand Swāmi and His sādhus, gathered great momentum and hundreds of thousands of disciples became followers.

19 Art and Religion

Sahajānand Swāmi was a lover of fine arts. All beauty emanated from Him,[1] in His human manifestation, and He displayed this aesthetic sense and tried to promote it in the groups of His Paramhansas and disciples. Architectural designing, sculpture, handicrafts were all developed by His Paramhansas and devotees under His personal care. Music, *rās* (a type of Indian dance wherein the dancers move round clapping and moving the steps of their feet in complete synchronisation with the music), Holi festivals, duels, bullock fights, and races were allowed to flourish. The reason for this was to provide a beginning to lift people to higher instincts and raise them to the understanding of finer faculties which are the glimpses of the beauty of Ātmā.

Brahmānand Swāmi designed many temples. The lotus-shaped pedestal on which the Vadtāl temple has been erected is an ingenious feat of great architectural design. He had an absolutely clear grasp of the design of the temples of Junāgadh, Muli, Vadtāl, etc. which were entrusted to him for construction. Sahajānand Swāmi merely gave instructions. No funds were available. But Brahmānand Swāmi could see great potentialities in the orders of his Master. In times of difficulties, he simply invoked the Master with his exuberant bhakti, and the difficulties were solved.

Funds were not at first available for the Vadtāl temple. The depth from which the fervent praises flowed from the heart of Brahmānand invoked the Master. Nārāyangiri sādhu, who

---

[1] Yad yad vibhutimatsatvam - Gītā, 10-41

lived at Vadtāl and who had ample wealth at his disposal, was inspired to help. With Nārāyangiri's co-operation the temple was completed. The ceremony of image installation was performed with great enthusiasm and jubilation in the presence of many thousands of devotees. Huge funds were collected as donations on this occasion by the disciples, who wanted to propitiate the Master. The Master offered to repay Nārāyangiri his amount from this fund. But he said with great respect, 'Lord! As all these disciples have offered you these donations for procuring Your blessings, I too humbly dedicate everything at Your lotus feet and crave Your benedictions.' The Master was pleased and conferred upon him His heartiest blessings.

The temple at Muli (Saurāshtra) was under construction when suddenly water and stone for masonry became scarce. Brahmānand Swāmi explored all possibilities nearby but was disappointed. He composed poems and mildly, but with intense devotion, rebuked the Master for putting him in a forlorn position. Smilingly the Master appeared behind him and touched his feet. Brahmānand awoke from his meditational worship and saw the Master behind him. He got up and prostrated before Him saying, 'Lord! Excuse me for rebuking you. But water and stones are scarce. The work has stopped. There are no sources nearby for procuring these things.'

The Master smiled and said, 'Beloved disciple! I enjoyed the sweet words of rebuke from your mouth. Nothing is sweeter to me than your words of utter devotion. I will guide you to a stone quarry nearby and also to a big reservoir of water.' And Brahmānand followed the Master. He was shown the stone quarry and the reservoir of water at a place which had previously been inspected by him without finding anything. The Master disappeared. However, the divine potentialities of the Master showed that everything required was there all the time. This stone quarry and the water reservoir are still in existence today.

The construction of the temple at Junāgadh was also a difficult task, inasmuch as the Shaivites, who were the officers of the State, were in great opposition to the building of this temple here. However, Brahmānand had earned the grace of the Nawāb, as a poet of fine ballads. The Nawāb gave all co-operation and overruled the decisions of his officers, thus fully helping Brahmānand. The temple, possessing lavish architectural beauty, was soon completed. Brahmānand, with an indomitable faith in the Master, always believed that ultimately the will of the Master prevailed. He therefore stood firm against all such difficulties and hardships and relied only on the divine working of his Master.

Sahajānand Swāmi's aptitude for fine arts as well as His divine love attracted many people. A devotee who was a tailor by profession had cut a fine waistcoat for his Master. The cutting, fitting and the embroidery woven on it were so mar-vellous that the King of Bhāvnagar called him in his Darbār and gave an order for such a waistcoat for himself. The devo-tee, with all modesty at his command, said, 'Sir! It was with the sheer depth of love that I could prepare this waistcoat for my Master. Mere craftsmanship cannot produce such a prod-uct. You may, therefore, kindly excuse me for refusing to accept your order.' The king was amazed, but felt that it is only innate love which brings out such faculties of fine art. The devotee was rewarded for his boldness and truthfulness.

The various dresses, ornaments, and flower garlands that were prepared for the Master by His devotees, bore imprints of great craftsmanship. Hearing the aishwarya (great lordship) of the Master, one female disciple who had never seen Him before, prepared dress and ornaments of sumptuous grandness for Him. An impostor learnt of this and appeared before the lady as Sahajānand incognito. The lady, hearing the name of Sahajānand, was overjoyed and gave away the rich dress and the ornaments to him. Afterwards she learnt that he was an impostor and was much grieved. But with an enhanced enthusiasm she again prepared garments and ornaments of lavish richness for the Master. When they were offered to Sahajānand Swāmi in Kāriyāni, He came down from the great pedestal and accepted them saying, 'Rich garments and ornaments of great value are offered to Me on many occasions but I have never before come forward to accept them with such fervour as now. The intrinsic love flowing from the heart of this woman has impelled Me to accept them with humility.'

The playing of rās with Paramhansas and appearing before them in as many forms as the number of Paramhansas, was one of the celebrations that they greatly enjoyed with their Master. The attraction of His divine form was so impelling that the Paramhansas could not resist the temptation of playing rās with Him. The folk dance which had become an antiquated art through negligence was thus revived for healthy existence.

The Holi festival was given an innocent colour. The prevalent practice of Holi dances had promoted vulgarity and demoralisation. Sahajānand Swāmi explained that all festivals had a religious background and significance and were arranged only to consolidate religious and moral faith. He exposed all vile practices, renovated the old festivals and explained the religious significance behind them, to promote moral and spiritual instincts. All established festivals were a valuable part of the culture of the land, and He brought this fact boldly to the attention of people.

Music was very greatly appreciated by Him. He was a lover of music, not simply because of its rhythm and sound but because it helped to invoke God. He believed music was to be played to propitiate God, to know Him esoterically and to blend one's life to living only in God. His Paramhansas, chiefly Premānand Muktānand, Devānand, Brahmānand were great artistes. People possessing great musical talents also craved to hear their music. They believed that music had reached its perfection only here. These Paramhansas were at times invited to sing in the assemblies of the great kings, but they used to decline the offer with great humility, as they had developed this art only through the grace of their Master, and their music was therefore to be offered to Him only.

Once Premānand was singing before the images in the temple at Junāgadh. The Nawāb of Junāgadh who entered the precincts of the temple heard the most absorbing Dhrupad Rāga with eloquent exposition, and was simply stunned. He himself was a great artiste and a lover of music, and had heard musicians of great talents in his assembly. There was no musician worth the name who had not attended his assembly and who had not been heard by him. But he felt that this music had reached its heights here, beyond which there was no further perfection. It did not emanate from the human heart, but from God Himself, the master of all faculties, who was singing through the human form. When Premānand finished singing, he came to where the Nawāb was sitting. The Nawāb could see that Premānand was greatly moved. Tears flowed from his eyes, and it was as if he were possessed by God. The Nawāb got up, saluted the great Paramhansa and with sheer humility said, 'Sir, the music I just heard was simply absorbing. I offer my salutations to you, the unparalleled exponent of this great art, which belongs to gods only.'

Premānand bowed to him with respect and said, 'The grace of my Lord engulfs me in His love and I do not know who sings. I am merely a tool for manifesting His great art.' The Nawāb was greatly amazed. He had so far never heard of any artiste who simply waived his personality and assigned everything to the grace of his Master. With further salutations the Nawāb left.

After some time singers of great fame from the State of Gwalior came to Junāgadh to display their art before the Nawāb. They sent a message to the Nawāb expressing their desire to sing before him. The Nawāb declined to accept their request and said, 'I thank you for coming here. But I have heard music of an absolutely divine nature. Beyond that there is no talent. Premānand, the Swāminārāyan fakir has this talent and it is given to him by the God of music.' The great artistes were thrilled. They knew the divine potentialities of this art which had so far remained completely unexplored. They were overjoyed to hear about it. They requested the Nawāb to introduce them to this fakir. The Nawāb gave them a note and some money, and instructed them to go to Gadhpur where the fakir was staying with his Master.

The artistes left Junāgadh. They reached Gadhpur after two days. As they entered the Darbār Gadh, the assembly of the Paramhansas was about to disperse. Sahajānand Swāmi saw them coming and instructed the assembly to wait. It was noon and the meals were about to be served. The artistes saluted the Lord and took their seats, obeying the quiet but smiling gesture of the Lord. He then asked them, 'Noble guests! Where do you come from and for what purpose?'

Once again bowing low, the visitors said, 'Sir, we come from Gwalior. We had gone to Junāgadh to display our musical talents before the Nawāb. But the Nawāb refused to hear us. He said there was no musical talent higher than the one possessed by Premānand, the fakir of Swāminārāyan. Beyond that there was nothing to be heard. We have, therefore, come to hear Premānand.' Muktānand, Devānand and Brahmānand, the veteran tabla (drum) players were pleased to hear this eulogy of their comrade. They became anxious to hear the orders of their Master.

Hearing the praise of His veteran disciple Premānand, the Master was pleased. Even though it was noon, He wanted to satisfy their desire. He therefore ordered His musicians to bring the necessary instruments and start the performance.

The atmosphere was stilled and everybody waited expectantly for a great display of art by Premānand. With the customary salutations, Premānand asked the Master, 'Lord, what rāga shall I sing?' Every action of these Paramhansas was motivated according to the desire of the Lord since they believed that His will would work within them and bring out the best in them.

The Lord, with a graceful glance at Premānand, said, 'Sing Bhairavi.' Hearing this the visiting musicians were amazed, as Bhairavi was a musical mode performed only during early morning hours. They chuckled at the ignorance of these Gujarāti people who they believed lacked even ordinary knowledge of musical modes. However, they were prepared to listen.

Premānand started the ālāp (the opening exposition) the others played the musical instruments in accompaniment. The traditional style of Premānand in elegantly exposing the resources of the Bhairavi rāga in a delectable voice, and his excellent diction in a modulated tone, stilled the audience. The lucidity and elegance with which he developed Bhairavi made an indelible impression upon the Gwalior artistes. It was as if the day was newly dawned and even the cuckoos began to sing. The veteran musicians were amazed to find the potentialities of Bhairavi so ably brought out. They bowed down, showering praises of the utmost appreciation. They realised the amazing greatness of Premānand as an artiste of unequalled calibre. They saluted him with great respect.

Premānand said politely that his art was due only to the grace of his Lord. The musicians realised that the choice of Bhairavi rāga was not due to the ignorance of the Lord, but the wisdom with which He wanted to bring out the unparalleled musical talent of His disciple, Premānand. The Lord then rewarded the musicians with gifts and blessed them.

Sahajānand Swāmi possessed such talented artistes, who were like gems in His fellowship. On suitable occasions He brought out their talents before those who would be benefited.

He believed that the promotion of every art promoted culture and the finer instincts of people. People of fine aesthetic faculties can more easily attain perfection on the spiritual path, since their artistic talent emanates from Ātmā. The ultimate goal is to realise Ātmā, for which this life is required to be developed into perfection.

Sahajānand Swāmi established the custom of holding congregations of devotees at fixed intervals at the temples built by Him. These congregations helped the devotees to maintain a constant contact with Him and His sādhus. They also helped people to learn His teachings, to cultivate a habit of living a life of austerity, and to develop fraternal feelings amongst the fellow disciples. Apart from the spiritual development that He desired to promote through these congregations, such gatherings of devotees helped them to learn the culture of different provinces, the habits, education, customs of their people and the geographical conditions of different lands. It fostered a feeling of unity amongst the people of different provinces and wiped out the barriers of narrow provincialism. Sahajānand Swāmi believed that a wider fraternity could not be built unless people tried to understand each other, to live, mix and exchange views with each other. His congregations promoted this feeling of fraternity, vital for spiritual progress. These congregations spread the message of Swāmi Sahajānand throughout the country and educated people for the great mission that He had initiated. It became an established convention to hold these congregations regularly at various temples, to promote and inculcate the teachings of Shree Swāminārāyan.

The aesthetic faculty so highly developed and exhibited by Shree Sahajānand Swāmi induced in His followers a great taste for developing various kinds of craftsmanship. When elegantly rich dresses and ornaments were offered to Him by His disciples, He immediately gave them away to the poor or the brāhmins. He thus taught His disciples to lead a life without possessions. The greatest possession is the image of God that one has to invoke within, without which all possessions, however great, limit the development of people. Apart from His many sermons, His disciples learnt much from the life and example of this, the greatest divine Reality that had so far manifested on earth.

20 Personal Characteristics

The transcendental love which is an innate attribute of God, was amply exhibited in the life of Shree Sahajānand Swāmi. Full of compassion, He did not discriminate against sinners. With great magnanimity He welcomed all and rejected none. His redemptive will had no span to measure the good and evil, but had only the desire to redeem every soul provided that it also possessed that craving.

He preached, He talked, He lived a life of utter austerity and self-denial. When He accepted luxurious articles, dresses, or garlands offered to Him by His disciples, He told them, 'It is for your pleasure and satisfaction that I accept your offerings. When I introvert and look within at the infinite greatness of God and the bliss emanating from Him, all the riches of this world look insignificant.'

Again, lest His disciples might follow Him in action, but without His divine spirit, He cautioned them thus, 'It is impossible to get release from the bondage of Māyā if one indulges in and enjoys panch vishayas (the five sense objects). I am immune from the pleasures of the riches and luxuries offered to me as I always behave as Ātmā and control my indriyas, manas, prānas and chitta; whereas you have no control over them and therefore are likely to be enmeshed in the pancha vishayas.[1]

---

[1] Vachanāmrit, Gadhadā Sec. I-18

Describing the equanimity in which He lived, He said, 'I remain equipoised between the attractive or repulsive pancha vishayas, between the rich and the poor. Enjoying the fruits of the kingdom of the three worlds, begging from house to house, riding over an elephant or walking on foot, have all the same charm for Me. I have lost the consciousness even of the highest attributes of Dharma, Jnān, Vairāgya and Bhakti that I possess, since all My cognitive organs are introverted within, where I see the light of chidākāsh and within that light I see God. One who thus introverts and tries to commune with God, loses all attachment in the best of panch vishayas.'[2]

In His discourses, He always disclosed the various aspects of His life to inspire His disciples to lead their lives accordingly. In one of the discourses He said, 'In my childhood days, I had formed a habit of visiting the temples for darshan, to hear religious and scriptural discourses, to serve the sādhus and to visit the various pilgrim places. And when I left home, I discarded all possessions, and liked to stay in jungles only. My association with Shree Rāmānand Swāmi afforded Me an opportunity to mix with many people. However the thought runs poignantly in My mind that I should remain detached from all attachments with all kith and kin in the manner in which people lose their attachment with their relations who have been laid on their death bed. Again, the various sense objects, either good or bad have no attraction for me. I act, behave and work only for your good and have no motive except to inspire you all in the devotion of God. Without this purest devotion, I have no interest in life, in people and in the world and would live a melancholy life like a great king who, having lost his only child, in old age, loses all interest in the world.'[3]

Again He said, 'The intense devotion that I have in God cannot be effaced even in the most dire circumstances. I have

---

[2] Vachanāmrit, Gadhadā Sec. 1-13.
[3] Ibid., Sec. II-55

no attraction to the great cities and the great palaces if they are devoid of devotion. I like to stay in a secluded place, either in the jungle, in a cave, under a tree, or on the bank of a river, for the meditational worship of God. I love you all because you all are the best disciples. Kāla, Karma and Māyā (time, action and illusion) cannot sever this uncommon tie of bondage between us, the result of your absolute love for God. Sometimes I feel like leaving you all, but when I see you so intensely devoted to God, I become hesitant. But I cannot be dragged to live amongst people who have no love and devotion for God.'[4]

The mumukshu or seeker should fulfil the requisite sādhanās which are the steps for realisation. The sublimity to which He desired to raise them is brought out in one of His discourses: 'Death is imminent to us all at any moment, even now. Therefore one should, in order to attain the eternal values of divine life, draw inward from all the sense-objects and reach the divine goal. The desire that emanates from the mind makes one perform actions. Therefore one should examine whether actions are performed to fulfil desire or are performed without attachment as a matter of duty. Again, the careful examination of the mind at every moment is essential in order to allay the fear that it will not betray one; this is a prerequisite for a seeker who wishes to perform desireless actions. Seated within the hearts of all, I always watch whether Muktānand and other saints and devotees are freed from vāsanā (unconscious desires) or not.[5] Thus a constant intuitional eye or conscious thought is required to be applied by a seeker over all his actions.'

For thirty long years He continuously moved from village to village, addressed large crowds, talked to His Paramhansas and devotees, and disclosed to them the way of redemption. It was inherent in His nature. He had come to redeem, He redeemed, and returned to His abode, keeping the gates of

---

4 Vachanāmrit, Gadhadā Sec. III-13.
5 Ibid., Sec. III-30

redemption open through His realised saints.

The compassion that filled His heart led Him to ask for a boon from Rāmānand that a thousandfold miseries, if they be the lot of his disciples, may fall on Him and the disciples be relieved of them. This feeling of absolute mercy sometimes made Him impatient to help people. Once He left a meeting of His saints and disciples and ran to help a farmer whose house was about to fall through torrential rains. He rested on His shoulders the supporting beam of the house until the farmer cleared out his belongings and cattle.

He forewarned His disciples that the S.Y. 1869 would be a year of the worst famine and that they should therefore sell their cattle stock and store cereals. Those who obeyed Him were not affected by the famine conditions. The others suffered badly. He remained in hiding, from one place to another, in order that people of idle curiosity might not gather round Him and be a source of trouble to His disciples. Congregations were banned and sādhus were asked to live on ajgarvritti, i.e. feeding on what they got without begging. However, those who remembered Him and chanted 'Swāminārāyan' mantra were spared the untold miseries of the famine.

He was a lover of learned pundits. Dinānāth Bhatt, a very great Sanskrit scholar of Gujarāt of those days, Prāgji Dave, a great scholar of Shrimad Bhāgawat, and 87 Bhatt, were some of the many who were always by His side in the assemblies. He showered on them freely all the opulence that was offered to Him by His disciples. He encouraged these pundits to undertake research in the studies of scriptures and to bring out illuminating facts. He loved and respected brāhmins and taught them to live according to their creed.

His supernatural actions were sometimes interpreted as magical or mesmeric powers and some people were therefore afraid to approach Him. Once two farmers who feared to meet

Him were travelling in their carts loaded with cotton. Suddenly they saw from the opposite direction Sahajānand Swāmi coming with His kāthi followers. They immediately hid their faces in the cotton heaps. Sahajānand Swāmi saw this from a distance and smiled. He decided to meet these farmers face to face, relieve them of their fear and lift them to the lofty heights of spiritual realms. He stopped near the cart and dragged their faces out of the cotton heaps and threw on them His graceful glance. Immediately they went into samādhi and saw the beautiful and blissful realm of the Lord. Their tiny world was lost and they experienced the unbounded joy of the divine abode and its Lord. When they awoke, they immediately prostrated before the Lord. With tears in their eyes and with folded hands, they said, 'Lord! You have showered unlimited grace on us. We have known today that you are the Ultimate God and are glad to be laden with the unrelievable burden of gratitude. We pray we may ever remain grateful to You for Your compassionate grace.' With these words they again prostrated before Him for further blessings.

Sahajānand Swāmi smiled and said, 'You are ever blessed by Me. Forget Me not and you will be led to My abode after death.' And then, waving His hand, He bade them good-bye and proceeded on His way.

With His Paramhansas He enjoyed sumptuous feasts without attachment as He could serve them in great profusion. At times He used to overfeed them and pour milk over them! The Paramhansas indulged in happy reminiscences of these divine episodes and enjoyed the blissful image of the Master. Sahajānand Swāmi never encouraged puritanism as that would deprive His disciples of the joys of life filled with the nectar of devotion. That blissful rās emanating from the divinity personified could be enjoyed only if the Master freely and openly associated with them. The rās, the Holi and Vasant festivals were all arranged not for sensory enjoyment but for deriving joy from the divinity manifesting before them. That was all for the benefit of the disciples, and the Master amply exhibited all the beautiful features of His life before them for divine reminiscence. This was the only nectar to be drunk by them up to the brink for ultimate transmigration into the divine realms.

21 Last Phases

In the earlier stages of His life, Sahajānand Swāmi did not want to build temples, inasmuch as intelligent and ignorant people would be led to the image worship and would fail to appreciate the value of the living God or Guru who alone could, within a short period, regenerate the spiritual aura latent in their hearts. The idolatry, except for the regenerated few, offered only the equipment for moral armour, and depreciated the value of love and knowledge. As Aldous Huxley puts it:

> The moralists cease to be realistic and commit idolatry inasmuch as they worship not God, but their own ethical ideals, inasmuch as they treat virtue as an end in itself and not as the necessary condition of knowledge and love for God – a knowledge and love without which that virtue will never be made perfect or even socially effective.[1]

But He had already imparted the requisite knowledge. He had taught them to live a life of transcendent love which overcame all worldly barriers and recognised only the ultimate Guru and His associates. This divine love inculcated the seed of compassion in one's heart, to uplift humanity from the miseries of life. Sahajānand Swāmi wanted every disciple to be the apostle of God, to work for Him and to save humanity from the perils of worldly living. Mere image worship alone would restrict the mental sphere beyond the recognition of

---

[1] Huxley, Aldous, The Perennial Philosophy, London, 1946.

ethical and moral values. But Sahajānand Swāmi encouraged that type of idolatry by which the devotee would realise the living Guru or Paramātmā in the image and work according to His will.[2]

The approach to a Guru is equally beset with danger, inasmuch as the necessary requisites of a realised Guru may not be thoroughly recognised and the mumukshu might be misled. The sacerdotal authority which spurious gurus acquire over other people leads to antinomianism, to reframing moral codes to permit all kinds of harmful indulgences. Such individuals undermine spiritual discipline and bring spiritual regress for credulous people. The mythological history of India includes many such gurus who had become spurious gods and wrecked all moral and ethical standards.

Knowledge is essential for the realisation of Brahman. Only the Brahmanised Guru can infuse this knowledge and kindle the light within. One must therefore strive for knowledge by approaching a Brahmanised Guru, in the Upanishadic tradition, and rise step by step. The wisdom to distinguish between Sat and Asat (truth and untruth) is also an essential factor in spiritual progress. Otherwise, as Huxley puts it:

> For ordinary, nice, unregenerate people to accept this truth by hearsay and to act upon it in practice, is merely to court disaster. All the dismal story of antinomianism is there to warn us of what happens when men and women make practical applications of a merely intellectual and unrealised theory that all is God and God is all.[3]

Explaining Pantheism, Shree P. N. Shrinivāsāchāri says that its 'fatal defect is the denial of the evilness of the evil, and the reality of the moral consciousness. The all-God-theory

---

[2] Vachanāmrit, Gadhadā Sec. I-68
[3] Huxley, Aldous, The Perennial Philosophy, London, 1946

destroys God and the Self that seeks God and gives man a logical and moral holiday.[4]

Sahajānand Swāmi in one of His discourses warns against the sacrilegious activities of such spurious gurus who preach that the 'whole universe is Brahman and therefore divine. The mumukshu should therefore realise that all the females and males are the forms of Nārāyan. If the mind is poignantly attached to them, he should meditate upon them that they are the forms of Brahman.' 'In interpreting the scriptures so pervertedly such a guru has an ulterior motive to satisfy his own and carnal desires. But the fruit of it is "the most devilish hell for him.... One should not hear scriptures from the mouth of such asat purush."'[5]

He thought that image worship would offer the best solution by promoting moral and spiritual regeneration of all. Except for the negligible drawback of being too idealistic to cultivate virtues at the cost of divine knowledge and love, He believed that idolatry did not offer any danger. He therefore decided to reopen this path of upāsanā (worship) for the masses by building temples.

Once in Panchālā when He had a serious illness, Muktānand Swāmi came to Him and examined His pulse. Muktānand was shocked at the illness of the Master. He began to shed tears which fell on the forehead of the Master. The Master looked up and asked Muktānand, 'You seem to be crying. Why?'

With folded hands and tears flowing from his eyes, Muktānand said, 'Lord! I feel that You are thinking of reverting to Your abode. The world would not know that the Highest Reality – Parabrahman -- had descended on this earth, since You do not leave behind You a traditional school to promote and preach Your doctrines and to worship Your

---

[4] Srinivasachari, P. N., The Philosophy of Vishishtadvaita, Adya, 1943
[5] Vachanāmrit, Loyā 11.

divine form. Even small people have built up their traditions to be followed by their disciples.' So saying, Muktānand paused.

The Master looked meaningfully towards Muktānand and said, 'Swāmi! What you say is correct. I have now decided to recover from illness. I promise you that I shall fulfil your desire and build up a lofty tradition for the best of the seekers.' The solemn words of the Master penetrated Muktānand's heart and he experienced a thrilling sensation. The history of temple building started with this significant incident.

Temples were built at Vadtāl, Bhuj,Ahmedābād, Junāgadh, Muli and Gadhpur during His lifetime. He personally took an interest in the construction work and at times participated and worked in carrying the stones and bricks. He explained that there was dignity in the service of God and of the devotees attached to God. The huge temples, with amazing architectural ingenuity, were designed by sādhus and were completed by the labour of sādhus and other skilled disciples. These temples today offer opportunities of worship to hundreds of thousands of people and have proved of great inspiration.

The next problem was the management and administration of the temples. Since the sādhus were restricted from even touching coins, they were prevented from undertaking this duty. Sahajānand Swāmi thought of entrusting the affairs of the temples to honest and intelligent disciples. One Gopi Bhatt, a brāhmin disciple, was given the management of the temple at Ahmedābād. He was also instructed to take care of the sādhus and to provide for their needs.

But after some time it was found that Gopi Bhatt was mismanaging the affairs of the temple for his own interest. He neglected the care of the sādhus. Complaints were sent to Sahajānand Swāmi who came to Ahmedābād. With the help of Brahmānand Swāmi, He skilfully managed to take back possession of the temple.

However, the problem of management persisted. Afterwards some of the leading sādhus and other disciples suggested that if the Master consented, His own relatives who had inherited the stamp of divinity, might be called here and entrusted with the affairs of the temples. It was ultimately agreed and two saints were sent to Chhapaiyā to call for the the relatives of the Master.

The meeting of the relatives after a long period of nearly thirty-five years, presented scenes of happy rejoicing. They all lovingly scolded Ghanshyām, who to them was still a small lad, for neglecting them for so many years. Everybody was in a joyful mood, recollecting the episodes of Ghanshyām in His days of childhood.

After this happy reunion, Sahajānand Swāmi chose the two sons, Ayodhyāprasād and Raghuvir, the former of His elder brother Rāmpratāp and the latter of His younger brother Ichhārām, and adopted them, installing them as the Āchāryās or the heads of the two dioceses, namely Ahmedābād and Vadtāl. With due reverence, the whole fellowship accepted them as their spiritual heads. The code of conduct and the duties of these Āchāryās were specifically prescribed. They were required to abide by these, failing which they could be forced to resign. The difficult problem of management and administration was thus solved. Temple activities were at last running smoothly.

These were also the early days of the British regime in India and the British officers had a very tough fight to clear the country of warlike elements. These officers, without Upanishadic wisdom, nevertheless watched with great interest the working of Shree Sahajānand Swāmi, who eradicated the antisocial elements from the lands of Gujarāt and Saurāshtra without holding a weapon. With His spiritual army, He killed the inner enemies of human beings and made them really humane. Sir John Malcolm, then Governor of Bombay, was prompted to meet this unique personality. He extended to Him the invitation to meet him at Rājkot. The invitation was courteously worded and expressed the keenest desire of the Governor to pay respects to this towering personality. Sahajānand Swāmi received the invitation but was unable to proceed to Rājkot at the time as He was ill. He therefore declined respectfully. But the Governor could not resist the temptation of meeting Him as soon as possible and sent another invitation, expressing his own willingness to come to Gadhpur if the Master was still unable to come to Rājkot. Sahajānand Swāmi immediately prepared to proceed to Rājkot and sent the news in advance.

The Governor gave a sumptuous reception for the Master and His retinue. The great dignity and the power attached to his position as Governor melted at the first sight of this Divine Personality. The Governor received the Master in his great apartment, which was profusely decorated, and offered Him a seat. He stood opposite Him with folded hands. Bowing once again he said, 'May the Lord bless me, and may the Lord bless my enemies.'

The audience was amazed to hear this wonderful boon that the Governor of a conquering race had asked for, and anxiously awaited the Master's reply. The Master, with a pleasing smile, gracefully said, 'The Lord will always bless you. The blessed soul always wishes for the good of all. So long as you represent the ideals of a true ruler, you shall continue to rule this land.' The Governor heard with rapt attention all the words of the Master spoken in Hindi. He was pleased, as the spontaneous message of the Master specifically instructed the rulers to uphold the rules of equity and justice. He felt that this was a man from another world, who had come to uphold not only the scales of justice but also to foster spirituality. He again bowed down to the Master.

Shortly afterwards, various costly gifts and sweets were

offered to the Master. The Master accepted them and immediately distributed them amongst the members of the assembly. The kings of various States who had accepted the sovereignty of the British, were present. They were amazed at the Master's humility, and realised His greatness. The Master then rose up and prepared to leave when the Governor again came before Him and requested the Master to give him any available gospel written by Him. Immediately Shikshāpatri[1] was produced and the Master gave it to the Governor, who respected the book by touching it his head. The Master and His retinue then left. A colourful military band played stirring music and the soldiers offered the salute.

The Master came back to Gadhpur. He had now decided that it was time to return to His divine abode, and exhibited signs of illness. He expressed His desire to Muktānand and Gopālānand and advised them to have patience. The whole fellowship was entrusted to the care of Gopālānand Swāmi, whose every word was to be implichitly obeyed as the command of the Master. He sent Brahmānand to Junāgadh, and asked him to send Gunātitānand Swāmi to Gadhpur immediately.

An atmosphere of utter melancholy prevailed at Gadhpur. Crowds of people poured into the town as they learnt of the sad illness of their Master. The piercing entreaties of the most beloved disciples did not detract the Master from His decision. In S.Y. 1886 on the 10th day of the bright half of Jyeshtha month at 11.00 a.m., the Master enacted the last episode of His life and returned to His divine abode, Brahmadhām. The people were engulfed in great pangs of sorrow and grief.

The funeral rites were performed by Raghuvirji, Gopālānand and Gunātitānand Swāmi, who held that the life of the Master on earth was absolutely divine and He was

---

[1] This Shikshāpatri was passed on by Sir John Malcolm to relatiaves after he died. Bodelian Library, Oxford, now preserves this historic treasure in its Museum.

completely free from birth and death. It was explained to all by these two veterans that even though the Master had passed away, He continued to manifest on earth for upholding Bhāgawat Dharma through His spiritual hierachy. The history of Bhāgawat Dharma which flourished with equal vigour under the most dynamic spiritual successors of Shree Sahajānand Swāmi, each a strong and impressive disciple of the Master, is both thrilling and interesting.

22 Spiritual Heritage

For the survival of Sampradāya, the spiritual heritage must be maintained. *Amarkosha* defines Sampradāya - as *Sampradāyo gurukramaha*. One after another, each Guru, having established harmony or identification with his predecessor, must lead the Sampradāya for its successful functioning. The Guru gives knowledge to the disciple and the disciple receives it to be again imparted to his disciple. However, the primordial guru is Parabrahman, Gurureva Parambrahma[1] and the first disciple is Brahman or Akshar. The relationship between Akshar and Purushottam is akin to sharir-shariri bhāv. But when each manifests separately and contemporarily, then the divine harmony between them is not apprehended by all. The co-operative identity between Brahman and Parabrahman is imperceptible inasmuch as the self-existent entity of Brahman is visible, and inspite of the feeling of separatism of Brahman from Parabrahman, Brahman is lost in Parabrahman by the feeling of absolute attachment. This is the relationship or divine harmony required to be maintained between Guru and shishya (pupil). In following the Gurukrama, shishya does not become the Guru or God, but exhibits all the redemptive attributes of God or conversely God or Guru works through him. This is the spiritual legacy, enjoyed by the shishya.

Swāminārāyan was the ultimate God and therefore in His life and philosophy, He amply exhibited that God does not merely create but sustains the jivas, and does not merely

---

[1] Br. Achintyānandji, Harililākalpataru 2-28-22

sustain them but elevates them. The knowledge of His Self in His humanised form that is both immanent and transcendent, with infinite greatness and profundity of powers, is the only path for ultimate salvation. But when He is not on earth, the saint who has bequeathed His spiritual legacy is equally redemptive.[2] This is how His redemptive will is put into action for elevating the jivas.

Swāminārāyan has enunciated the Divine Law that either God or His saint always manifests on earth for the ultimate redemption of jivas. It is not simply the redemptive will but the redemptive action of Shree Swāminārāyan that He had come not merely to sustain but to elevate the jivas, which He had passed to His successor to sustain and take on the upward ascent. The law of redemption is thus made operative.

In order that the continuous manifestation of God is felt on earth, the instrument for such revelation should either exist, emerge or descend. Such an instrument is either pure Brahman or one which has identified itself with Brahman, having been fully Brahmanised. Pure Brahman has absolutely no trace of Māyā, as its content is only Parabrahman.[3] He is the body or the divine abode – Brahmadhām – of Parabrahman and sustains Him and the infinite number of released jivas. Still by its concomitant power He inspires Prakriti-Purush, all the cosmic gods and the demigods. Akshar Brahman therefore was the first divine hierarch, who bequeathed the redemptive will and action of Shree Swāminārāyan. Shree Gunātitānand Swāmi, the incarnation of Akshar Brahman, was the first divine hierarch of Shree Swāminārāyan after He reverted to His abode.

But Brahman in the humanised form would naturally reveal various human limitations. How then is this incompatibility with total divinity to be reconciled? In His usual laconic style, Shree Swāminārāyan defines Brahman as a saint first, since He

---

[2] Vachanāmrit, Vadtāl 10   [3] Ibid., Sārangpur 6

felt that the monadic intelligence of jivas would not be able to conceive the vast and infinite attributes of Brahman which are to be realised and experienced by the awakened jnatritvashakti or chidrupa shakti inherently attached to jiva. He says:

> He is the real sādhu, who has the knowledge of his self as Ātmā, who implicitly observes all the precepts attached to his āshram (stage in life) and who has the knowledge of God. The other attributes attached to a sādhu he may reveal or he may not, according to the conditions of time and place, but these three are the essential conditions required to be fulfilled by a true sādhu.[4]

Elaborating still further, He says:

> 'The saint who has full control over his cognitive and conative organs, and is never led away by their influence, who always indulges in activities relating to God, observes fully the five precepts, namely nirmān, nirlobh, nisswād, nishkām and nissneh (humility, non-avarice, indifference to taste, desirelessness, emotional detachment) and who being Brahmanised still offers worship to God, is to be worshipped together with God with equal devotion.[5]

The *Brahmasutra Upāsatraividhyate* explains the threefold forms of worship to be offered to God, namely God in full resplendence with all His attributes, God with His vibhuti or the best devotee, and finally God in His Parā Swarup.[6]

Such a saint represents and manifests God totally in all His resplendence, infinite attributes and profundity of powers. In one of His Vachanamrits, He says:

> Everybody desires to worship God, but one who has

---

[4] Vachanāmrit, Sārangpur 12.

[5] Ibid., Gadhadā Sec. III-26

[6] Gunavishishtasya, vibhutivishishtasya, parasya brahman upāsyāt.
        - Shatānand Muni, Shikshāpatri Bhāshya, p. 449

nown God, has realised Him and who has been fully Brahmanised, totally manifests God within himself. His realisation gives him a divine vision with which he visualises that the architect of the whole cosmos and all the cosmic forces is the God visible before him in human form, and these cosmic forces are sustained by Him only. There is no other entity beyond Him to whom such doership can be assigned.

Again, such a saint by virtue of his realisation is in a position to maintain the equanimity between the duality of honour and insult, the charms of beauty and the repulsion of decayed forms, the heaps of gold and the heaps of earth. Only such a pure Brahmanised Guru can sustain God and become the channel for the working of the Divine Law of Redemption.[7] Such a saint or Guru, is the embodiment of Hari or Govinda.[8]

Such a jnāni or saint carefully observes the five main precepts and abstains from the sense-objects like the wise mumukshus. However, inwardly he is above Māyā and has overcome all the sense-objects. He experiences a state of deep sleep towards the world[9] even in his waking state (yasyām jāgrati bhutāni sānishā pashyato munehe).

The abstaining from sense-objects as if fearful of them does not amount to bādhitānuvrutti, as it is not the persistence of the trace of avidyā, but is an aspect benevolently preserved for the benefit of the followers.

Describing the absolutely Brahmanised condition of such a saint, Shree Swāminārāyan says:

Such a saint has the vision to see here as well as yonder like one who sees the āmlā fruit in his palm. He has gained a pure Brāhmic vision which evolves shuddha

---

7 Vachanāmrit, Gadhadā Sec. I-27.
8 Vedras, p. 146.
9 Ibid., p. 144

chitta and destroys the vāsanāmaya chitta. The shuddha chitta which is passive and sentient, knows itself as Brahman. With this knowledge it realises the transitory nature of the world. The chitta is focused on Brahman only. In this released state one remains above the pains and pleasures of the world, conscious of being separate from the body. Just as a baked seed loses its ingredients for further generation, such a saint whose activities relate to God only, is not bound by his actions.[10]

He is the saint, jnāni or the Guru. He is the cause of final salvation. He is Brahman. By his Brahma Vidyā, his disciple attains a sentient body — a new life,[11] which resuscitates the gurukrama.

Ātmā is realised only by the grace of such a Guru. The luminosity of Ātmā dissolves Māyā in the way in which the icy stones are melted by the rays of sun. Māyā persists only until the Ātmā is not realised – ātmajnānāt jagat bhāti. Such a released soul always enjoys the proximity of Nārāyan and even although embodied, has no attachment towards the body. Just as the blind cannot see the beauty of the physical world, the released soul does not see his body. With Brāhmic vision he sees Brahman only.[12]

Since embodiment is the association with the body, one may feel that it is incompatible with the release which is disassociation from the body. However, it is not the body but the association of a vāsnāmaya chitta which creates bondage. Chitta is the monadic form of mahat tattva, the great evolute from Purush and Prakriti and sustains jagat in a subtle form.[13] The body which is composed of five elements, namely earth, water, light, wind and space, can be overcome by controlling

---

10 Vedras, p. 166-7.
11 Ibid., p. 182
12 Ibid., p. 151
13 Vachanāmrit, Gadhadā Sec. I-12

the quintessence of the five elements, namely smell, taste, beauty, touch and sound respectively. It is therefore manas, buddhi and desire which emanate from chitta that create bondage. The persistence of these elements, which is nescience, is incompatible with release. Chitta therefore takes away all knowledge. Its nescience is removed when it is offered to a Brahmanised Guru.

The manifestation of a Guru in the process of a divine hierarchy is therefore vital for dispelling the darkness of his followers and to resuscitate the sampradāyic teachings. However, if the contention is entertained that nescience persists with the association of the body, the living Guru, a representative of God, cannot offer ultimate deliverance, and consequently release would become impossible. The approach to a Guru therefore could become futile.

The various schools of thought explain this particular aspect of Shree Swāminārāyan's philosophy in different ways. According to Shatānand Muni, 'Nitya Muktas' who are conspicuous by virtue of their sustaining the Bhāgawadbhāv, are fit to be worshipped, since their identity is lost in this Bhāgawadbhāv.[14] The ultimate worship in this mode of Bhakti is offered to the Lord through such Nitya Muktas. They descend on earth only by the wish of the Lord,[15] and not of their own desire or attachment, of which they have none.

Another school of thought holds that the eternal Brahman only continuously manifests on earth in one form or another, since He is the ultimate body which sustains Parabrahman fully in all respects. The Nitya Muktas and others enjoy in gradation the bliss of Parabrahman according to the degree in which they have realised Him in regard to His infinite greatness and profundity of powers. The aprithaka siddhabhāv between Brahman and Parabrahman is therefore

---

[14] Shikshāpatri Bhāshya, p. 449
[15] Vachanāmrit, Gadhadā Sec. 1-71

unique and justifies the total revelation of Parabrahman through Brahman only. The salvation scheme is thus made perfect.

The spiritual hierarchy is thoroughly maintained through either of the above mediums. The maintenance of this hierarchy has enlivened this Sampradāya since the total revelation of Parabrahman is being felt and experienced through such Gurus. The recently living personality Swāmi Shree Jnānjivandāsji was the fourth in spiritual lineage of the original founder Shree Swāminārāyan.

Swāmi Shree Jnānjivandāsji (Yogiji Mahārāj)

Born in a poor family in the village Dhāri, near Amreli (Saurāshtra) this child, a prodigy in spiritual activism from a small age, exhibited no signs of worldly attachment even when he grew up.

He went to school, responding to the routine of a family life, but he had no interest in learning, as for him the chanting of the 'Swāminārāyan' mantra only was the best learning. However, he scored well in school, where his profound devotion impelled him to impart spiritual learning to his fellow students.

He left home at the age of fourteen and joined the Swāminārāyan Temple of Junāgadh (Saurāshtra). His rustic and unsophisticated living did not disclose the potentialities of the divine harmony with God that he enjoyed even at this age. He was assigned various duties which he carried out as willingly as if he was serving God Himself. Some time afterwards, he was initiated into Vaishnavi Dikshā and renamed Swāmi Jnānjivandāsji. As he focused all his cognitive faculties only on God even while performing the duties assigned to him, the sādhus of the temple also called him by the loving name of 'Yogi'.

After some years, he left the Swāminārāyan Temple of

Swāmi Shree Jnānjivandāsji

His Supreme Divine Holiness, Swãmi Shree Pramukh Swãmi Mahãrãj Shãstri Shree Nãrãyanswarupdãsji

Junāgadh and joined Swāmi Shree Yagnapurushdāsji, a God-intoxicated saint who had inherited the spiritual legacy of his Guru Shree Prāgji Bhakta, and desired to reveal Gunātitānand Swāmi and Shree Swāminārāyan in their divine and transcendental forms of Akshar and Purushottam or Brahman and Parabrahman.

The strength and tenacity that Swāmi Shree Yagnapurushdāsji possessed by his all-absorbing divinity, and the truth of the tenets that he preached, made way for the all-out emergence of a new school of thought, which reconciled Swāmi and Nārāyan as Akshar and Purushottam.

Swāmi Shree Jnānjivandāsji enjoying esoteric bliss by his total accord with Paramātmā, realised the truthfulness of the mission of Swāmi Shree Yagnapurushdāsji, and joined him to further that mission. He came to see the futility of dogmatic truths, followed merely to maintain tradition, and felt that real knowledge is available only by the process of cultivating Ātmic consciousness inspired by a saint in divine contact with God. For revealing this truth he preferred to work under Swāmi Shree Yagnapurushdāsji.

This movement gradually developed a great momentum. The spiritual ties between Swāmi Shree Yagnapurushdāsji and Swāmi Shree Jnānjivandāsji were closely woven. However, the exuberance of bhakti for his Lord as well as for his Guru Swāmi Shree Yagnapurushdāsji, made him a humble disciple only. His Brāhmic consciousness was completely obliterated in the profound devotion of his dedication of self at the lotus feet of his Guru, as he enjoyed the absolute bliss emanating from the divine self of the Guru, who was to him the personal manifestation of the Lord Himself. His vision, conditioned by this intense devotion, recognised none except God. Just as the mirror reflects our own image, His God-conscious vision reflected the image of God in every devotee. The followers of Swāmi Shree Yagnapurushdāsji respected him as they did their Guru.

The truth of a tenet is in its realisation and not in its interpretation, however learned or intelligent that interpretation may be. As people began to realise the inherent truth of Shree Swāmināṝāyan's philosophy as explained by Swāmi Shree Yagnapurushdāsji who had the aparokshānubhav (direct experience), they joined this new school of thought. As the movement developed fully, Swāmi Shree Yagnapurushdāsji, who was by now eighty-seven, thought of reverting to the Divine abode. He therefore entrusted the mission to the care of Swāmi Shree Jnānjivandāsji, his direct spiritual descendant.

Swāmi Shree Jnānjivandāsji, affectionately known as Shree Yogiji Mahāṝāj, followed the footsteps of his Guru. The compassion that filled his heart impelled him to retrieve the people from their attachment to worldly life. He travelled incessantly from village to village and from town to town to transfuse in everyone the divine contact of God which he was enjoying. His profound saintliness, absolute celibacy, exuberant devotion, total detachment – all these redemptive attributes made an indelible impression on the hearts of true seekers. He often said in great humour that one who comes in the clutches of the divine is never spared for worldly enjoyments. The great interest that he evinced in the life of every disciple, and the infinite flow of compassion from his heart for them, one and all, bound them spiritually to him with links that grew stronger every day.

The tremendous influence that he exercised on educated youths by his all-absorbing love curbed their exasperating vitality and channelised it into the spiritual field. Many of these youngsters who once denied belief in God and moral codes, became the meek servants of God by his influence; some of them adopted the robes of sādhus.

He spoke little. But his mode of living was a great message

itself for a divine life. His humour and light sarcasm penetrated within, as they were laden with perfect spiritual wisdom, and kept the disciple always awakened against the vicissitudes of a worldly life. To him, the value of life was not merely in renunciation but in a harmonious living to the tune of God.

In every town and village, he started spiritual centres which were regularly attended by his disciples. He did not encourage mere spiritual discourses but desired mental awareness to be cultivated in life so as to prevent worldly forces from penetrating within and disturbing the inner peace. The band of workers that he raised bring out boldly – by their living, service and sense of love and devotion – the fact that man is made in the image of God.

His tours in East and South Africa were undertaken only with a view to infusing in the hearts of those people the principles of ethical religion. The Africans hailed him as 'moongu' or God, as he visited their wretched huts and patted their backs with affection. Even though they did not understand his language, his face radiant with love of God, inspired them. A discarded race meant only for menial jobs was thus redeemed from the troubles of their lot.

Many of the Indians who had migrated there had become confirmed addicts of wine and meat-eating. This hedonist way of living recognised no moral or ethical code. However, Shree Swāmiji's preachings, his way of living, his unbounded love and heart full of compassion all had a great impact on them. They gradually began to realise the potential values of human life and the obligations attached to it. They could see that Swāmiji never imposed his sacerdotal authority on anyone for the observance of moral codes. On the contrary, he accepted even the vilest sinners, and his compassion towards them transformed them into devout devotees. The history of his tours in Africa was marked by many notable instances, incidents in which the free play of his divinity brought about a fusion of the conflicting elements of life.

He was living for God only. His God-intoxicated life vibrated the atmosphere in tune to his living. Bliss emanated from his person and wherever he moved people thronged around him in thousands. Even at a ripe age, his spiritual activism propelled the wheels of ethics and morality.

One of his final great tasks on this earth was to establish the Shree Swāminārāyan Mission in England. In May 1970, at the age of eighty, he travelled to London, where he dedicated the first Shree Swāminārāyan Temple. On 14 June 1970, the inhabitants of London witnessed a great Rath Yātrā (procession) to celebrate this event. In spite of heavy rain clouds, the procession was blessed by sunshine, and not a drop of rain fell.

Afterwards at the Temple in London, Shree Yogiji Mahārāj performed the Murti Pratishthā (dedication of images).

Soon after his return to India, he passed away to His divine abode Akshardhām on Saturday 23 January, 1971.

His successor, Swāmi Shree Nārāyanswarupdāsji, was born Wednesday 9 December 1921 at Chānsad (District Barodā). In his pre-initiation days he was known as 'Shāntibhāi'. He came in contact with Swāmi Shree Yagnapurushdāsji when only a youth, and was invited to join the Fellowship at the age of sixteen. He was initiated into the Bhāgawati Dikshā and given the name Swāmi Nārāyanswarupdāsji. On first seeing him, Shree Yogiji Mahārāj commented, 'A divine soul has come to lead the Fellowship to greater and greater heights.'

His spiritual potentialities were rapidly apparent to Swāmi Shree Yagnapurushdāsji, who eventually appointed him head of the Fellowship, working under the spiritual guidance of Shree Yogiji Mahārāj. Under his able guidance, Swāmi Shree Nārāyanswarupdāsji advanced in spiritual identity until Shree

Yogiji Mahārāj, during his own last days, instructed the whole Fellowship to work under the command of Shree Nārāyanswarupdāsji, who had reached the greatest spiritual heights and became a pure vessel for the total revelation of the Lord.

Now popularly known as Shree Pramukh Swāmi, his divine personality has completely filled the gap left by the passing of Shree Yogiji Mahārāj, and the Fellowship experiences the divine working of the Lord through him. He is the fifth great hierarch of the Lord, and continues the spiritual heritage for the redemption of humanity.

PART TWO

23 Vachanamritam

The Concept of God

Vachanāmritam is the scriptural text containing the discourses by Shree Swāminārāyan delivered in the assemblies of saints and bhaktas. There are 262 such discourses held at separate places – at Gadhadā, Sārangpur, Kāriyāni, Panchālā, Loyā, Ahmedābād and Vadtāl. From amongst the thousands of such discourses, these selected 262 are chronologically arranged and ably compiled and edited by Gopālānand Swāmi, Muktānand Swāmi, Shukānand Swāmi and Nityānand Swāmi, His saint-disciples of unparalleled scholastic genius. Because of the clarity of expression and lucidity of the exposition of the subjects mainly centred on the knowledge of absolute truth, the text is thoroughly comprehensive. The discourses are scattered and brief. Polemical references are avoided, except only where they are necessary in order to understand thoroughly the problem of natural theology.

Vachanāmritam is a revealed text, inasmuch as the words have come straight from the mouth of Shree Swāminārāyan who was the Ultimate Reality Himself. He spoke with an authority of His own while explaining the divine forms of Brahman and Parabrahman, and the path of ultimate redemption – upāsanā.

These esoteric words of wisdom, delivered with great compassion, penetrate straight to the heart of a mumukshu or seeker. Since the true seeker has a desire to know the Ultimate Reality, problems of absolute truth are discussed fully and specifically in this text.

According to Shree Swāminārāyan, God is transcendent, immanent, suprapersonal and personal. For the redemption of many jivas He manifests on the earth either Himself or through His saint in harmony with Him, as provided by His own divine law.[1] This knowledge of God or His saint in His absolute divinity and profundity of powers is not immediately available to jivas because of their imperfections and finiteness. Spinoza correctly puts it, 'that which is in itself and is conceived by means of itself, i.e. that the conception of which can be formed without the aid of conception of any other thing.' God in person has to reveal Himself to give the knowledge of Himself. By this revelation in human form, finiteness or limitation is not imposed on God nor is His transcendence renounced nor His divine powers restricted. This is very explicitly explained by Shree Swāminārāyan in this text.

The path of bhakti (devotion) is shown by Shree Swāminārāyan for the journey of the jiva to the ultimate boundless realm of Brahmadhām, the abode of released souls. The empirical self assimilated with the physical body has to realise its purer self, which is Brahman. The concept of bhakti in Shree Swāminārāyan's philosophy consists in the apprehension and fulfilment of Ekāntik dharma which includes swadharma, i.e. ahimsā and brahmacharya; jñān, i.e. the knowledge of one's own self detached from the empirical self, and vairāgya, which aims at detachment from enticing sense-objects and also everything evolved from Prakriti which appears to offer extravagant joy. The supreme God, who is the most beautiful divine personality, who is devoid of all evil and full of all goodness, is to be sought as one would engage for a marriage. This matrimonial love for God is the essence of true bhakti.[2]

---

[1] Vachanāmrit, Vadtāl 19.   [2] Ibid., Gadhadā Sec. II-10

Shree Swāminārāyan says, 'Shraddhā is one of the sixteen sādhanās for attaining that exalted position of service at the lotus feet of Lord which the released souls have been enjoying in Akshardhām.' According to Erich Frank, 'It is only in the experience of faith that God is felt.'[3] The theory of knowledge expounded by Shree Swāminārāyan clearly explains that jiva with his inherent knowledge (chidrupa shakti) can know God. The chidshakti of jiva is the attribute of Parabrahman. Therefore with this attribute the jiva can know Parabrahman. Or, in the words of Shree Swāminārāyan, Parabrahman inspires within the knowledge of His own Self.[4]

Shree Swāminārāyan has referred to Himself in this text as God – Parabrahman. He did not speak out of any ego, or in the ways of Vāmdev[5] or Prahlād[6] who had attained cosmic consciousness. He spoke because He *was* God. To eliminate any doubt from the minds of the sceptics or rationalists, He made His position clear while addressing the Paramhansās in one of His discourses, when He said, 'Oh, ye Paramhansās! The great and the learned out of you may come near Me. I desire to reveal before you the knowledge of My form. I do not do so out of any ostentation or to exalt my position.'[7] And then in the same sonorous voice He continued:

My cognitive organs (jnānendriyas) and conative organs (karmendriyas) are always drawn inward and remain in the inner recesses of my heart (hridayākāsh) wherein I see immense light. In that light there is God seated – young, and with a dark complexion, and that is I. You are all seated there before Me, but this town of Gadhpur, this verandah, etc., are not visible to Me. When you get this knowledge of My form in all its infinity and profundity,

---

[3] Frank, Erich, Philosophical Understanding and Religious Truth, London, 1945

[4] Vachanāmrit, Gadhadā Sec. 1-51 – Brihadaranyaka, 1-4-10

[5] Rushir Vāmadevaha pratipede aham Manur Suryash cha iti.

[6] Vishnu Purāna

[7] Vachanāmrti, Gadhadā Sec. II-13.

you will be relieved of all worldly bondage. You all see Me and feel that you all know Me, but when you get this vision you will be able to overcome all the vices and passions connected with the physical self. That light is the light of Akshar Brahman and the God seated in that self-luminous Akshardhām is Parabrahman – that is I.[8]

Spoken in an ecstatic mood and in all spontaneity, these words of Shree Swāminārāyan, full of compassion, were not to impose His authority or to instruct His followers, but to expose the hitherto unrevealed fact or phenomenon before them for the redemption of jivas. He wanted to inspire the jivas to start a spiritual enquiry about the unknown Reality, the relevation of which had so far remained beyond the understanding of many, even those with subtle insight. Because of the divine personality that He possessed and the dynamic will with which He started the spiritual and ethical regeneration for the redemption of many jivas, Shree Manilal Pārekh in his book *Shree Swāminārāyan* referred to Him as 'God in redemptive action'.

Nowhere is the description of God so vivid and so authoritative as in this text given by Shree Swāminārāyan – the God, who came down from the realms of infinity into finity, without losing His character of infiniteness, transcendence, immanence and divinity. Shree Swāminārāyan is close to Huxley's concept when he describes God as immanent as well as transcendent, suprapersonal and also personal. Huxley says that transformation of consciousness, which is 'enlightenment', 'deliverance', 'salvation', comes only when God is thought of in this manner.

Shrimad Bhāgawat says God has created buddhi, indriyas, manas and prānas for jivas to enable them to transmigrate into ever higher regions and to know Him by realising their own

---

[8] Ibid.

Ātmā.[9] This being so, why should God remain beyond the reach of those who have focused their buddhi, indriyas, manas and prānas in Him? For this purpose therefore He assumes the human form, mingles with human beings and becomes known to those who purify themselves by serving the feet of such a saint who is in absolute communion with Him. The purified buddhi devoid of vāsanā, is the integral part of jiva and is also known as Jnātritvashakti. The jiva through this jnātritvashakti or consciousness, pervades the whole body. It is only by this buddhi or intellect that he can know God. As Thomas Aquinas puts it, 'Intellect and reason are not two powers, but distinct as the perfect from the imperfect... The intellect means an intimate penetration of truth, the reason, enquiry and discourse.'

According to Shree Swāminārāyan, God does not descend – He simply manifests. When He manifests in human form, He assumes the body of parā prakriti.[10] But as it is difficult to apprehend this divine revelation in its proper perspective by the intelligent as well as the non-intelligent, by rationality as well as doubt, Shree Swāminārāyan explained in the assembly of His devotees and saints thus, 'Some say, God when in human form has a body composed of twenty-four tattvas evolved out of prakriti, and some say that there are no tattvas in God as He is fully sentient (chaitanya-swarup). But God is divine inherently and apparently, even when appearing in human form.'[11] 'When He manifests on the earth, He leaves none of His powers or attributes behind in His divine abode. Therefore His very contact transfigures the prakriti and the twenty-four tattvas into total divinity.'[12]

---

[9] Buddhindriyamanaha prānān janānām asrajat prabhuhu

Mātrārtham cha bhavārtham cha hyātmane kalpanāya cha

    – Shrimad Bhāgawata, 10-87-2.

[10] Na tasya prākrutā murtirmānsmedosthi sambhavā. - Vāraha, A-75-44.

[11] Vachanāmrit, Gadhadā Sec. II-17.

[12] Ibid., Vadtāl, 7.

During the discourses on Bhāgawat, while explaining the meaning of the phrase *yatra trisargo mrishā*, He said:

The sattva, rajas and tamas, the three gunas which constitute the nature of Māyā, the five bhutas, namely the earth, water, fire, wind and space, the four antahkaranas, namely manas, buddhi, chitta and ahamkār, all these do not exist in the form of God. By His own divine form He dispels the darkness of māyā and shines forth as the Eternal Reality. Even when He assumes human form, He possesses the same attributes which He has in His transcendental divine form residing in Brahmadhām. This divine form of Brahmadhām and the human form on the earth are one.[13]

It is by His divine grace that He appears before the human eyes in the form which is sought by them.[14] Shatānand Muni therefore describes this divine phenomenon as 'swarupaikya' and says that there is no difference between the human form of God here and the one residing in Brahmadhām.[15] They are one.

Ultimate salvation rests upon realising this knowledge of God in His infinite divinity and profundity of powers.[16] Shree Swāminārāyan therefore on one occasion, with great compassion, revealed in plain words His divinity in the assembly thus, 'That Parā Swarup of Purushottam, having absolute mercy on jivas for their ultimate redemption, has manifested on the earth and is visible before you. He is the form of worship for you all.... This Para Swarup of Purushottam, and the one which resides in Akshardhām are one.'[17]

---

[13] Ibid., Panchālā 7.

[14] Vachanāmrit, Gadhadā Sec. I-78

[15] Divya murti narakrutostasya bhedo na kinchana.
                              – Satsangijivanam, *3-29-37*

[16] Nirgunatvam bhavatyeva tajnānādeshcha sarvathā. – Ibid.

[17] Vachanāmrit, Gadhadā III-38.

This problem of Purushottam has been discussed in this text with intricate subtlety, inasmuch as the versatility of the human mind has built up various notions regarding God according to different approaches, either intelligent, rational, intuitional or dogmatic. It is difficult to erase such notions which tend to close the inner receptivity permanently. The method of Shree Swāminārāyan was a consistent approach to explain this rational theology through knowledge, understanding, and intuition. He did not encourage belief in mere revelations since glimpses of revelation are short-lived and they do not lift the soul beyond temporary ecstatic joy. These revelations, in the words of Erich Frank, are mere superfluity; he says, 'Even if a man thinks that in his own soul he has felt the immediate presence and proximity of God; even if in mystical ecstasy, he believes he has seen God directly, such an experience lasts only a short moment and cannot be retained.'[18]

God in His human form exhibits all the shortcomings of the human being in order to mingle with the people. At times, in this association He reveals the flashes of His divinity with a feeling of absolute commiseration to uplift the rigid, the downtrodden or the doubtful, who cannot realise by intuitional knowledge His divinity in human form. Otherwise He supresses the aura of His greatness, mixes with people, loves them so that His divine association or their involvement with His divine self, will remove their avidyā or ignorance. He exhibits human shortcomings, but the wise with their intuitional knowledge, realise Him in His absolute divinity and attain Him. Those who have no wisdom judge Him by the exhibition of His human nature and become infatuated. They therefore cannot overcome His Māyā. It is with this intuitional knowledge that Shree Swāminārāyan desires His disciples to

---

[18] Frank, Erich, Philosophical Understanding and Religious Truth, London, 1945.

know Him, for which He bestows His grace (buddhiyoga) or gives the association of a saint who has fully realised Him. This 'spiritual grace', as Huxley puts it, 'cannot be received continuously or in its fullness except by those who have willed away their selfwill to the point of being able truthfully to say, "Not I, but God in me".[19]

The life and teaching of Shree Swāminārāyan reveals how this knowledge is attained, with which the jiva transcends Māyā or the vortex of Prakriti.

---

[19] Huxley, Aldous, The Perennial Philosophy, London, 1946.

LIFE AND PHILOSOPHY OF LORD SWAMINARAYAN

24 Commentary on the Vachanāmritam

Even though Vachanāmritam is written in simple Gujarāti language, it is difficult to understand. The matters discussed are intelligible to mystics only. The subject deals throughout with self-realisation and unitive consciousness with God, attained only through upāsanā. Gunatitānand Swāmi,[1] the pontifical head of the Swāminārāyan Temple at Junāgadh, had a unique divine harmony with Shree Swāminārāyan. Out of the five hundred Paramhansās of Lord Swāminārāyan, Gunatitānand Swāmi was the foremost, not only on the administrative side of the fellowship, but also on spiritual matters. Lord Swāminārāyan therefore advised all His Paramhansās to go to Junāgadh once every year, and learn Brahma Vidyhā from Gunatitānand Swāmi. His sermonising was rather trenchant but penetrating and mostly related to the topics in Vachanāmritam.

As these discussions are of great importance in order to understand the philosophy of Shree Swāminārāyan, we give below some important extracts out of many:

'Nārāyan says to Prahlād, "It is difficult to conquer Me by weapons. I may be conquered only if one chants My name, thinks of Me, and sees Me in His eyes, always and at all

---

[1] He was believed to be the incarnation of Akshar Brahman. Hindu mythology relates that the divine abode always incarnates with God on earth, as Lakshman the incarnation of Shesha was with Rāma, and again Balarām with Krishna. Shrimad Bhāgawata describes Balarām as Sheshakhyam dhāma mamakam.'

times."' (I-3)

'One should be attached to such a sādhu who has established a unitive consciousness with God and who lives his life in accordance with the tenets prescribed. The attributes of dharma, jñān, vairāgya, bhakti and upāsanā will develop only under the tutorship of such a sādhu. Otherwise even the wise will degenerate.' (I-7).

'It is difficult to eradicate vāsanā, since it is Māyā attached to jiva as his causal body. However, the observance of the primary tenet laid down in Shikshāpatri, namely assuming oneself as Brahman and devoting oneself to the upāsanā of the Lord, will totally eradicate the vāsanā attached to jiva.' (I-130)

'God, under the garb of a sādhu, possesses thirty redemptive attributes, and under the garb of a king, thirty-nine attributes. But mere supersensitive powers do not lead to Godheadship.' (I-148)

'The best devotee is proficient in the knowledge of Brahman and Parabrahman. However, one who is of a meditative disposition and has love towards God will also progress unhampered.' (I-157)

'Constant attachment to a saint who possesses all the redemptive attributes, will produce in one those attributes of wisdom. But such a saint is rare and hard to find.' (I-161)

'The highest benedictions of God are showered upon one who knows God, knows His saint and acts according to the tenets prescribed by them.' (I-166)

'It is better to sing the praise of God, and it is still better to remember the divine episodes of His life. Meditational disposition is a further step forward, but the best thing is to sustain God in one's own Ātmā.' (I-201)

'God, His abode, the released souls and the jiva are the four eternal entities, excepting which everything that is evolved out of prakriti is ultimately perishable. Out of these, jiva is bound by Māyā in the form of sexual attachment, which is implacable.' (I-226)

'I desire to give you knowledge with which you will be able to resist passion with the strength of Girnār mountain, ego with the strength of Meru, and vāsanā with the invincible strength of Lokālok mountain. This divine knowledge will help you to distinguish between the Ultimate Reality – God and His various other incarnations.' (I-323)

'Jadbharat remained unattached in this world since he believed such an involvement would hamper spiritual progress. People called him mad, as according to them only those who carefully discharged their worldly duties were wise. But according to the spiritually wise, such people have not known the true wisdom.' (I-334)

'One who reads scriptures or sings the praise of God or holds discourses in order to elevate his ego, attains nothing. But one who does these things assuming his self as Brahman and sustains God within, whose exoteric manifestation is visible to him, has attained proficiency in Sāmkhya as well as Yoga.' (I-343)

'The knowledge that Shreeji Mahārāj (Lord Swāminārāyan) is the cause of all the causal aspects and that all the incarnations emanate from Him, is upāsanā. That Ultimate God or the Highest Entity is nirdosh i.e. devoid of all the gunas or the vices which evolve out of Prakriti. The profoundity of His powers and the infiniteness of His swarup constitute His mahimā or greatness. This mahimā is required to be perfectly visualised in order to give impetus to spiritual progress. Shreeji Mahārāj has specifically prescribed in Vachanāmritam that with this knowledge of His divine form one should assume himself as Brahman and offer worship to Him.' (II-2)

'In introverted meditation there are four obstacles, namely

women, wealth, social status, and the actions propelled by gunas.' (II-9)

'All actions performed for attaining mundane greatness or rewards should be regarded as worthless. The grace of the saint is proffered only to those who have an aptitude for satsang. The real saint is never propitiated by even the most enticing objects of this world. He has no affinity even towards his disciple, beyond getting him removed from his miseries and transmigrating him to the everlasting world.' (II-24)

'One who is either a sādhu or a grihastha (householder), who has the greatness of the world in his heart, cannot erase this from the hearts of his disciples. His preachings will enhance his own desires and he will wish the same to be imposed on others.' (II-33)

'Two paths, namely Rājayoga and Brahmayoga, are prescribed for spiritual development, out of which Rājayoga is likely to lead to success. However, Brahma Vidyā is the main lore to be studied and ultimately that leads to final realisation. But it is difficult to be adopted and executed successfully. Still it is the only ultimate path.' (II-38)

'The Ekāntik sādhu who has established harmony with God, exhibits exuberance of love towards jivas for their ultimate liberation. The others who satisfy the desires of their disciples know not the true path of love, as the showering of desired results would spell spiritual regress.' (II-92)

'Withdrawing inwardly for meditation, and with that inner sight examining thoughts emanating from the mind, is the only process for attaining the eternal and ultimate bliss of God. Vachanāmritam lays great stress on pratilom, the process of withdrawing inward.' (II-123)

'Whoever obeys my orders receives the benedictory grace of Mahārāj (Lord Swāminārāyan) . But those who have no knowledge do not realise the significance of this. Mahārāj and

His Ekāntik saint (He refers to Him only) offer only God's bliss. They do not desire to proffer aishwarya which would ultimately entail endless miseries. We want every disciple to establish harmony with God, but at no time should our compassion for the disciple impel us to offer the disciple his desired objects[2] which could lead him towards their enjoyment. One who prefers sense objects is not the true Saint of God, and one who bestows aishwarya is not God. One who craves for mundane pleasures is not a devotee, and one who satisfies such desires of the devotee is not God. Prahlād realised the significance of this truth. The true devotee should therefore centre all his desires upon attaining God only.' (III-24)

'Māyā cannot draw into her vortex one who has realised the knowledge of Brahman and Parabrahman. A fish with fins as sharp as blades would cut the net and free itself. Similarly a realised soul can free the infinite jivas from the web of Māyā. You have the proximity of such a Saint, which is your great fortune. Shed lethargy therefore and make the best use of the time offered to you.' (III-27)

'Krishna was staying with Yudhishthir, but Yudhishthir had no knowledge that Krishna was God. Similarly Parabrahman manifests before you today in human form but His greatness and divinity are to be realised. Great benefit has been proffered on us as we live in proximity with God. However, so long as we do not develop the attributes of a saint, the benefit cannot be maintained. One should therefore try to develop a ceaseless mental contact with God, since the true devotee does not for a moment divert from the lotus feet of God.' (IV-1)

'Redeeming the jivas from the bondage of Māyā is the task entrusted by God to His graced disciples. When King Parikshit was cursed by the Rishi, in spite of Bhagwān Veda Vyās he

---

[2] A boon bestowing any desired result.

was redeemed of the curse only by Shukdevji.' (IV-9)

'The God of the divine abode has manifested Himself here on the earth. To Him there is no temporal here and everlasting beyond. One who realises this goes beyond Māyā.' (IV-57)

'Brahmacharya is the chief sādhanā out of the many that Shreeji Mahārāj has prescribed. His manifestation on the earth was for the eradication of avidyā – māyā.' The quintessence of His preachings is centred around this object only. Avidyā persists as long as the Ātmā is identified with the three bodies, namely gross, subtle and causal. The contact of a Brahmanised Saint will relieve one of the upādhi of the three bodies.' (IV-85)

'When one feels he is jiva, he has all the vices. But when he thinks himself as Akshar, he is relieved of all the vices. When one assumes Aksharbhāv, how is the transmigration to Akshardhām warranted?' (IV-100)

'It is by knowledge of God and also by meditational worship that one enjoys the bliss of God. Therefore Sāmkhya and Yoga are both vitally necesary for establishing contact with God.' (IV-117)

'The attachment to sense objects is an impediment in spiritual progress. But merely having the awareness of this knowledge does not relieve one of this attachment. It is like the ocean which does not dry up. But during the ātyāntika pralaya (the state of final rest) it dries up. Therefore one who attains that ultimate knowledge is totally relieved of his attachment. That ultimate knowledge is the knowledge of Brahman, i.e. this saint.' (IV-7)

'Detachment from sense objects purifies the indriyas – both conative and cognative, as also the jiva.' (V-23)

'If the disciple is not relieved of the miseries of births and death, he has not sought a true guru.' (V-46)

'It is difficult to suppress one's greatness attained by the proximity and contact of God, satsang, and the fulfilment of Ekāntik bhāv. However, by bending low and respecting others, one should preserve and enjoy the extravagance of such an elated position bestowed upon him.' (V-86)

'The ultimate knowledge is to seek release from Māyā. One who has attained this knowledge of Brahman and Parabrahman, remains detached from the influence of Prakriti and Purush (which when combined evolve the forces of Māyā). He is Brahman – Gunātit. Shreeji Mahārāj desires everybody to attain this Brahmanised state.' (V-207)

'The outward marks of tilak on the forehead should not be applied if one cannot observe the tenets of *Shikshāpatri*. Otherwise miseries will befall him. However, one will be released if he cannot observe the tenets but confesses that he cannot observe them and still has attachment towards God and His saint.' (V-315)

'One who offers devotion to God has to face three obstacles, namely heinous elements of society, deceitful members of the fellowship, and his own cognitive and conative organs. Such pernicious elements should be carefully avoided.' (V-333)

'God, being the great commiserator, knows no faults or evils of his devotees. He forgives them of their evils, for if He discards them they will fall from the path of salvation. He acts with great magnanimity. This has been indicated in Vachanāmritam at various places, for Shreeji Mahārāj had such an integral commiseration for the jivas.' (V-365)

'The most intense vāsanā is hridayagranthi, which is deep attachment or unfulfilled carnal desires. Only the Brahmanised Saint knows the perils of sexuality. Others, even although they have renounced the world and become sādhus, sustain a hidden desire to fulfil carnal desires.' (V-400)

'How can the greatness assigned to saffron coloured robes be explained until the jiva is purified?' (V-405)

'God and His Brahmanised saint in human manifestation exhibit by their actions and talk that they have nothing in common with the sophisticated world. The others upon whom greatness is imposed naturally try to reconcile their behaviour with the pattern of society.' (V-412)

'One who changes opinion according to different talks, suffers from a great deficiency. The wise, like Muktānand Swāmi, would first patiently hear and then express their views if deemed necessary. One who practises inward withdrawal gains power to withstand such influences.' (V-418)

'The various tenets relating to Dharma should be observed carefully. The slightest infringement will involve great perils.' (VI-4)

'The Vachanāmritam is full of the quintessence of the four Vedas, six Darshanas and eighteen Purānas. It should therefore be carefully studied.' (VI-19)

'The wise were always dearer to Shreeji Mahārāj, since they possessed the faculty to distinguish between Sat and Asat, kārya and akārya, bhaya and abhaya, bandha and moksha. Krupānand Swāmi was one such wise person.' (VI-64)

'The various desires emanate because of attachment towards sense objects. The desire to drink poison or burn one's own house or children never arises in the mind as that involves personal loss. One should therefore entertain desires strictly in accordance with the scriptural codes.' (VI-103)

'The ego of virtues, ego of proficiency in actions, and the ego of being the oldest in the fellowship, should all be discarded.' (IX-67)

'Religious discourses, talks, sankirtan and seva are the four essentials wherein one should ever hesitate to feel satisfied.' (X-132)

'One should perform purified actions and remain pious

until death. There is no sacrifice greater than to observe Brahmacharya. There should be no retreat in observing the precepts.' (X-I5I)

These are but a few extracts taken from a series of long discourses all spoken in an extempore mood, and recorded with restriction because of the limitations of time and place. Reading them as a whole gives a comprehensive idea of the philosophy of Shree Swāminārāyan.

25 The Theory of Knowledge

Generally the three pramãnas or the sources of knowledge for knowing God, are accepted by various philosophical schools. They are perception or pratyaksh, inference or anumãn and scriptural or shabda.

Knowledge of God cannot be attained through the sense organs since the finite organs cannot approach or know the infinite. Inference or anumãn draws knowledge from vyãpti or pervasion of the object, as, for example, the appearance of smoke gives the inference that fire is there. But it requires repeated observations to establish the fact beyond doubt. Therefore inferential knowledge together with perception, also being Dharmabhuta jnãn or attributive consciousness, falls short in the attainment of the knowledge of God.

Therefore it is only the scripture or the shabda-pramãna which is recognised as the special source of knowledge of the Infinite. But scriptures too are required to be studied at the feet of a Guru who has the fullest realisation of his self, and as such has attained the knowledge of God. The Shrutis proclaim beyond doubt that the realisation of the self and the attainment of the knowledge of God are not obtained merely by such hearing (bahunã shrutena) or by subtle intelligence (medhayã) or by delivering discourses (pravachanena). The scriptures which are an authority by themselves, establish the existence of God.

The integral knowledge of God consists in knowing God in

all His fullness with His divine attributes. So the mere academic knowledge of scriptures cannot deliver the jiva from its ignorance. Knowledge is the attribute of self (the chidrupa shakti) having a relationship with jiva similar to light and luminosity. That consciousness of self (the jnātrutvashakti) knows. It is monadic and finite so long as it is confined to the body. It attains pervasiveness (vibhutvam) when the shackles of the body are removed or the empiric state of mind is dissolved. It then attains Brāhmic consciousness[1] by concentrating this jnātrutvashakti on the humanised God or the immediate divine form of God, whose outer contact and knowledge are a prerequisite for Brahmanisation. The senses and the mind cannot reach it, as it is an object beyond sense-perception and beyond the limitations of time and place. Since it is an interrelated process of knowing God through self, and knowing self through God, the immediate relationship of jiva with God on the earth is fundamentally necessary. The divine law therefore provides that either God manifests on the earth or He reveals Himself through His realised saint for the redemption of jivas.[2] Therefore the relationship between the finite and the infinite is to be established.

As the Shrutis say 'Without knowledge there is no salvation. He only attains salvation who knows Him. No other ways of conquering death are known.[3] Who is therefore to be known, how, and by whom? If God of the infinite realms is to be known here by jiva of the finite realm, the proposition naturally appears contradictory. Since 'if the infinite is infinite, and finite is finite, knowledge would become impossible.'[4] The finite is therefore to be raised to infinity by awakening its

---

[1] 'Brahmanisation' or 'Brāhmic consciousness' is used for the identity or sādharmya with Brahman the Akshar and not with Brahman the Purushottam, who transcends Akshar.

[2] Vachanāmrit, Vadtāl 19.

[3] Rute jnānānna muktihi. Tameva viditvātimrutyum eti. Nānyaha panthāhā vidyate ayanāyā.

[4] Srinivasachari, P. N., Philosophy of Vishishtādvaita, Adyer, 1943.

Brāhmic consciousness, which brings about its harmony with the ultimate Reality – Parabrahman.

Explaining 'Knowledge' Shree Swāminārāyan says, 'One who has merely seen God when in human manifestation, heard God or touched God, cannot be said to have known God, since knowledge starts from Atman. This esoteric knowledge reflects through manas and indriyas, but becomes conditioned or vitiated inasmuch as the manas and indriyas are attached to worldly things.'

In such a case, as Wildon Carr, explaining the philosophy of Bergson says, 'Intuition, then, is a direct apprehension of Reality which is non-intellectual.'[5] Shree Swaminārāyan, however, holds that mere intuition does not lead one to the fuller apprehension of the Ultimate Reality – God. It is only when God, the sustainer of the jad and chetana prakriti, the creator and the controller of all, assumes a human form for the redemption of jivas, that He becomes knowable and that too by His own grace.[6] The monadic self then is slowly infinitised as it realises the human God, the Ultimate Reality, Parabrahman.[7]

However, if the indriyas and mind do not approach God in human form, in His fullness that He is totally divine, they cannot reach Him.[8] 'It does not happen, not in any way, since the mind is full with many occupations, ideologies, which have a bearing more towards world than towards God.' And as Eckhart says, 'Indeed, I tell you. Any object you have in mind, however good, will be a barrier between you and the inmost truth.'[9]

But when a jiva with pure and sincere indriyas and manas, and having immutable faith approaches God,

---

[5] Carr, Wildon, The Philosophy of Change, London, 1914.

[6] Vachanāmrit, Loyā, 7.   [7] Ibid., Kāriyāni, I.   [8] Ibid.

[9] Huxley, Aldous, The Perennial Philosophy, London, 1946

when in human manifestation, God inspires in him the knowledge of His Self through His jnānshakti, draws the jiva nearer to Him and destroys his veil of ignorance. Thus the purified self apprehends God in all His infinite attributes. As the divine vision of the self, awakened through the grace of God, flows from within through mind and sense organs, they all become conditioned to this divinity.[10]

This is an invisible transformation made possible by His grace, without which no knowledge can help in knowing God.

The inner consciousness should be kept constantly in touch with and be merged in the human form of God or the Brahmanised Guru existing on this earth. This is intuitional knowledge, or antardrushti.[11] The tailadhārā vrutti or unbroken stream of this consciousness of God, transfuses divinity in ourselves and the chittavrtti becomes purified. The vāsanāmaya chitta is destroyed. The grace of God which infuses the Brahma drishti, is secured. God is realised in human form. Though in human form, He still transcends by His infinite powers and attributes, and remains unparalleled in His eternal entity. The Vedas therefore describe Him as 'neti-neti', i.e. infinite entity without a parallel.

But it may be argued that God seated inside as a witness can also inspire the knowledge of His Self. Why then should He descend on the earth and assume the finiteness and limitations of the human form? To which Shree Swāminārāyan replies, 'The infinite virtues and attributes of God are better visualised only when He reveals Himself in human form. His profound divinity radiating from His person, attracts the sense-organs and the mind. His redemptive virtues penetrate within, and drive out the desire for enjoying sense-objects.'[12]

---

[10] Vachanāmrit, Kāriyāni I.

[11] Vachanāmrit, Gadhadā I-49.

[12] Ibid., Sārangpur 7.

Thus a purification process for attaining self-perfection starts only when He descends and influences the mind and sense-organs. And then He commands, as did Krishna to Arjuna, 'Shed all your notions and concepts and surrender yourself to Me. I will purge you from all your sins and lead you to salvation.'[13]

Spinoza has also left the question of the knowledge of God by man unexplained: 'The infinity of God is in conflict with His complete cognisability on the part of man; for how is a finite transitory spirit able to conceive the infinite and Eternal? How does the human intellect rise above modal limitations to become capable and worthy of the mystical union with God?[14] Such a question was put to Shree Swāminārāyan by His disciple Swāmi Purnānand.[15] He then explained:

Within the gross and subtle elements which are evolved out of Prakriti, ubiquitous Prakriti is seen permeating and pervading. Since the primordial cause of all these evolutions is Prakriti, Prakriti is felt predominantly as the basic element within them. One therefore feels that there is nothing but Prakriti pervading everywhere. But the cause of Prakriti is Akshar, so Akshar pervades through Prakriti. Therefore if this cause is realised, Akshar will be felt pervading everywhere. And beyond Akshar is Purushottam – the Parabrahman, the teleological architect of the millions of macrocosms. Parabrahman as a final cause is therefore immanent as well as transcendent. Since He is immanent as a witness seated in the heart of all, why should He not be cognised if one with a subjective approach serves the lotus feet of a satpurush who has realised Him? It is He who seeks

---

[13] Gitā, XVIII-66.

[14] Falkenberg, Richard, and Armstrong, A. C. History of Modern Philosophy, London, 1895.

[15] Vachanāmrit, Gadhadā Sec. I-51.

the jiva – the self and transforms it to the sublime greatness of Brahman. It is like a diamond cutting a diamond.[16]

According to Shree Swāminārāyan the finiteness attached to the jiva through karmas from times immemorial can be removed when the actions of the jiva become devotional or are performed for propitiating God. The jiva then attains brahmanatvam and becomes the sharir – body of God.

However, the principle of finite and infinite is not sacrificed in these arguments. Even when the finiteness of the released jivas is redeemed, it is retained in other jivas who are in a state of bondage through ignorance. At the same time the infinite does not lose its infiniteness inasmuch as the infiniteness is in immortalising and Brahmanising the jivas (Brihatvāt cha brahmatvāt cha). Still the Brahmanised jiva does not attain parity with the infinite Parabrahman who dwells in the jivas which are infinite in number, and transforms them to the extent of their realisation of His infiniteness, which in spite of being realised, remains neti-neti or incomprehensible.[17]

Knowledge of God as described in Sāmkhya, Yoga, Vedānta and Pancharātra Shāstras

According to Shree Swāminārāyan, Sāmkhya, Yoga, Vedānta and Pancharātra should be read together, as reading each separately does not give a consistently full knowledge of God. Each is supplemented by the other, and is explained by Shree Swāminārāyan in that context.

Sāmkhya explains that before the cosmic evolution there were only two entities, namely Purush and Prakriti. Purush is always dormant, and before creation Prakriti was in a state of equilibrium and, as such, motionless. But the influence of Purush disturbs the equilibrium of Prakriti, and it then

---

16 Vachanāmirt, Gadhadā Sec. I-51.

17 Vachanāmrit, Gadhadā Sec. II-67.

evolves. When the ubiquitous Prakriti evolves, it produces mahat and other elements twenty-four in all. As these tattvas are evolved out of prakriti they are vikrutis.[18] This cosmic evolution has two aspects – expansion and contraction. The tattvas that have evolved out of Prakriti, are therefore transitory and have a cause-effect relation with Prakriti, the original cause. This system, according to Shree Swāminārāyan, is faulty since it considers the various manifestations of God, and Aniruddh, Pradyumna and Sankarshan, are to be understood as the evolutes of Prakriti and therefore subject to change.[19] As Dr. Rādhākrishnan explains, 'The God whom the Sāmkhya admits, is not pure subject, but has in him the potentiality of object.... All things that constitute the universe are subject-object. Both in God and in the lowest matter, we have the two tendencies of Purush and Prakriti.'[20] Sāmkhya says that only nirgun Vāsudev is above Prakriti and therefore is not the object of perception as well as conception. He is cognisable only by Ātmā.

Shree Swāminārāyan, however, interprets the Sāmkhya system by eliminating therefrom the conception that the manifestations of God are separate from Vāsudev – the Nirgun Brahman. He says that everything which has evolved from Prakriti is transitory. Ātmā only is pure Brahman. Nirgun Vāsudev manifests on the earth for the redemption of many jivas and is therefore the Ultimate Reality. He is in the manifested human form, the object of meditation and devotion for the mumukshu. But because of His manifestation in human form, He cannot be said to have evolved out of Prakriti.

The Sāmkhya however offers one solace to the mumukshu inasmuch as that he accepts that even the best of sense objects,

---

[18] Mulaprakrutir avikrutir mahadādhyāhā prakrutivikrutayaha sapta Shodashakāsh cha vikāro na prakrutihi na vikrutihi purushaha – S. Karika.

[19] Vachanāmrit, Panchālā 2.

[20] Radhakrishnan, Dr S., Indian Philosophy, part II, London, 1929-31.

having evolved from Prakriti, are perishable. He is not therefore captivated by them. With this abstinence from the sense objects, he should follow the yoga which prescribes the meditation on and devotion to God in personal manifestation here on the earth. Since God has to liberate people by the process of involution, He has to descend on the earth for this purpose.

God is conceived in yoga sutras only as a means for removing the obstacles from the path of the yogi, so that he can easily concentrate and attain liberation from the bondage of prakriti. In this yoga system, Hiranyagarbha, Virāt etc., are conceived of as the amshas or parts of God. Therefore in this system the achyutabhāv – indivisibility of God is impaired. Commenting on this apparently faulty conception of God, Shree Swāminārāyan says :[21]

The ultimate God is without an equal by His pre-eminence, and reigns supreme. Prakriti, Purush, Hiranyagarbha, Virāt, etc., are His devotees and they meditate upon Him. God, by His antaryāmi shakti, being concomitant in them, they are each described as God in scriptures. Shrutis therefore say, 'everything is Brahman and nothing is apart from it'. [22]

Again, 'This whole universe is Brahman since He is the creator of the universe. By His ubiquitous power, He is immanent in it and also separate from it.[23] Therefore the imposition of Godheadship on Prakriti, Purush, Hiranyagarbha, Virāt, etc. becomes consistent because of the concomitance in them of the antaryāmi shakti of the supreme God.

21 Vachanāmrit, Panchālā 2
22 Sarvam khalu idam brahma - Chhandogya, 3-14-1.
    Neha nānāsti kinchana. - Bruhadāranyaka, 4-4-19.
23 Idam hi vishvam bhagavān ivetaro
    Yato jagatsthānānirodhasambhavaha - Shrimad Bhāgawata, I-51-20.

Advaita Vedānta accepts the Eternal Brahman as the cause of the whole universe. It describes God as immanent, all pervasive and nirgun (free from qualities). Under this system God is held to be formless. To remove this deficiency in the knowledge of God in Advaita Vedānta philosophy (since God who is eternal has a divine form and possesses all divine qualities), Shree Swāminārāyan prescribes the reading of Pancharātra Shāstra, which clearly describes that God has a divine form. But the apprehension of God according to the Pancharātra system affords again a difficulty. According to Pancharātra, when God descends on the earth in human form, all the human attributes are imposed on Him. He cannot therefore be visualised as absolutely perfect, immanent and all-pervasive. As such Sāmkhya, Yoga, Vedānta and Pancharātra should be read together for having the complete knowledge of God.[24]

Shree Swāminārāyan says that God has described His divine form in the Vedas. However, this was not properly understood and the various seers described Him differently according to their individual experience and realisation. Sāmkhya described Him as beyond twenty-four tattvas. Yoga described Him as the twenty-sixth, the twenty-fifth being the Ātmā. But both these shāstras could not give a comprehensive idea of God, as to whether He possesses form or is without form, or whether He has the divine attributes or is super-imposed with human attributes when in manifestation on the earth. Nārad Pancharātra described God as having a divine form, and as being the cause of ultimate salvation. These various accounts are like milk which looks white, smells sweet and feels cold or hot, but only when drunk gives one a proper idea of its flavour. Even though the eyes, nose and the touch have cognised it as milk, these organs have not been given a proper idea what it tastes like. Similarly each of the four systems of philosophy has described God in its own way, but

---

[24] Vachanāmrit, Gadhadā Sec. I-52

only after a comprehensive reading of all the four systems together, can one know God and realise Him. Otherwise each system falls short of giving a clear concept of God and therefore obscures the ultimate truth.[25]

Sagun and Nirgun Brahman

When Shree Swāminārāyan speaks of Sagun and Nirgun Brahman, He does not confuse this with the two Brahmans of Shankar. Brahman is one and unparalleled and is not distinguished as causal (kāran) Brahman and produced (kārya) Brahman. Brahman, according to Shree Swāminārāyan, is the supreme cause. Nirgun and Sagun are the phases of His power (aishwarya) described in Shrutis as *anoraniyān mahato mahiyān*. He is the inner self or soul of Akshar, Prakriti, Purush and the various evolutes therefrom. But still He is purest and devoid of all evolutionary changes, unattached to them and fully enlightened. He is attached to Himself only and is without a parallel. Subtlety, purity, non-attachment, power, enlightenment are the various attributes of His Nirgun swarup. This nirgunabhāv or the phase of His aishwarya, has the power of transforming matter into divinity. The horses and the chariot which carried Shree Krishna and Arjuna to the abode of Bhumā Purush, were transformed into divinity by Shree Krishna by this power to go beyond the Lokālok and the tamas of Māyā which are impenetrable by human beings.[26]

The Sagun phase, which is mahatomahiyān, is the manifestation of the vast and the infinite greatness of Parabrahman before whom the millions of universes look like atoms. Shree Krishna gave the vision of His cosmic form to Yashodāji when He opened His mouth. The Vishwarup darshan given to Arjuna and Virāt darshan to King Bali, are the phases of His Sagun aishwarya. Sagun and Nirgun aishwarya are therefore the phases of God, which according to His desire appear and dissolve like clouds appearing and

---

[25] Ibid., Vadtāl 2.   [26] Vachanāmritam, Kāriyāni 8.

dissolving in the sky during the monsoon.

The Divine Law provides for the manifestation of Parabrahman here on the earth for the ultimate redemption of jivas. The upāsanā of this divine form of Parabrahman who manifests on the earth is the ultimate cause of final liberation. But if one thinks that redemption requires that the human form of God before him must first reveal His divine form seated in the divine abode, he will not be redeemed.[27] Shree Swāminārāyan stresses that God is to be realised here on the the earth by attaining the Brāhmic vision. Knowledge of the divine self of God is mukti or release from māyā. So long as the released soul possesses the prakrit body and works here in tune with the wish of God, he thus becomes a jivan mukta or one who has lost the consciousness of the physical body. Therefore holding the prakrit body is not incompatible with release, which has been attained by the knowledge of one's own self and the Parabrahman here.

This knowledge of the purified self is attained only through satsang (association of the wise) – which implies the contact of Sat or Ātmā with Paramātmā.

---

[27] Ibid., Gadhadā *Sec.* l-9.

26 Satsang-the Path of Enlightenment

Satsang is the only means for ultimate redemption or absolute Brahmanisation. Shree Swāminārāyan says 'The eternal truth Sat is Ātmā and Sat is Paramātmā. The contact of Ātmā with Paramātmā is Satsang.[1] This fellowship established by Shree Swāminārāyan is known as Satsang. Mortification of all the physical desires and service at the lotus feet of the Brahmanised Guru are the sādhanās prescribed by Shree Swāminārāyan for becoming a true satsangi.

Such a Brahmanised Saint works as a purifier, and, as Brahman, Brahmanises.[2] The attachment towards such a Saint should be deep. He should be worshipped with the same idolatry which one offers to God. He is a cathartic agent, and purges the sādhak from all sins as does a sacred pilgrimage. Such a Saint lives in God and is therefore the instrument of God's manifestation. His is a dedicated life for the uplifting humanity and relieving them from the threefold miseries, namely ādhi, vyādhi and upādhi. His principal desire is to relieve the sādhak from the ignorance attached to jiva. When the mumukshu approaches him, he explains the cardinal truth that 'Thou art the Ātmā, the eternal truth and the knower, and thy body, mind, indriyas and prānas are all perishable.[3] This preliminary knowledge distinguishing the Ātmā and the body

---

[1] Vachanāmrit, Gadhadā Sec. III-39

[2] Brahmavid brahmaiva bhavati.

[3] Vachanāmrit, Gadhadā Sec. I-16

as separate is essential for setting apart Sat from Asat or Chit from Achit. It is the first step in the divine ladder to reach the eternal abode.

The manas is the source of the undercurrent of thoughts principally based on carnal desires. Buddhi is a factor of knowledge which pervades the whole body through the cognitive organs. Doubt, decision, recollection, and torpidity arise from buddhi as it tries to reason. Chitta is the cosmic intelligence or mahat, and is pure, predominantly with shuddha sattva. The ego-centred jiva with vitiated manas and buddhi cannot visualise God. Chitta is pure, but with the evil influence of manas and buddhi, it becomes polycentric. God, therefore, remains beyond the reach of manas, buddhi, chitta and ego.[4] Therefore the state of pure consciousness is required to be developed by the negation of the unconsciousness which is the nature of the empiric self – and which is a barrier in the uprising of the pure consciousness. Shree Swāminārāyan says that:

> The subjective experience of God seated within as antaryāmi, is not attained by jiva who is deprived of his purity by the vitiating influence of body, mind and sense objects. When the jiva discards this evil influence and meditates upon Brahman, he becomes enlightened with the redeeming attributes of Brahman. But the recollection of this meditational worship of Brahman is mostly hampered by the outward influence.[5]

The immediate presence, therefore, of a Brahmanised guru is absolutely essential to infuse stillness within. For attaining a pure and blissful state of Ātmā, the jiva should try to live an orderly life with a control established on mind, chitta and all other cognitive organs.

The association of Ātmā with body has become so

---

[4] Vachanāmrit, Panchālā 4.

[5] Ibid., Gadhadā Sec. II-31

indistinguishable that one has to separate them by an awakened consciousness, and live a life led by Ātmasattā. This consciousness resists the forces of māyā when fully awakened and does not allow association with the Ātmā. By this process of introverted chittavrutti, the empirical self attached to sense objects is gradually freed from this attachment. With the chittavrutti constantly kept attached to the purified Ātmā, shining like radiant sun, Ātmā assumes the form of Brahman. He thus becomes a channel for the working of Parabrahman. In the words of Dr Rādhākrishnan, 'The Purṇāvatār brings out the Māyā of mystic love when the enchanter descends into human love by establishing himself in its centre and by the cunning art of spiritual alchemy, transfigures the bodily self and Brahmanises it.[6] Such a devotee, when in an ecstatic mood, utters, 'I am God and the world has surged out from me,' and forgets his Brāhmic consciousness too. In reality it is God who speaks through him. The utterances of Vāmdev and Prahlād exhibit the manifestation of God through such Brahmanised devotees. The Brāhmic consciousness does not become extinct but is suppressed. It is the vishishta aikya with visheshan and visheshya relation, but they do not have swarupaikya or absolute unity.

It is only through the bondage of divine love with Brahman, that association with Parabrahman becomes possible. That love should not be adulterated by indulgence in worldly objects. According to Shree Swāminārāyan, one who enjoys the proximity of the humanised God in waking, dream and deep sleep states, and also derives during these states an equal enjoyment from the sense objects, has a superficial love for God, which does not lift him to the sublime height of Parābhakti. Parābhakti recognises only self mortification which elevates the life and establishes God in the centre. Such a devotee loses awareness of self, transcends cosmic consciousness and is merged in Brāhmic consciousness. Such

---

[6] Radhakrishnan, Dr. S., Indian Philosophy, part II, London, 1929-31

single-pointed devotion towards God forbids deflection towards other objects whether worldly or other-worldly.[7]

However, it is difficult to attain such undeflected repose in God, as the flickering chittavritti is drawn towards various sense objects. But just as in Yoga, the control over prāna leads to nirvikalpa samādhi, in bhakti the control of chitta by intense and purified devotion, controls prānas and leads to nirvikalpa samādhi.[8] However, the force of devotion should be immensely powerful in order to reject the worldly desires which intervene and block its flow. The constant thinking on God in chitta, the unswerving meditation of God in the mind, and developing the ego to attain God, would create an equanimity to establish harmony with God. The desire to attain God and the dissipation of worldly desires will augment the perfection of bhakti yoga.

The consciousness that 'I am Atma' is required to be developed to keep apart the drashtā or the Ātmā from the physical body. With this consciousness one should probe into the inherent nature of manas, buddhi, chitta and ahamkār from which the worldly desires emanate. As long as these desires persist in the mind, one should not resort to dhyān or meditation.[9] The desire to enjoy the sense-objects will be gradually eliminated by the awakened consciousness, which will reveal endless miseries entailed in the enjoyment of sense objects. Simultaneously it will also reveal the eternal bliss to be experienced when sense-objects are discarded. The identification with Ātmā should be established by this thought force. A gradual teaching or conditioning of the mind to this state of 'no-mind' or void, should be adopted. Otherwise the irretrievable mind offers a greater resistance if it is forcibly uprooted from the sense-objects, and reverts to its original state with an increased appetite. So long as the attachment

---

[7] Vachanāmrit, Gadhadā Sec. 1-26

[8] Vachanāmrit, Gadhadā Sec. 1-25

[9] Vachanāmrit, Sārangpur 12.

towards sense-objects persists in the mind, one should avoid meditation. When the mind is purified by the thought consciousness, in its probing it loses its restless desires and becomes fit to sustain the divine form of God in meditation.[10]

The process of stabilising the mind cannot be attained in a short time. The mumukshu should not therefore lose courage. The undercurrents of thoughts surging from the subtle body should be ignored when the drashtā, in the state of awakening, is busy offering worship to God. And when the drashtā is in the state of meditation, the outward disturbances should be totally ignored. The awakened thought-consciousness thus keeps apart the drashtā from the body-consciousness and helps in meditation; this thought-consciousness compares the fruits of the enjoyment of sense-objects and of indulgence in the Ātmic self.[11] Repose in God is possible when harmony with God is established.

Therefore the intensity of desire for enjoying sense-objects can be mitigated only by developing this Ātmic consciousness wherein one acts only as Ātmā, and does not succumb to baser instincts emanating from the mind. This formless Ātmā should then be identified with Brahman or Akshar. When fully Brahmanised, it loses its temporal instinct and attains God.

This yoga of the mind – wherein thought-consciousness has awakened – offers into the sacrificial fire all the desires, attachments and vāsanā. It is known as jnānyagna. It is also termed as intuitive vision – antardrshti, in which state, the activities either external or internal, relate to God only.[12] The sadhak who can freely indulge in external activities without disturbing the internal contact with God, has attained control over mind and over his cognitive as well as conative organs. He is described in *Gitā* as the amsha of Paramātmā.[13] One who

---

[10] Ibid., 12.
[11] Vachanāmrit, Sārangpur 12.
[12] Vachanāmrit, Gadhadā Sec. II-8
[13] Gitā, XV-7.

successfully performs this jnānayagna ultimately attains the Brāhmic consciousness and becomes the instrument for the revelation of God. The devotee in this state of Brāhmic consciousness realises the infinite greatness and powers of Parabrahman, which although being narrated by Parabrahman remain endless.[14]

This status of being beyond the influence of three gunas, exalts the devotee to the sublime regions of Brahmadhām. Kingship does not elevate him and pettiness does not derogate him. He feels his greatness because he has attained the Highest. His Brāhmic vision is stretched far and wide. He therefore looks upon the immense richness of the millions of universes as no more than a spadeful of grass. The object of happiness to him is Parabrahman only.[15] The inherent desire to enjoy the sense-objects entirely vanishes from his heart as he establishes a repose in God.[16]

Such a devotee, whose love for God has no bounds, even if he is concerned with worldly objects, is not affected by them. He is in a state of upāsanā or pure consciousness, wherein his cognitive and conative organs are drawn inward (pratilom) and he enjoys the bliss emanating from the divine form of Paramātmā. It is like one who through complete fatigue enjoys the blissful state of deep sleep, and in that state rejects conjugal enjoyment. If in this state of deep sleep – a state of ignorance – one can discard the enjoyment of sense-objects, the devotee who has attained upasham or a state of enlightenment, can discard the sense objects with grace, since he derives enjoyment from Paramātmā only. However, if he is concerned with sense-objects, it is only for sustaining his body and not for the fulfilment of desires, of which he has none. The

---

[14] Dyupataya eva te na yayurantamananta tya tvamapi.

- Bhāgawat, 10-87-41.

[15] Vachanāmrit, Loyā 10

[16] Vishayā vinivartante. - Gitā, II-59.

immense love for God surging from his heart rejects even the best of sense-objects, like the torrential flow of a river which throws out the biggest objects coming into its flow. Such a devotee, having his internal vision fixed on God, loses cognition of the world and worldly objects, and passes into a state of complete oblivion wherein nothing except God exists.[17]

But Shree Swāminārāyan says that this state of upasham which has been attained by a constant practice of pratilom (withdrawing inwards), offers a danger when the manas, indriyas and prānas revert to their original state (anulom) in which case the desire emanating from them conceals all knowledge. The resurgence of desire is incompatible with knowledge. But this desire is inherent within, and is not completely annihilated so long as one is not fully Brahmanised.[18]

Shiva, Brahmā, Parāshar, Shringi, Rishi Nārad, and others were confronted by sense objects and had succumbed to this inherent desire for enjoying them. As a consequence, they were dislodged from the nirvikalpa state. The wise and the ignorant both enjoy bliss – the former, the bliss of the nirvikalpa state, and the latter the bliss of the state of deep sleep. But when the indriyas of the wise relax or revert from the Ātmā, and of the ignorant from deep sleep, they are both confronted with sense-objects, and the danger of a fall becomes imminent.[19] Therefore the contact of all sense-objects, internally as well as externally, should be carefully avoided, and Brahman should be contemplated unceasingly, with a sense of wisdom, distinguishing the empiric self from pure Brahman, which is one's real Ātmā. So long as a devotee is not fully Brahmanised, he may at times feel the contact with God,

---

[17] Vachanāmrit, Ahmedābād 3.

[18] Vishayā vinivartante nirāhārasya dehinaha
    Rasavarjam rasopyasya param drushtvā nivartate. - Gitā, II-59

[19] Vachanāmrit, Vadtāl 20.

but is likely to fall from that blissful state if he does not totally avoid the contact of the sense-objects.

The slightest desire, even for a loftier goal, deflects one from contemplation of Brahman. The nirvikalpa samādhi, according to Shree Swāminārāyan, is the complete identification of one's Jivātmā with Akshar Brahman. And in this Brahmanised state, the Brahmanised self sustains God. This is an inseparable state, wherein the Brahmanised devotee holds Parabrahman with sharir-shariri bhāv. Again, the object of enjoyment of the devotee in this state, is Parabrahman only. Brahman is therefore not only an essential element in the salvation scheme, but a fundamental truth of ethical religion, since unless the formless Jivātmā meditates upon Akshar Brahman, it does not become the divine body of God, and consequently cannot enjoy God. This is the nirvikalpa samādhi – pure and highest and *gloria excelsis* from where spiritual regress is not possible.

Anything which is lower or lesser than this pure Brāhmic condition, is a savikalpa state. Even if one desires to become like Nārad or Sanak or Shukdevji, or become the inmate of the hermitage of Shree Nara-Nārāyan Rishis, or attain the status of the soul of Shvetdweep, he is still in the savikalpa state.[20] Akshar Brahman being the highest abode-Param Vyoma-in which there is none else than God, is the highest attainment for a mumuksu. The complete identification with Akshar Brahman is the nirvikalpa samādhi or the highest mukti.

---

[20] Vachanāmrit, Gadhadā Sec. I-40.

27 Mukti or Liberation

Mukti, according to Shree Swāminārāyan, is not the merging of the self with the Absolute, but is the exclusive service of God by assuming a divine (aprākrita) body.[1]

Shree Swāminārāyan says that jivanmukti is attainable here only, and the holding of a physical body is not incompatible with the release of the soul from māyā or the shackles of Karma – shubh or ashubh. Since Ātmā is the knower, his awakened knowledge separates him from the physical body. With the Ātmasattā, he works through the body. The ānand of the unitive consciousness of this Ātmasattā with Brahman or Akshar is derived only after the extinction of the empirical self. It is not necessary to be physically disembodied to enjoy this bliss, as it is knowledge of one's own self as Brahman, attained and established, that blots out the world within.[2]

The archi mārg or the Brahmapath is the direct and straight divine path from here to beyond or from the spatial and temporal world to the eternal Brahmalok. This path is also known as sushumna[3] which starts from Brahmarandhra and stretches beyond the Lok of Prakriti and Purush into Brahmalok. The sushumna in the physical body resides in the heart and stretches up to Brahmarandhra, the seat of the thousand-petalled lotus.[4] When the empirical self goes beyond

---

[1] Tatra brahmātmanā Krishna sevā muktishchāgamyatām. - Shikshāpatri, 121.

[2] Vachanāmrit, Gadhadā Sec. II-66.

[3] Ibid., Sec. I-65

[4] 'Sushumnā is the greatest and to it all others are subordinate; for by the power of yoga (yogabala) prāna is made to go through it, and, passing the chakras, leave the body through the Brahmarandhra.' Avalon, Arthur (Sir John Woodruffe), The Serpent Power, Madras, 1919.

the cosmic gods like Varuna (god of water), Sun, Moon, Wind, Prajāpati, Indra, Agni (god of fire), which preside over the various cognitive and conative organs[5] it reaches Brahmarandhra. It is the process wherein the indriyas revert into manas, and manas into prānas, and prānas into the jiva residing in the heart. The jiva goes with the prānas into Brahmarandhra from where it leaves the body and passing through the archi marg or Brahmapath, which is the sushumna of the brahmānd, reaches Brahmadhām. This redeemed soul, according to the Upanishads, is escorted by the atimānav purusha to Brahmadhām. But according to Shree Swāminārāyan, it is Parabrahman who, with other released muktas, comes to fetch His beloved devotees as an expression of grace. He feels a little reluctant to send the atimānav purush or trans-human person to fetch the devotee who has taken refuge and surrendered totally at His lotus feet.

The Brahmalok is infinitely far and beyond the eight spheres or circles, namely the earth, water, fire, wind, ether, intellect, Pradhān Purush and Prakriti Purush. However, this infinite and eternal Brahmadhām is visualised nearer and within by one who meditates upon it and feels that just as the jiva resides in the body, Paramātmā resides in the jiva which is Brahmadhām personified.[6] The empirical self has to discard the identification with the three bodies. It is only by the contact of and meditation upon the personal Brahman, that the jivātmā is purified and is released from the vāsanā ling-sharir and attains Brāhmic state or mukti. It is only then that this absolute pure Brahman has the immediate approach to Parabrahman.

When God descends on the earth with a redemptive will, mukti is attainable here and now. Prapatti or total dedication

---

5 Vachanāmrit, Gadhadā, I-65.

6 Ibid., Sārangpur, 10.
Aham brahma param dhāma brahmāham paramam padam
- Bhāgawata, 12-5-11

at the lotus feet of this God in human form is the way of total redemption. According to Shree Swāminārāyan, anthropomorphism is in no way ascribed to worldly man, but to God only, who assumes human form for the redemption of humanity as a whole. He says :

Ātmā cannot be realised by merely thinking about it or by meditating upon it. It is only by the meditational worship of God, when He descends on the earth, and by His upāsanā, by chanting His name and by remembering the divine episodes of His life, and by observing one's own dharma, that Ātmā can be realised and total redemption attained; but without upāsanā, death cannot be transgressed and Brāhmic consciousness cannot be attained.[7]

The devotee who attains such mukti enjoys the ecstasy of union with Brahman, and feels the whole cosmos filled with the ānand of superlative knowledge, wherein he enjoys harmony with God. His conative and cognative organs cease to stretch towards the sense-objects.[8] Such a devotee does not see others except God, does not hear others and does not cognise anybody.[9] This relapse into the ocean of pacific divinity, makes for oblivion to external influences. However, he performs all duties disinterestedly and with perfect equanimity.

A devotee should not have the slightest desire to attain the sārupya, sāyujya, sāmipya and sālokya mukti. A devotee who desires such mukti is sakām or arthārthi. The nishkām bhakta prefers seva even in the redeemed state. The sevya-sevak bhāv between God and the devotees is an absolute necessity. The extinction of the self in the state of mukti, according to others, is like the absolute unconsciousness of a stone or like the state of deep sleep. The theism of Swāminārāyan is based on the

---

7 Vachanāmrit, Gadhadā Sec. II-35

8 Ibid., Sec. I-24.

9 Chhāndogya, Kh. 7.23-24

doctrine of eternal service of the Lord in Brahmadhām or when He manifests on the earth, rather than on the attainment of Ātmasattā.[10] Mere Ātmasattā or pure consciousness without the contact of God, permanently hinders the path of total redemption.

Again the stages of redemption differ according to whether one worships cosmic Gods or Gods of the other loks.[11] It is only when the upāsak meditates upon Akshar Brahman, attains Brāhmic state, and realises Parabrahman, that he is freed from the influence of the gunas and is enlightened. This is Parāgati or ultimate redemption. Again, in this stage of mukti the released soul does not remain still or dormant but has spiritual activism, with which he sings the praises of God in His full splendour.

This is the highest attainment possible here on the earth. However, the apprehension of God in all His splendour here, does not in any way preclude the spiritual journey to Brahmadhām, which is beyond the lok of Purush and Prakriti.[12] But such a devotee, even within the framework of the physical body here, enjoys the ecstasy of divine joy and is totally absorbed in singing the praise of God. In fact, God becomes his vital nerve and he cannot sustain life without Him.

The bliss of enjoying God after the transmigration of the soul to Brahmadhām or in the trans-empirical state, is graded according to the knowledge and realisation of God that the devotee may have attained here. It differs with the various released souls according to their realisation, yet each of them still feels that he is enjoying complete bliss. Even though this gradation in the status of the released souls (due to their inherent capacity of realisation) is apparent, none of the

---

[10] Vachanāmrit, Gadhadā, Sec. II-35

[11] Anekajanmasamsiddhas tato yāti param gatim.   - Gitā, VI-45

[12] Vachanāmrit, Gadhadā, Sec. - I-21

released souls individually feels elated or degraded by this gradation, since each of them completely enjoys the bliss. Thus no such awareness of distinction is felt amongst them; however the awareness of the transcendence of God is always before them. This consciousness of the transcendence of God keeps them always subservient to God. The niyamya-niyamak bhãv persists as sãsyatã and control of evolution and all cosmic functions is retained by God only.[13]

The meditational worship of Brahman or a Brahmanised Guru through whom God is worshipped (only during the condition when God is not manifesting on the earth with all His divine aspects), and the observance of the Pancha Vartmãn (nishkãm, nirlobh, nisswãd, nissneh and nirmãn) which forbids indulgence in passion, covetousness, taste, attachment and egoism, are the cardinal requirements for total deliverance as prescribed by Shree Swãminãrãyan. This process or sãdhanã would naturally extinguish the vãsanã lingdeh or the causal body. As such the resurgence of any instinct, even out of shuddha sattva, does not arise in the trans-empirical state which is a pure and absolute Brãhmic state. Each released soul out of the infinite, unmindful of the others, enjoys in his own way, and the enjoyment of the bliss of Paramãtmã is full and saturated for him as he experiences fully the plethora of divine joy. Thus the disparity in status or condition amongst various released souls does not in any way create any distinction between them, which is the feature of the empiric state here on the earth.

It is not merely the theological deification that Shree Swãminãrãyan desired to arouse in the hearts of His disciples. He wanted them to know Him with a purified vision by observing the rules of swadharma and cultivating jnãn and vairãgya. Knowledge is not outside but within, and God is not beyond but here and immediate. God in human form should

---

[13] Aparimitã dhruva — Bhãgawata, 10-87-30

be realised by an implicit faith in scriptures as also in the nectar words of the Guru, and then by following the path of upāsanā and bhakti as shown by them.

Intense bhakti is not attained simply by Vedic study, tapas or meritorious deeds. Since it is the integral experience of the bliss of Parabrahman, it is attainable only by Ātmā Brahmanised by the contact of Brahman. Ātmā is powerless so long as it is confined in the body and is subject to ignorance of its self, and its pervasiveness is circumscribed within the body. When it is freed from ignorance and attains its full freedom – Ātmasattā – it becomes the cosmic soul and its pervasiveness stretches throughout the whole cosmos. Brahman, however, is the totality of all Ātman and covers the millions of macrocosms.[14] There is nothing which is devoid of the Brahman or chidākāsh.[15] The contact of this Brahman manifesting on the earth in the form of a guru, destroys the vāsanāmaya chitta and imparts Brahmadrishti.[16]

When Ātmā is merged in Brahman which is full of light and knowledge, the mumukshu realises the transitoriness of the world and cultivates repugnance towards māyāmaya bhog or sense-objects. He then develops the consciousness of his self as Brahman, and remains steadfastly attached to the Guru. The Guru, who is one with Parabrahman and is indistinguishable from Parabrahman by the apruthaka-siddha bhāv or visheshan-vishesya bhāv, bestows on the disciple the grace with which he attains Parabrahman.

Shree Swāminārāyan has therefore promised mukti here and now, in this life. In fact He has bestowed this grace upon many of His disciples, who during their life-time have lived a Brāhmic life. At all times during His discourses, He used to infuse in them the knowledge of the divinity which they

---

[14] Vedras p. 165

[15] Vachanāmrit, Gadhadā Sec. l-46.

[16] Vedras p. l66.

possessed by His contact. 'I behold unto you the divinity of the released souls of my Brahmadhām. If there be any trace of untruth, I swear by you all.'[17] The immediacy of Brahman and the enjoyment of the integral bliss and ānand emanating from Parabrahman, elevate the devotee to the status of a mukta, even though still embodied. To him who has realised Brahman, the eight spheres encircling the universe are conquered or penetrated, and apparently to such a devotee the transmigrational journey from here to Brahmalok is superfluous since he is always in Brahmalok.[18] The subjective experience of Brahman elevates him. However, the Brahmanised Ātmā has to migrate to Brahmalok after death since it cannot consistently be assimilated with jad prakriti or matter. Many have been led to this Brahmadhām by Shree Swāminārāyan who comes to fetch His devotees with His released souls, and gives darshan to many others in the waking state. Contemporary writers recorded many such incidents in their writings.[19] The phenomenon has not ceased and has been recurring even now. As put by William James, Such mystic experience is not the aberration of the diseased mind as explained by the materialists, but is the genuine experience of God, which illumines the intellect, purifies the will and exalts the feeling.'

Shree Swāminārāyan has spoken as God, not as a philosopher, thinker or seer. He has spoken from the unseen regions, where He wanted to lead His disciples. The mystic experience of the divine vision which He bestowed on thousands convinced them of the reality of His utterances. The immutable faith of His disciples in His words, and their determination to live a life according to the tenets expounded by Him, helped to promote the cause which He wanted to

---

[17] Vachanāmrit, Gadhadā Sec. II-21.

[18] Vachanāmrit, Sārangpur 10

[19] Nishkulānand Swāmi, Bhaktachintāmani, Gadhadā, 1881.

foster. His contemporaries, amongst whom many were sceptics, agnostics, solipsists and subjectivists, questioned His Divinity, opposed Him, interfered with His work, but they all surrendered when they experienced His aishwarya (Lordship), absolute compassion, and His dynamic will to redeem humanity. The unparalleled philosophical wisdom that He bestowed upon His disciples, many of whom were from a class believed irredeemably ignorant, is a bold testament to His divine working.

He did not believe in manifesting supernatural powers as such, but did not hesitate to exhibit them whenever it was necessary to do so. He trained His disciples to study scriptures, to associate themselves with the saints of the holy order, and to lead a pious and lofty life. He gave light. Those who received it were enlightened. Others, who relied on scientific enquiry into the mystical working of this Divine Personality, with the span of life so insignificant for measuring the will and working of God which has so far remained beyond human perception and conception, were discarded. 'The more the scientist-philosopher seeks to marvel at the mystery of nature, the more veils are left behind. Ignorance increases with knowledge and the riddle of the sphinx remains unsolved.'[20]

Shree Swāminārāyan, however, says that the feeling of scepticism inherent in many can be wiped out only when the Ātmā is freed from the upādhi of the causal body, is purified and has realisation of Paramātmā. The realisation gives a vision of the Viswarup of God resplendent with divine beauty and divine powers, wherein one beholds millions of universes, each having fourteen lokas and various gods and goddesses residing therein. Sometimes He assumes a smaller form and rests on the leaf of a banyan tree. Markandeya Rishi, meditating upon this form of God, had the vision of His

---

[20] Srinivasachari, P. N., The Philosophy of Vishishtādvaita, Adyar, 1943

Viswarup. One who has such realisation feels the scriptural descriptions of God and His various lokas are thoroughly truthful and is relieved of the tinge of sceptical thinking which holds back his intellect[21] whenever he cannot understand the cosmic working.

According to Shree Swāminārāyan, intellectual reasoning in order to know God and His saint with all their attributes and profundity of powers, and meditating upon such a form when known, would give the devotee the revelation within (sadya mukti or immediate release) relieving him from the process of gradual evolutionary progress which Sāmkhya provides or the Kramamukti (the release through stages) which the archā worship offers. Mukti is attained only by the spiritual grace that is being offered continuously and in all its fullness by Him.

And the recipients, in the words of Aldous Huxley, 'who have willed away their self-will to the point of being able truthfully to say, 'Not I, but God in me',[22] will be totally redeemed. Ultimate mukti or Brāhmic consciousness is attained not simply by sādhanās but by grace – Kripā. It is God who seeks the self. Again it is the self who, in order to propitiate God, has to develop vivek, vairāgya and dharma. This is the spiritual endeavour that God expects him to perform for external as well as internal purification. Otherwise the fullest dedication is the complete cause of the release from māyā that God grants him. There should not even be the slightest desire even for Ātmānubhav, which is bestowed by God only through grace, irrespective of any imperfection that the devotee may have, provided only that his dedication to Him is complete and his manas, buddhi, chitta and ahamkār are centred on Him only.[23]

---

[21] Vachanāmrit, Ahmedābād 1.

[22] Huxley, Aldous, The Perennial Philosophy, London, 1946

[23] Vachanāmrit, Gadhadā Sec. III-5.

It is atyāntiki mukti that He grants, and not the release from or annihilation of death, which is generally termed mukti. Atyāntiki mukti offers bliss and the kainkarya or seva of Parabrahman in His Brahmadhām.

28 Satsangijivanam

Written in the style of *Shrimad Bhāgawat*, *Satsangijivanam* was composed in five chapters by the veteran scholar and saint Shree Shatānand Muni in a mood of divine inspiration from Shree Swāminārāyan. This scripture depicts the life and philosophy of Shree Swāminārāyan. As compared to the Vachanāmritam, which is unique in its detailed exposition of spiritual experience and the establishment of divine communion with God, *Satsangijivanam* combines spiritual, metaphysical and religious aspects of Bhāgawat Dharma as explained by Shree Swāminārāyan. The erudite author has very devotionally interwoven the divine episodes of the life of his Lord, Shree Swāminārāyan. In all there are 17,627 verses, written in lucid style in rich Sanskrit.

Suvrat Muni, a learned Brāhmin from Kurukshetra and a foremost disciple of Shree Shatānand Muni started the recital of this scripture in Jagannāthpuri before King Pratāpsinh.

Sat sampradāya or cult inherits the spiritual legacy of its founder who may be either God or a saint in rapport with Him. The presence of such a Guru enlivens the sampradāya and rejuvenates its ethics. These ethical truths are bequeathed to posterity. But they can be realised only at the lotus feet of a Guru, as *Chhāndogya* explains, 'He who has found a preceptor, knows.' If the spiritual thread between the Guru and Shishya (disciple) is lost, the sampradāya turns into an antiquated body which ultimately becomes merely fanatical.

Satsangijivanam traces the thread of the divine hierarchy in

Uddhava, the chief disciple of Shree Krishna, who had a spiritual union with Shree Krishna.[1] He was ordained by Shree Krishna to spread His message of Bhāgawat Dharma in his next birth. Uddhava, in his next birth as Ramānand Swāmi[2] was initiated during a dream into Bhāgawati Dikshā by Shree Rāmānujāchārya in Shree Rangam. He was then asked to leave Shree Rangam and spread the message of Bhāgawat Dharma from a place which he found suitable. Rāmānand was therefore the founder of this sampradāya which is known as Uddhavi Sampradāya.[3]

The unitive consciousness that the disciple has with his Guru or the devotee has with God, qualifies him for being the sadāchārya. He alone can correctly interpret and preach the meaning of Shrutis to the mumukshu. The knowledge of Brahman and Parabrahman rests in spiritually experiencing the Brāhmic consciousness and enjoying the beatitude of Parabrahman. But mere mental knowledge does not carry the devotee beyond the mundane spheres. The necessity of a satpurush or a sadāchārya is acknowledged with due respect. Vedānta, as is commonly understood, is not merely a pessimistic denial, but is an optimistic establishment of the ontological Brahman within the self or Ātmā. The sampradāya, therefore, correctly acknowledges the values of Brahman and Parabrahman for infusing Brāhmic consciousness 'within its followers, and requires the guidance of such a Guru. Otherwise it would function only as a traditional school teaching aphorisms and holding polemical discussions to maintain its own front.

---

[1] Sākshād Uddhava hi Krushnād api anur anyunaha
Krushnābhaktipravartakaha. - Satsangijivanam, II-A. 37-89

[2] Rāmānāndabhidho yo atra vartate vaishnavāgranihi
Tam mama aikāntikam bhaktam avagaccha tvam Uddhavam.
-Ibid., II-A. 37-43.

[3] Ato naha sampradāyo ayam sarvavaishnavasammataha
Ouddhavākhyo astu iti shrutvā tathā uchus te ākhyitā api.
- Ibid., II-A. 37-9I

The *Vedas*, being impersonal, their authority is self-established. The *Upanishads*, as part of the *Vedas*, the *Brahmasutras*, the *Gitā*, *Vishnu-sahasranām*, *Vidur-Niti*, and *Vāsudevmahātmya* from *Skanda Purāna*, are the scriptures recognised as authority by Shree Swāminārāyan for explaining the tenets of this sampradāya.

According to this text, the essence of bhakti is in renouncing the sense-objects, cultivating detachment from worldly pleasures, and applying the mind totally to the blissful self of Paramātmā. The culmination of bhakti is in attaining the ideal of Jadbharat.[4] The sādhus and the devotees of this sampradāya are expected to reach this ideal, the fulfilment of which is by cultivating complete abstinence from attachment to sense objects, and developing absolute devotion to Shree Hari.[5]

The Brahman is not distinguished as sagun or nirgun. He is nirgun as He is devoid of gunas evolved out of Prakriti and is therefore beyond the pleasures and pains born of karmas.[6] Since He possesses the six redemptive attributes (He possesses infinite redemptive attributes but these six are the chief) namely jnān (knowledge), shakti (strength), bal (power), aishwarya (lordship), virya (the quintessence of redemptive power) and tejas (light), He is described as sagun. Sagun and nirgun bhāv are the two different phases of the aishwarya of Parabrahman who reigns in His Brahmadhām, and manifests on the earth as and when He wishes. This manifestation is a result of His will (since He is satyasankalpaka).

However, He does not descend or incarnate on the earth by vacating His Brahmadhām. By His potential redemptive will,

---

4 Shanti ye sādhavo asmākam tyktagrāmyasukhā iha
  Bharatashyārshabhasyeva bhaktis teshām mamāpi cha.

- Ibid., III-A. 29-II

5 Vishayato viratish cha Harau ratihi. - Ibid., II-A. 29-2I

6 Na prakrutā gunās tasmin santityuktaha sa nirgunaha.

- Ibid., III-A. 29-21

He makes Himself visible from His Brahmadhām before human beings in a human form. And still He is totally divine, the inspirer of knowledge to all, and the impeller of all actions of human beings according to their karmas.[7] His vibhutvam or purnatvam is in His power to interpenetrate and work as antaryāmi in all the jivas and it is not destroyed even while in human manifestation.

The knowledge of the supreme Brahman therefore validates that He is Ekadeshastha, i.e. residing in His divine abode and still omnipresent by the will of His manifestation and is all-pervasive by His jnān and tejas, i.e. immanent in all by His power of sustaining the lives of, and inspiring knowledge to, all jivas. Even in human incarnation, when necessary, He exhibits His powers, as recorded in the history of the various incarnations. God in human form is not limited by human disabilities, although He assumes human form to mix with His disciples. God therefore does not assume a second form, but manifests from His abode by His divine will, according to the requirements of time and place.

Although the philosophy of religion recognises priority of reason over faith, the theophanic revelations of God before the devout disciples, as a result of His propitiated will, impart spiritual experience to devotees even if they may be few. This revealed theology has therefore a unique place in Hindu philosophy, which also recognises natural or rational theology for the elevation of the thinking faculty. The approach of Hindu philosophy is for the correct way of living and not merely for an advance in thinking or knowledge. It is a search for the spiritual experience of the Ultimate Reality. And the Guru, either in the form of God or a seer, is the correct preceptor to lead one to a proper knowledge and experience of Ultimate Reality – God. The mystic experience that he transmits to his disciple is a record of his unitive experience

---

[7] Prakāshākāsh cha sarveshām svatantro divyavigrahaha.

- Ibid., III-A. 29-II.

with God. God therefore descends on the the earth to fulfil the cravings of His devotees.

The spontaneous appearance of Shree Krishna in as many forms as the number of Gopis in answer to their divine call to play rās, the assumption of four forms by Vishnu for alleviating the distress of the devas by churning the ocean (as Kurma He held the Mandarāchal on His back; as Ajit, He churned the ocean; as Dhanvantari He brought the nectar; and as Mohini, He distributed the nectar amongst the devas), and again the appearance of Vishnu in the form of Trivikram who spanned the whole cosmos within only three steps, all these phases of divinity are but revelations emanating from the divine form of Brahman seated in His Brahmadhām, as a result of His redemptive will. These revelations and also the incarnated form of Brahman, are but one and not distinguished from the Brahman of the Brahmadhām.[8] During the phase of His manifestation in human form, human aptitudes, limitations, anger, covetousness, passion, death, etc. may be displayed by Him for the successful working of His redemptive will.[9] Those who cannot visualise the inherent divinity in His human form are devoid of understanding. Therefore Brahman, the transcendental Highest, even in many phases of His divine working on the earth, is one. This is swarupādvaita.[10]

The text goes on to describe the ways of attaining spiritual experience by directly apprehending Brahman. By Brahmopāsanā, the Yogi attains nirvikalpa state. This Brāhmic

---

[8] Narākrutis tathā krushno jñātavyo divyavigrahaha
Divyavigraha evasau naranātyadharash cha vai.
- Satsangijivanam, III-A. 29-76

[9] Ajnatvam pāravashyatvam vibhibhedādikam tathā
Tathā prakrutadehatvam dehatyāgādikam tathā.
- Ibid., III-A. 29-107

[10] Ekasmin advitiye bhāgawati cha parabrahmani dvaitabuddhi
Kartavya naiva tasmin anur api cha kudhiha sacchidānandarupe.
- Ibid., III-A. 29-144

consciousness mitigates bhedadrishti and identifies the yogi with Brahman (*Brahmavid brahmaiva bhavati*), i.e. he is superimposed with the attributes of Brahman.[11] He is then known as mahāmukta.

By the force of the meditational worship of Brahman, the causal body is destroyed and the released soul attains the divya vigrah or bhāgawati tanu, enjoying the bliss of Paramātmā. But the entity of the released soul does not get extinct and so the Shrutis describe them as *nityo nityānām chetanash chetanānām eko bahunām*, etc.

The word Brahman, however, raises confusion, as it refers both to the divine abode and also to God. But when the word Dhām is suffixed to it, it refers to the divine abode or Brahmadhām. When it is used singly it refers to Brahman – the God. With the *brahmashabdam dvayam proktam*,[12] the text elucidates the Shrutis of Mundaka used to explain the above complex[13] in terms of Brahman the abode and Brahman the God. Brahman as abode is also referred to as Akshar and Brahman as God is referred to as Parabrahman.

All jivas are inherently Brahman, but as they are obscured by the limitations of Māyā their buddhi or intelligence is affected. The jiva attains its fully fledged form of Brahman when his avidyā-karma is destroyed. There is thus a vital difference between jiva, Ishwar, Brahman and Parabrahman[14]

---

[11] Brahmaiva brahmavid iti shrutivarnyaha sa yogir āt
Mahāmukta iti proktas tattvavidbhir dvijottama.
- Ibid., IV-A. 21-16 17.

[12] Brahmashabdam dvayam yatra proktam syat tatra tu dvija
Ādyam tu Bhagavaddhāmā Jnātavyam bruhad aksharam.
Dvitiyam tu svayam Krushnaha sarvakāranakāranam.
Aksharāt para ityukto divyāngash cheti budhyatām.
- Satsangijivanam, IV-A. 21-52. 53.

[13] Sa vedaitatparamam brahmadhāma - and, sa yo ha vai tatparamam brahma. Mundaka, 3.2l and 9.

[14] Bhedo hi vāstavo nunam jiveshabrahmanām Harehe!
- Satsangijivanam, IV-A. 21-54.

as propounded by the Shrutis – *nityo nityānām* etc. Again the Shruti *Brahmavid Paramapnoti* also clearly specifies that even the Brahmanised souls have to serve Parabrahman with sevaka-sevya bhāv. Shrutis further describe Akshar as the body of Paramātmā wherein Paramātmā resides as antaryāmin and whom Akshar does not know.[15] This Shruti extols the nature of Paramātmā as the supreme self, infinitely transcendent, with whom even Akshar has no identity, let alone Ishwars and jivas.[16] The infinite greatness of Paramātmā remains unfathomed even by Akshar and other released souls who possess the attributes of Paramātmā, to the extent they have realised Him in their Brahmanised state.

However, in the Brahmanised state, the ecstasy of the mystic union with God is not denied, as the Brahmanised soul has an integral experience of the joy of Parabrahman. His Brāhmic consciousness or Brahmānubhav has erased the cognitive and conative feeling related to the empirical self. With the realisation of this self as Brahman, he visualises before him, around him and within him the unitive consciousness with Parabrahman.[17] Parabrahman works through such a released soul whose empirical ego is extinguished and who has realised that his life or the ego-centric prāna is Parabrahman only. Sometimes in the ecstasy of this divine union he utters, 'I am Parabrahman, the Infinite who constitutes everything.'

The text concludes by enunciating the fundamental principle of Shree Swāminārāyan which is essential to be realised for the purest devotion, and says, 'The conceptual

---

[15] Yo aksharam antare sancharan yasyāksharam shariram yam aksharam na veda. - Subalopanishad, Kh. 7.

[16] Aksharasyāpi chen nāsti brahmanaha Krushnaruptā
Kutas tarām tad ishasya jivasya tu kutas tamām
-Satsangijivanam, IV-A. 21-59

[17] Brahmaikam eva vikshante jivesādin pruthag na tu.
- Ibid., IV-A. 72-40.

knowledge of one's own self as Brahman should be realised and in that Brāhmic state only worship should be offered to Parabrahman. Such a devotee attains nirvikalpa samādhi and attains Paramdhām which is beyond.[18] So long as the empirical ego persists, the meditational worship is tarnished. Concentration on personal Brahman, or a Brahmanised Guru and assuming his form, extinguishes this ego. Actions performed in this state are not characterised by ignorance but are purely devotional and ultimately help in the final realisation of one's own self as Brahman.

The text further explains the word *Triyugi* used for God, as explained by Muktānand Swāmi during his discourse with some pundits at Vattapattan (Barodā). These pundits held that according to scriptures there cannot be any incarnation of God in Kali Yuga. The scriptures describe Bhagwān as *Triyugi* i.e. one who incarnates only in three yugas, namely Satya Yuga, Tretā Yuga and Dwāpar Yuga.

Muktānand Swāmi was of an absolutely quiet disposition and had a profound knowledge of scriptures. He felt that these pundits, in spite of their learning, knew scriptures. only superficially. He therefore explained the meaning of *Triyugi*.

According to Amara Kosha, the meaning of Yuga is a pair. The three yugas or the six features, namely the evolution and the destruction of universes, the cause of births and deaths, salvation, brahmavidyā or knowledge, the cause of ultimate release, and avidyā or ignorance, the cause of bondage of samsrti, are known to God only. Again the six redemptive attributes, namely jnān, shakti, bal, aishwarya, virya and tejas are possessed by God only. Bhāgawat explains that in Satya Yuga, people were of a thoroughly meditative disposition and thus there was no need for God to incarnate on the earth. Therefore in the rest of the three yugas – Tretā, Dwāpar and Kali – God incarnates.

---

[18] Brahmarupena tato bhajettam...   - Ibid. IV-A. 72-44.

Yuga is born within, according to how one performs actions with preponderant influences of the three gunas, namely Sattva, Rajas and Tamas, or with the mixture of any of them. When Kali or the tāmasic actions predominate within, God is not likely to manifest or be perceived within. However, even in Kali Yuga, if one has developed internally the attributes of Sattva guna, (jnān, vairāgya, bhakti, etc.), God is likely to manifest before him or inspire His knowledge within. Thus the word *Triyugi* should be correctly interpreted and understood. God has no restrictions and is not bound by any rules as He is Param Maheshvaram, capable of developing sattva guna in the hearts of people even in the dark age of Kali Yuga.

Muktānand thus successfully refuted the arguments of the various pundits and established the Law of Karma which evolves gunas and develops yugadharma within. There is no hard and fast rule that a particular yuga would evolve only its dharma, inasmuch as the actions characterised by guna predominate, and develop accordingly the particular yugadharma. It may be Satya, Tretā, Dwāpar or Kali according as the actions are sāttvic, sāttvic-rājasic, rājasic-tāmasic and tāmasic respectively.

Chapter V of the text contains rituals, sacraments, vrats, and the prāyashchitta vidhi for infringement of the various sacraments.

29 Shikshãpatri

This is an integral part of Shree *Satsangijivanam* wherein Shree Swãminãrãyan has given precepts and the code of behaviour for sãdhus, brahmacharis, grhasthas, widows, and women dedicated to a life of renunciation. Sir Monier Williams, in his book *Religious Thought*, hails this *Shikshãpatri* as 'a collection of two hundred and twelve precepts, some original some extracted from Manu and other sacred shãstras and many of them containing high moral sentiments worthy of Christianity itself... they are calculated to give a fair idea of the purer side of modern Vaishnavism.'

Written in the form of an epistle, the book has been composed with a pure vision to establish amongst the devotees of this fold a code of conduct to be strictly observed for ultimately controlling the cognitive and conative organs. Shatãnand Muni, explaining the purpose of this small epistle, writes, 'the control over the cognative and conative organs is necessary for performing purified actions. Karma yoga is better than renouncing of karmas. The purified actions lead to Bhakti. No other fruit is higher to the virtuous than the dedicated devotion to God. Bhakti should be coupled with Dharma for ultimate realisation. Bhakti should be performed by assuming one's own self as Brahman devoid of three bodies – the gross, subtle and causal. The empirical self always thrives on the enjoyment of sense objects which hinders meditational worship.'

The underlying principle of this epistle is that unless these religious tenets are observed strictly, upãsanã and bhakti are not fulfilled. The heart of a devotee should be like butter soft and pure, so that it becomes unable to retain any vitiating element generated from the mature play of the cognitive as well as conative organs. Here is the full text of Shikshāpatri

SHIKSHĀPATRI

Shikshāpatri-Mahātmya

When knowledge degenerated and ignorance prevailed in the world, and when people became confused in the performance of their duties, and Shāstras were misinterpreted to uphold karmas which inflicted injuries on living beings, the Lord of Akshardhām incarnated on the earth out of compassion and gave us this Shikshāpatri, the Mother of Mukti, on whom I meditate. (1)

To extricate the people who rot in the muddy whirlpool of Samsār and to purify them, O Shikshāpatri, you have incarnated on the earth. It is only you who can dispel the intense darkness of ignorance of the people. Therefore O Shikshāpatri, I meditate on you! (2)

This Shikshāpatri, which is like a stick for the application of collyrium and which removes darkness in the form of ignorance from the heart, should be worshipped for the vision of true knowledge. (3)

This Shikshāpatri has been evolved by Bhagwān Swāminārāyan who resides in Akshardhām, especially for all His disciples living in various countries. Therefore, O sanctifier, you are the saviour from the cycle of births and deaths! O Mother! I meditate upon you who have been so wisely incorporated in the holy scripture by Shree Shatānand Muni. (4)

I resort to you, O Shikshāpatri, evolved by the wish of Bhagwān Swāminārāyan and incorporated in the Satsangijivan scripture by Shree Shatānand Muni. (5)

You are the quintessence of all the nectar churned from the

ocean of scriptures, and therefore those who drink this nectar become fit for immortality. (6)

Shree Sahajānand Swāmi, who is the only resort of the Satpurushas and who gave this nectar to Mukundānand and other disciples on this earth has brought you about, O Shikshāpatri! I worship you, the dispeller of demonic evils and the healer of the pains of this Samsār! (7)

O Nārāyan! May you live in my heart, You who are the redeemer of living beings who rot in the cycles of births and deaths, You who have undertaken the writing of this Shikshāpatri to impart to people the spiritual wisdom of their ultimate redemption. May You always enlighten me. (8)

O son of Dharma! May You always reside in my heart, You who always love your disciples and always bear a smiling face which attracts everybody. (9)

This Shikshāpatri, which is the bestower of all benevolence and which shines brightly upon the earth, is the second sacred divine form of Shree Swāminārāyan Bhagwān. (10)

O Shikshāpatri! I accept you as the second divine form of my Lord Swāminārāyan who is worshipped by all His disciples and who is the cause of everything. You have been evolved by Him, and therefore you are the giver of all desired fruits. I therefore worship you always as the very form of my Lord. (11)

'This nectar in the form of Shikshāpatri I have given to this world for the welfare of the people. May it therefore be served with due reverence by all My disciples.' One should therefore always bear in mind this divine order of the Lord and always abide by the precepts laid down in Shikshāpatri, which will ultimately lead one to the eternal abode. (12)

SHIKSHĀPATRI
(The Epistle of Precepts)
by Swāmi Sahajānand

I meditate in my heart on Shree Krishna, the gay divine flute player who sports in Brindāvan, on whose left is Rādhā and in whose bosom dwells Lakshmi. (1)

I, Sahajānand Swāmi, write this Shikshāpatri from Vrittālaya (Vadtāl) to all my followers residing far and wide. (2)

Ayodhyāprasād and Raghuvir, the respective sons of my brothers Rāmpratāp and Ichhārām, born of Dharmadev; the Brahmachāris headed by Mukundānand, grihasthas such as Mayāram Bhatt, and others who are my followers; married women with husbands alive or dead; and all saints such as Muktānand and others may all accept my benedictions – benefactors of Swadharma as prescribed by the scriptures, and the happy remembrances sanctified by the name of Shree Nārāyan. (3,4,5,6)

Listen, all of you, with due attention to the benefits inherent in this writing, the Shikshāpatri. (7)

My followers who strictly observe the Rules of Ethics (non-injury, etc.) as enjoined by the scriptures, shall derive happiness here and hereafter; those who wantonly transgress rules and behave wilfully shall suffer great distress here and in the life hereafter. (8,9)

Hence it is incumbent upon all my disciples to follow scrupulously the commandments of this Shikshāpatri, both in letter and spirit, and never transgress them. (10)

Code of conduct in general for disciples of all classes: *(II – 48)*.

None of my followers should ever kill any living creature, nor should they intentionally kill insects such as lice, bugs and the like. (11)

No one should kill animals (such as goats) even for the

purpose of performing sacrifice rites or for propitiating any deity, for non-violence alone is avowedly held to be the highest ethical code. (12)

No one should ever commit homicide for any object, whether it be for women, wealth or even a kingdom. (13)

No one should ever commit suicide, in a fit of anger, or being vexed by some sinful act, by means such as taking poison, strangulation, or a headlong plunge down a well, even in a place of pilgrimage. (14)

No one should ever eat flesh or meat, even the remnant of offerings in a sacrifice, and no one should drink alcoholic liquor, wine, or any intoxicating beverage, even if it has been offered to deities. (15)

No one should mutilate any part of his body or that of others with a weapon, as a punishment for performance of misdeeds either by oneself or others, in a state of excitement, or as an atonement for misdeeds. (16)

No one should steal, even for benevolent purposes, nor should anyone take things like fuel, flowers, and the like without the consent of their owners. (17)

None of my followers, male and female, should commit adultery or practise gambling and similar vices, and they should abstain from drinking or inhaling intoxicants such as Bhang (hashish), tobacco, snuff and the like. (18)

Except at Jagannāthpuri, no one should eat and drink what is unacceptable at the hands of a person under the scruples of caste system, even if it be the remnant Prasād of the offering to Shree Krishna. (19)

No one should ever impute any false charge to anybody with the object of promoting self interest, nor should anyone ever abuse anybody. (20)

No one should ever vilify Gods, places of pilgrimage,

Brāhmins, chaste women, saints and the Vedas, nor should any one listen to any such talk. (21)

No one should accept an offering made to a deity to whom flesh and wine are offered, and before whom goats and such beasts are sacrificed. (22)

If my followers should happen to pass by temples of Shiva or other deities, they should bow down with due reverence to the idols therein. (23)

None of my followers should ever dispense with the conduct prescribed in the code of Varnāshram - Dharma, and should never accept any code of behaviour not sanctioned by the scriptures. (24)

No one should ever listen to religious discourses from a person whose preaching might lead one to fall away from devotion to God and one's duty. (25)

No one should ever utter truth that might bring about humiliation to himself or to others, and should give up the company of ungrateful persons, and never accept bribes from anyone in social affairs. (26)

No one should associate with thieves or vicious persons, addicts, heretics or alchemists. (27)

No one should keep contact with those who hanker after women and wealth, or practise sinful acts under the cloak of hypocritical devotion or so-called wisdom. (28)

No one should listen to or pay any credence to scriptures skilfully contrived to deny the existence of the Supreme Eternal Reality and His incarnations. (29)

No one should drink unfiltered water or milk, nor bathe in water containing germs. (30)

My disciples should never take medicine mixed with liquor or meat, or which is prescribed by a physician not known to them. (31)

No one should allow bodily excretions or filth to fall in places where such nuisance is prohibited by the scriptures or by a public authority. (32)

No one should enter or pass through private property, nor stay in a place without the owner's permission. (33)

None of my male devotees should listen to discourses from the mouth of a woman nor enter into discussion with women, kings or their courtiers. (34)

No one should insult preceptors, superiors, persons of social status, learned men, and those with weapons. (35)

Duties relating to Dharma should be performed immediately, while duties relating to social affairs should be performed after due deliberation. The learned should impart their learning to others, and should constantly keep the company of saints. (36)

No one should approach a Guru, deity, or a king empty handed, and no one should commit a breach of trust or indulge in self-praise. (37)

None of my followers should wear any garment which is likely to expose any part of the body to view. (38)

No one should practise devotion to Shree Krishna while disregarding religious tenets, nor give up worship of Shree Krishna for fear of calumny to the ignorant. (39)

All males and females coming to the temples of Shree Krishna for darshan, either daily or on days of religious festivals, should keep themselves aloof from the opposite sex. (40)

All my Brāhmin, Kshatriya and Vaishya followers (Dwija or twice-born, as they are called) initiated into the devotion of Shree Krishna by the spiritual master, should always wear a double kanthi of Tulsi beads around their necks, and should put an upright tilak mark on their forehead, and their chest and both arms. (41)

The tilak should be made of Gopichandan stick or of consecrated sandalwood paste mixed with saffron and kumkum that has been offered to Shree Krishna. (42)

In the centre of the tilak, a round mark should be made of Gopichandan or kumkum which is duly offered to Rādhā and Lakshmi. (43)

Sat-Shudra devotees of Shree Krishna, observing Dharma, should also wear a kanthi and imprint a tilak mark like Dwijas. (44)

The devotees who belong to the lower substrata of society should wear a double kanthi of sandalwood beads, and should put only a round kumkum mark on the forehead. (45)

None of my brāhmin devotees should ever give up the family tradition of imprinting Tripundra and wearing Rudrākshmālā. (46)

The Vedas proclaim Nārāyan and Shiva as one and as Brahmaswarup; therefore they should be generally known as such. (47)

In the event of an ordinary mishap, my followers should never fall back upon the permitted relaxation sanctioned by scriptures which is reserved for severe calamities. (48)

Rituals of daily worship to be observed by the followers:

All my disciples shall wake up before sunrise and, after meditating on Shree Krishna, should retire for discharging bowels. (49)

They should then sit at one place and brush their teeth, then bathe with clean water, and then put on clothes duly washed and untouched. (50)

They should then sit on an undefiled place in seclusion,

facing either east or north, and perform Āchamanam. (51)

All my male disciples should then put tilak on their forehead and a round kumkum mark as aforesaid; married women should make only a round mark of kumkum on their forehead. (52)

Widows should not have a tilak or a round kumkum mark. They should offer mental worship to Shree Krishna. (53)

My disciples should then reverently bow down to the image of Rādhā and Krishna and chant the holy name of the Lord in accordance with their usual and normal procedure; only after this should they start their daily routine. (54)

Those devotees living a consecrated life like King Ambarish should also follow the course of rituals as already described. (55)

They should worship the idol of Shree Krishna made either of stone or of metal, or a Shāligram, with offerings procurable within one's own time and means, and then chant His holy name. (56)

Afterwards they should read hymns or a religious text suited to their ability; those who are unacquainted with Sanskrit may sing a song in praise and adoration of Shree Krishna. (57)

They should then offer food to God, and should take Prasād only from the offered dish. Thus in a spirit of supreme love and dedication they should serve Shree Krishna. (58)

Those devotees who live a consecrated life are known as nirgun; all their deeds are purified in their constant and devout contact with the Lord who is ever nirgun. (59)

Those votaries should never drink water, eat roots, fruits or the like, without offering the same to Shree Krishna. (60)

Ethics of Conduct-continued: (61 – 92)

My devotees disabled by old age or other adversity should hand over to some other devotees the images of Shree Krishna which they may be worshipping, and worship the Lord to the best of their ability. (61)

My devotees should worship only those images of the Lord that are given by the Āchārya or installed by him. Only obeisance should be offered to other images. (62)

All my followers should go to the temple every evening, and there sing aloud songs in praise of the Lord. (63)

They should read and hear narrations from the life of the Lord with utmost reverence and on festival days they should sing songs of Shree Krishna to the accompaniment of musical instruments. (64)

All my devotees should invariably follow the course prescribed above, and also study religious works in Sanskrit or vernacular to the best of their knowledge. (65)

A man must be thoughtfully assigned a work for which he is best suited, never otherwise. (66)

One who has engaged servants should take proper care in respect of their feeding and clothing, according to his means. (67)

A person possessing virtues should be so respected and addressed, taking into consideration the prevalent custom, time and place, but should never be otherwise treated. (68)

A preceptor, a king, an elder, a renunciate, a learned man, and an ascetic should all be duly honoured on their arrival by rising up and bowing to them. (69)

No one should sit in a posture with one foot placed on the thigh or with both knees bound with a cloth-strap, in the presence of a preceptor, an idol of God, a king or in an assembly. (70)

My disciples should never enter into futile debate with the

Āchārya and should respect him and serve him with money, clothes, and the like according to their means. (71)

On hearing of the arrival of the Āchārya, my disciples should proceed up to the outskirts of the town to receive him with respect, and on his departure should accompany him to the outskirts to bid him farewell. (72)

My devotees should desist from performing any acts which are contrary to the scriptural tenets, however fruitful they may be, for verily Dharma alone yields all desired results. (73)

My disciples should never follow any unrighteous deed which may have been performed by great persons of the past. They should follow their righteous deeds only. (74)

My disciples should not disclose the secrets of others. Those deserving of merit should be accorded appropriate respect, but in no case should the bounds of courtesy be ignored by observing a false decorum of equality. (75)

During the four months of the monsoon, all my devotees should take up additional religious duties, and those who are physically invalid should take up additional religious duties at least during the month of Shrāvan. (76)

The recitation or listening attentively to the sacred narratives from the life of the Lord, the singing of hymns in His praise, adoration and worship of the image of God, chanting His holy name or His Mantra, the performance of pradakshinā, and Sashtang Dandvat Pranām (prostration before the Lord's image); these eight additional duties are held to be the best. Any one of these may be observed devoutly as additional duty during the period of monsoon. (77,78)

All my disciples should observe fast on Ekādashi, as also on Janmāshtami and on Shivrātri days; these festivals should be celebrated with great reverence. (79)

On these days of fasting my disciples should not sleep

during the daytime as this nullifies the vrat as does conjugal enjoyment. (80)

Shree Vithalnāthji, son of Shree Vallabhāchārya and the exponent of Vaishnavism, has prescribed the days of Vrats, and my disciples should observe these Vrats and perform festival duties accordingly; they should religiously adopt the practice of adoration and worship of the Lord as laid down by Shree Vitthalnāthji. (81,82)

They should visit the sacred places, chief amongst these being Dwārkā, and perform proper rites; according to their means they should be charitable and compassionate towards destitute persons. (83)

My devotees should hold the five deities (Vishnu, Shiva, Ganapati, Pārvati and Āditya) in great reverence. (84)

In the event of an affliction through the influence of an evil spirit, recourse should be taken to the chanting of Nārāyan Kavach or the Hanumān Stotram, but in no case should invocation of any inferior deity be resorted to. (85)

During the solar or lunar eclipse, my devotees should immediately suspend all usual activities and be ready in a purified state for the chanting of God's name or His Mantra. (86)

When the eclipse is over, they should bathe with their clothes on. Householders should give alms according to their means, and the saints should worship God. (87)

All our devotees belonging to the four castes should observe sutak (a period of ten days following birth or death in a family, during which all religious rites are suspended) immediately following the birth or death of kith or kin, in conformity with the scriptures. (88)

My brāhmin devotees should cultivate the qualities of tranquillity, self-restraint, forbearance, contentment, and similar virtues; the Kshatriyas should cultivate valour, fortitude, and other appropriate qualities. (89)

The Vaishya class should take to agriculture, trade, money - lending and similar pursuits; those of the Shudra class should serve the above-named three Varnas. (90)

The Dwijas (twice-born) should perform the purificatory rites (sixteen in all) and also perform daily rituals and obsequies (Shraddhā at the proper time) according to convention and their means. (91)

One should expiate his sins, whether great or small, done knowingly or otherwise, according to his ability. (92)

Authentic Scriptures (93,102):

The four Vedas, Vedānta Sutras by Vyās, Shrimad Bhāgawat, Shree Vishnu Sahasranām, Shree Bhagawad Gitā (from Mahābhārat), the Code of Ethics enunciated by Shree Vidurji (Vidurniti), Shree Vāsudev Mahātmya from the Vishnu Khand of Skand Purāna and Yāgnavalkya Smriti, are the chief amongst all religious scriptures, and I hold these eight scriptures as authoritative and of special significance. (93, 94, 95)

All my disciples who earnestly desire to attain emancipation should listen to all these eight scriptures. My brāhmin devotees should study these scriptures, teach and narrate them to others. (96)

Amongst the aforesaid eight treatises, my followers should hold the Mitākshar commentary on Yāgnavalkya Smruti as the guiding authority to determine matters of usage, mutual dealings, code for expiation, and Nitya Naimittik Karmas. (97)

The 5th and 10th Skandās of Shrimad Bhāgawat Purāna should be regarded as best for acquiring knowledge of the glory and greatness of Shree Krishna. (98)

The 10th and 5th Skandās of Shrimad Bhāgawat and the

Yāgnavalkya Smruti are authoritative treatises on Bhakti, Yoga, and Dharma in the order given. (99)

Shree Bhāshya on the Shāriraka Sutras, and the Bhāshya on Bhagawad Gitā, both by Shree Rāmānujāchārya, are accepted by Me as authoritative for acquiring a comprehensive knowledge of philosophy. (100)

The quotations from these scriptures which describe the transcendent glory of Shree Krishna and which give a superlatively elegant exposition of Dharma, Bhakti and Vairāgya, should be regarded as fundamental truths, compared with various other quotations even though they may describe the glory of Shree Krishna or the form ·of Dharma, Bhakti and Vairāgya. The quintessence of these chosen scriptures is devotion to God with observance of Dharma. (101,102)

Dharma is the ethical code prescribed by Shrutis and Smritis. Deep attachment to Shree Krishna, together with a fully developed awareness of His grandeur constitutes the concept of Bhakti. (103)

Non-attachment to all objects of the senses except to Shree Krishna, is Vairāgya. The comprehensive knowledge of jiva, Māyā and Ishwar is Jnān. (104)

Jiva, which is very subtle, resides in the heart. He is Chidrupa, and by virtue of his sentiency pervades the entire body. He is unpierceable, indivisible, and intangible. (105)

Māyā is trigunātmik, i.e. full of sattva, rajas and tamas qualities, full of darkness, and is the Shakti of Shree Krishna, responsible for creating attachment towards the body and its relations. (106)

As jiva resides in the heart, Paramātmā resides in jiva by His Antaryāmi Shakti. He is independent, and is the giver of benefits and consequences to all, according to their Karmas. (107)

That Paramātmā Shree Krishna (who resides as Antaryāmi in the heart), who is Supreme, Parabrahman, Bhagwān or Purushottam, and who is the cause of all manifestations, is the Lord of all, and He is to be worshipped for final emancipation. (108)

Where His manifested form is associated with Rādhā, the dual form is known as Rādhā-Krishna, and when associated with Lakshmi, as Lakshmi-Nārāyan. (109)

When associated with Arjuna, He is called Nar-Nārāyan, and He is also known by various other names when He is with Balbhadra and other devotees. (110)

At times, Rādhā and other devotees such as Lakshmi and Arjuna, are by the side of Shree Krishna. But at times when by sheer devotion they are absorbed in His heart, Shree Krishna should be considered as being alone. (111)

Hence these forms of Shree Krishna should not be discriminated as separate forms. When He is described as possessing four arms, eight arms, or a thousand arms, He is said to assume these forms by His free will. But He always has two arms. (112)

All human beings on this earth should worship Him, knowing that there is no other way for ultimate salvation than devotion to Him. (113)

It follows therefore that erudition, knowledge, and such other virtues of learned persons have their fruition in devotion to God and association with realised saints, for without devotion and Satsang even a learned man would degenerate. (114)

Lord Krishna, His incarnations and His idols alone are to be meditated upon, but a human being or a deva, even though he may be a devotee or knower of Brahman, should never be resorted to as an object of meditation. (115)

Assuming the self as Brahman, separate from the three bodies, one should always offer devotion to Shree Krishna. (116)

My devotees should listen with full reverence to the tenth Skandha of Shrimad Bhāgawat daily or at least once a year, so too should learned persons. (117)

My devotees should perform the Purascharan for the tenth Skanda of Shrimad Bhāgawat or Vishnu Sahasranām in a holy place, for such performances help one to attain all desired results. (118)

In the event of any calamity through nature or sickness, one should try to take precautions to save oneself or others, but should not behave in such a manner as to suffer from the consequences thereof. (119)

The internal dealings, ceremonies for expiation of sins, and the prevalent customs, should always be made adaptable according to place, time, age, means, caste and ability. (120)

The creed of our philosophy is Vishishtādvaita – qualified non-dualism – and the Goloka Dhām is the desired abode for souls who, in the released state, assuming Brahmabhāv, serve Lord Krishna. This is ultimate Mukti or liberation. (121)

The following are the special and common duties specified by Me for all my male and female disciples. First I specify the special duties to be performed by My disciples of different grade, class, āshram and sex. (122)

Special Duties (123-202)

Special Duties of the Āchāryas (123-132)

The Āchāryas, the sons of my elder and younger brothers, should never preach to females other than those of their kindred. (123)

They should never touch or talk to females not closely related to them, nor should they be cruel to any living being, nor accept money from others as deposits in their charge. (124)

They should never stand as surety for others in their general dealings; they should subsist on alms to tide over the period of austerity but should never incur debts. (125)

They should never sell food grains offered to them as alms by their followers. However, old cereals may be exchanged for new, and such an exchange does not amount to a sale. (126)

They should perform a special ceremony on the fourth day of the bright half of the month of Bhādrapad, which is the birthday of Ganapati. On the 14th day of the dark half of Ashwina month, they should perform a similar ceremony for the propitiation of Hanumān. (127)

The Āchāryas, namely Ayodhyāprasād and Raghuvirji, appointed by Me as the religious heads of My disciples, should initiate the male aspirants in our holy order and fellowship. (128)

These Āchāryas should behave according to their appropriate Dharma (duties). They should respect the saints and should study the scriptures with a spirit of reverence. (129)

They should perform with due rites the worship and devotion of Lakshmi-Nārāyan and other idols installed by Me in large temples. (130)

Anybody who enters the temple with a desire to have food should be so served with food and treated hospitably, according to the means available. (131)

A pāthshāla for teaching Sanskrit should be established, and a learned brāhmin preceptor should be appointed therein to impart the knowledge of Sadvidyā, for verily the propagation of the scriptural lore is an act of great benediction. (132)

Special Duties of the wives of the Āchāryas (133 – 134)

The wives of the Āchāryas, Ayodhyāprasād and Raghuvirji. with the permission of their husbands, should preach to females only and initiate them, giving them Krishna mantra. (133)

They should never touch, talk to or even show their faces to males other than those who are closely related to them. (134)

Special Duties of the Householder Disciples (135-156)

Our disciples who are householders should not under any circumstances associate themselves with widows who are not closely related to them. (135)

The householder disciples should not remain in private company with either their mother, sister or daughter (who may be of young age), except in the strictest emergency. They should never give away their wives to anyone out of a sense of emotional extravagance. (136)

My disciples should not keep any contact with a woman courtesan. (137)

My devotees should entertain and serve guests with food according to their means, and should perform in a proper way the sacrificial rites and oblations to ancestors. (138)

My disciples should serve their parents, preceptors, and sick persons while they live, to the best of their ability. (139)

They should take up such vocations as may be suitable to their caste. The agriculturist farmers should not castrate bulls. (140)

According to their means, my disciples should store food grains and save money against their future requirements, and those who own cattle should store a stock of fodder. (141)

My disciples should keep cows and other animals only if they can afford to take sufficient care of them and maintain them with grass, water or other needs. Otherwise they should abstain from keeping cattle. (142)

My disciples should not undertake business transactions (either for the purchase of land or for lending money, even with their sons or friends) except by a written document. (143)

My disciples should enter into a written understanding, with a witness attesting his signature thereto, for the amount that may be required to be paid on marriage occasions, either of their own or others, but should never rely on spoken agreement. (144)

My disciples should regulate their expenses according to their income and must never indulge in extravagant expenses, for expenses incurred in excess of income beget future misery. (145)

My disciples should maintain legible regular accounts of their income and expenditure written daily in their own hand. (146)

My disciples should donate one-tenth of their income or food grains that may be their agricultural income. Those who have insufficient means should donate one-twentieth of their income, either in money or in kind. (147)

The regular observance of Ekādashi vrat or other special vrats should be considered fulfilled only when the necessary concluding celebrations are performed according to the scriptures. Only then will they yield desired results. (148)

In the month of Shrāvan they should worship, or

engage the services of pious brāhmin devotees, for the worship of Shiva with Bilva patras and the like. (149)

My disciples should never borrow money from the Āchāryas or from the treasury of the temples; nor should they take utensils, ornaments, or clothes and the like for their own use from the temples. (150)

My disciples who visit the temples or approach the saints or preceptors for darshan should not eat food served by others, either in the temples or on the way. For this deprives one of the fruits of righteous actions. (151)

My disciples should pay wages regularly either in money or in kind to labourers hired by them and agreed with them, but in no case should they give them anything less than the agreed rates. They should never conceal a debt that may have been redeemed by them nor should they suppress their own descent and the giving of their daughters in marriage (Kanyādān). They should never maintain dealings with wicked persons. (152)

In the event of a famine, or harassment from the wicked, or tyranny of a king, which is likely to harm one's prestige or wealth or even one's own life, my followers should in such circumstances quit that place at once, even if it be their native place, and migrate to some other place where there is no such harassment. (153, 154)

My disciples with means should perform ahimsaka Yagnas (sacrifices without killing) for propitiating Vishnu, and should feed Brāhmins and ascetics on the day following Ekādashi fast or on religious days in places of pilgrimage. (155)

My disciples with means should celebrate the religious festivals in temples with great pomp and enthusiasm, and should give alms to deserving Brāhmins. (156)

Special Duties for Rulers (157-158)

My disciples of the royal families should, in conformity with the scriptures, extend full protection to their subjects and treat them as members of their own family. They should rightfully consolidate religious tenets on the earth within the sphere of their rule. (157)

My disciples who are rulers should be fully aware of the seven different constituents for successfully governing their state, the four expedients necessary for a victorious conquest of the enemy state, the six diplomatic qualities, and the important places to send spies. They should also skilfully understand those who are well versed in social affairs, and distinguish between people who deserve punishment and those who do not deserve punishment by their personal attributes.[1] (158)

Special Duties for Female Disciples (159 – 174)

Special Duties for Married Women (159 – 162)

The female followers should serve their husbands, be they either blind or ailing, poor, or impotent, in the manner in which they worship and serve God; under no circumstances should they speak harsh words to them. (159)

They should not, under any circumstances, develop contact with any young, handsome or virtuous man. (160)

---

[1] (i) Seven constituents: (1) the king; (2) the ministers; (3) the friends intimate, artificial and hypocritical; (4) the treasury; (5) the nations; (6) the forts; (7) the army.

(ii) The four expedients: (1) conciliatory discussion; (2) alms giving; (3) developing enmity between the heads of armies of the enemy; (4) taking away the kingdom, treasury, and executing enemies.

(iii) Diplomatic qualities: (1) to adopt conciliatory measures; (2) to initiate quarrels; (3) to besiege the enemy; (4) to divide one's own army for a two-pronged attack.

No devout wives should dress in such a manner as to expose their breasts, navel or thighs and thus attract the glance of males. They should never move about without putting on their sari and should never go to see vulgar shows. Again they should never maintain contact with debauched women or courtesans. (161)

Women whose husbands are away from home should not decorate themselves with rich dresses or ornaments nor visit other houses, and should abstain from indulging in light gossip or frivolity. (162)

Special Duties for Widows (163 – 172)

The widows should serve God with the same fidelity with which they served their husbands, and should always remain under the authority of their father or son and not behave freely. (163)

They should abstain from the touch of any male who may not be their nearest relative. During the period of their youth they should avoid contact or conversation with one who may not be their nearest relative except in unavoidable circumstances. (164)

There is no sin if they casually touch a suckling child, just as there is no sin in touching an animal. Similarly the touch of an old man in unavoidable circumstances also does not involve any sin. (165)

Widow disciples should not learn anything from people who are not closely related to them. They should observe bodily austerity by observing fasts or vrats. (166)

Widows should not give anything in charity if their available funds are sufficient only for their own subsistence. (167)

Widow disciples should take food only once a day, sleep on the floor, and refrain from looking at animals in coition. (168)

Widow disciples should never dress like married women or like renounced women, nor should they dress in a manner unbecoming to the traditions of the place they live in or with their family customs. (169)

They should always avoid the company of a woman who is habitually disposed to assisting abortion; they should not indulge in speaking about or listening to amorous talk about males. (170)

Young widows should never keep the secluded company of young men, even if they are closely related to them, except under unforeseen exigencies. (171)

They should never take part in the Holi festival, nor dress in rich or transparent clothes made of golden fabrics. (172)

Common Duties for Women Disciples (173 – 174)

The womefolk should never take a bath without their clothes, and they should never conceal their periodical menses. (173)

During the period of menses they should avoid touching anybody or even clothes for three days. They should enjoy the usual rights on the fourth day after taking their bath. (174)

Special Rules of Conduct for Ascetics (175 – 196)

Special Rules of Conduct for brāhmin Ascetics (175 – 185)

The Naishthik Brahmachāris (who have to observe eightfold celibacy) should avoid all contact or talk with females, nor should they intentionally look at them. (175)

They should never indulge in talk about females nor listen to such talk, nor should they ever go for their bath in places usually frequented by females, or where females reside. (176)

They should not touch or look at pictures of females or their idols made either of wood or metal, except those of Goddesses. (177)

These Brahmachāris should not draw pictures of females, nor should they touch any garment worn by a woman nor look at animals in coition. (178)

They should neither touch nor speak nor look at a man in the attire of a female, nor should they ever preach, talk, or sing devotional songs keeping females in view. (179)

They should not abide by the order of even their preceptors if such orders tend to dislodge them from their vows of celibacy. They should ever lead a steadfast, contented and humble life. (180)

They should instantly stop a woman who deliberately makes advances towards them, by talking to her or if necessary by reprimanding her. (181)

Nevertheless at times when the life of a woman or their own life is at stake, they should protect their life and also the life of the woman by talking to her or even by touching her. (182)

They should not massage their bodies with oil, nor should they arm themselves, or put on dress which provokes fear. They should conquer taste and subjugate their desire to enjoy palatable food. (183)

They should not take meals from a Brahmin's house where the meals are served by a woman. But if the meals are served by males they can go to such houses for food. (184)

They should study the Vedas and other scriptures, and serve their preceptors, and should avoid the company of males disposed to female habits, just as they avoid the

272 LIFE AND PHILOSOPHY OF LORD SWĀMINĀRĀYAN

company of women. (185)

Special Duties for brāhmin Disciples (186 – 187)

My brāhmin disciples should never drink water taken out by a leather pail, nor should they ever eat onions, garlic, or other forbidden foods. (186)

They should not take their meals without performing their daily rites, namely bathing, Sandhyā-Vandanam, Gāyatri (chanting hymns to the Sun God), Vishnu pujan (worship of Vishnu) and the Vaishva Deva (offering rice to the god of Fire). (187)

Special Rules of Conduct for Non-brāhmin Ascetics (Sādhus) (188 – 196)

Our ascetics should, like the Naishthik Brahmachāris, always avoid the eightfold contact with women and persons disposed to female habits, and should conquer passions such as lust, anger, avarice, etc. (188)

They should ever endeavour to control their senses and particularly the palate (Rasanā). They should never hoard money nor ask others to do so on their behalf. (189)

They should never keep with them other people's money as deposits, and should cultivate patience. They should never allow a female to tread in their place of residence. (190)

Except in sheer exigencies, our sādhus should never go out alone at night time nor even during the day without the company of their fellow sādhus. (191)

They should never use a cloth which is very valuable or dyed or printed gaudily, and they should never accept valuable shawls or other garments. (192)

They should not go to the house of any householder

disciples except for begging food or for holding meetings for spiritual discourses. They should spend their time in devotion and should not waste their time idly. (193)

My saints should go to such places for their meals where the food is served only by males, and the contact of females is totally out of sight. (194)

If no such facilities are available, my saints should beg cereals and cook for themselves. (195)

All my saints should adopt the code of behaviour practised by Bharatji, the son of Rishabhdev Bhagwān, who behaved like an ordinary illiterate brāhmin in order that he might not be involved in the alluring contacts of the world or in worldly relations. (196)

Common Rules for all Saints in General (197 – 202)

The brahmachāris and the sādhus of this fold should completely abstain from taking betel leaves, opium, tobacco or other forbidden substances. (197)

They should not dine on occasions on which certain purificatory ceremonies relating to the conception of a child are performed, or on the eleventh and twelfth days after the death of a person, on which days the obituary rites are performed. (198)

These sādhus should not sleep during the day except when they are ill, nor should they indulge in worldly talk nor listen to such talk deliberately. (199)

These sādhus should not sleep on a cot unless they are prostrated with acute illness. They should cultivate frank and upright manners amongst themselves. (200)

They should always bear the abuses and insults hurled upon them by the wicked and also their beatings. Not only should such evil acts be forgotten, but they should also

Process of Cosmic Evolution
as explained
by Lord Swaminãrãyan

TRANSCENDENTAL HIGHEST	**PURUSHOTTAM**	THE SUPREME LORD
INFINITE AND LIMITLESS	**AKSHARDHÃM**	THE DIVINE ABODE
	or	
	AKSHAR BRAHMAN	
PRIMORDIAL PURUSH		PRIMORDIAL PRAKRITI
FIRST PRODUCED	**PRADHÃN PURUSH**	LIMITLESS IN NUMBER
THE GREAT	**MAHATTATTVA**	(COSMIC INTELLIGENCE)
SÃTTVIC AHAMKÃR	**RÃJASIC AHAMKÃR**	TÃMSIC AHAMKÃR
	TWENTY FOUR TATTVAS	SEE NOTES
	VIRÃT	
	BRAHMA	
PRAJÃPATI		MARICHA etc.
	KASYAPA PRAJÃPATI	
INDRA-DEVAS	**DEMONS**	**UNIVERSE** (MOBILE AND IMMOBILE JIVAS)

bless the wicked for a change in their manner of living. (201)

They should not act as agents or as spies, nor should they indulge in backbiting, or act as eye-witnesses. They should shed attachment towards their body and also towards their relations. (202)

Conclusion (203 – 212)

I have thus narrated succinctly the duties (Dharma) of the different classes of My disciples. However, for further elaboration of their duties they should refer to the various scriptures of our Sampradāya. (203)

I have compiled this Shikshāpatri, the Epistle of Precepts, and have incorporated therein the quintessence of all the scriptures, the observance of which will yield the desired results. (204)

Hence all my disciples should observe all the rules laid down in this Shikshāpatri and should never take up freedom of behaviour. (205)

Those of my disciples who live in accordance with the precepts laid down here will attain all the four desired objects (Dharma, Artha, Kām and Moksha) on this earth. (206)

And those of my male and female disciples who do not follow the tenets of this Shikshāpatri are considered as excommunicated from the fellowship. (207)

All my disciples should, as a rule, read this Shikshāpatri daily, and those who cannot read it should listen to its recital with great devotion. (208)

If one does not find someone to read this Shikshāpatri, he should worship it daily, holding every word of it as the personified form of My divine self. (209)

This Shikshāpatri should be given only to those who possess aptitude for spiritual learning; it should never be given to those who are devoid of such learning. (210)

I have written this Shikshāpatri, which is the bestower of highest bliss to all souls, on the fifth day (Vasant – Panchmi) of the bright half of the month of Māgha of the Samvat year 1882 (AD 1826). (211)

May Lord Shree Krishna, the destroyer of all miseries of His devotees, the defender of Dharma and Bhakti, and the bestower of all cherished objects, spread His auspiciousness everywhere. (212)

This is the code of conduct laid down by Shree Swāminārāyan. The metaphysical part of certain verses has been referred to in the earlier chapters of this book.

In verses[1] where Lakshmi with Nārāyan, Arjun with Nārāyan, and Rādhā with Krishna, are described as Lakshmi Nārāyan Nar-Nārāyan and Rādhā-Krishna respectively, the intention is to join Swāmi with Nārāyan as Swāminārāyan or Akshar with Purushottam as Akshar-Purushottam. This principle of upāsanā has been very clearly elucidated in Vachanāmritam, where Akshar, assuming a second form, serves Purushottam.[2] The evolution of Akshar-Purushottam Upāsanā has its seed in the Vachanāmritam and is a strong foundation for full spiritual development. Shree Swāminārāyan says, 'The devotee should understand that Akshar is always by the side of Purushottam when incarnated on the earth, and therefore the principle should be so preached and understood.[3]

Shikshāpatri ends with the benediction 'May the Lord bless all for a devout life.'

---

[1] Shikshāpatri, 109-110.   [2] Vachanāmritam Gadhadā Sec. 1-21.
[3] Ibid., Sec. 1-71.

APPENDIX

NOTES ON COSMIC EVOLUTION

Purushottam : The Ultimate Reality or the Transcendental Highest.

Akshar : Also spoken of as Brahman – the divine abode of Purushottam.

Primordial Purush : Purush is sometimes referred to as Akshar or even as the Highest Reality (Purushottam) by scriptures. But Lord Swāminārāyan explains Purush as separate from Prakriti – indivisible, eternal, infinite, unaffected by the factor of time, self-luminous, omniscient, possessing divine body, cause of cosmic evolution, Knower of Māyā and her evolutes. Purush was dormant, but was inspired by Purushottam through Akshar to start the cosmic evolution, which he does by activating Prakriti, then in a state of equilibrium. Shrimad Bhāgawat explains: 'Purushottam by assuming the form of Purush, activated Prakriti to release from her womb the various universes.' Shree Swāminārāyan differs and explains that Purushottam does not assume the form of Purush but inspires Purush through Akshar. Purush is different from Akshar and Akshar is different from Purushottam.

Primordial Prakriti : Māyā is, in the beginning, motionless

	and in a state of equilibrium. But when disturbed by Purush she becomes active.
Pradhãn Purush	'First produced' - described as lower nature of lower Brahman.
Mahat Tattva	Cosmic intelligence. The universe is within it in an unmanifested form. It is luminous, unaffected by qualities and full of pure sattva.
Sãttvic Ahamkãr	The ego of beneficent attributes.
Rãjasic Ahamkãr	The ego of earthly positions.
Tãmasic Ahamkãr	The ego of maleficent instincts.
Twenty-four tattvas	Five bhutas or gross elements: the earth, water, fire, wind and space.
	Five cognitive organs: nose, tongue, eyes, skin and ears.
	Five conative organs: mouth, hands, legs, anus, and the genital organ.
	Five principles of the elements: smell, taste, form (or colour), touch and sound. Four Antahkarans (inner instruments): manas (mental), buddhi (intelligence), chitta (mind), and Ahamkãr (ego).
	Notes: The function of manas is to think.
	The function of buddhi is to decide.
	The function of chitta is to reveal wisdom.
	The function of Ahamkãr is to possess.

Vrat	The universe, is also known as Vishwaswarupa, which is described in Bhagawad Gitā as the form manifested before Arjuna by Shree Krishna.
Brahmā	The creative divinity that surged out from the navel of Virāt.
Prajāpatis	These are all the different agencies through which the evolution of the universe takes place in different ages.

The human body is formed of twenty-four tattvas. Every human being performs actions inspired by three gunas, namely: sattva, rajas and tamas. Predominance of sattva guna which is also described as light or knowledge, inspires one to perform benevolent actions. The predominance of rajas guna will inspire one to perform actions which will be full of motion, self projection, activity, vehemence, etc. The predominance of tamas guna will result in performance of lazy, irritating actions full of heat, arrogance, ignorance.

The human body has three states: the gross body, which has a state of waking, the subtle body which has a state of dreams, and the causal body which has a state of deep sleep. This state of deep sleep is also described as the state of ignorance. And ignorance is blissful. In the state of deep sleep we forget worries, calamities, and pains and merely enjoy the bliss of Brahman leading us with all compassion into this state.

The lore enunciated by the Rishis is known as Brahmavidyā, a lore for redemption, and is so all-inclusive in its various aspects that it regards everything which has emanated from Brahman as Brahman. But at the same time it warns the sādhaks not to take everything as Brahman for granted, but to realise all as Brahman by shedding the impurities of life.

Upanishads describe annam (food) as Brahman, Prānas (Vital airs) as Brahman, Manas (mind) as Brahman, Vijnān (intellect), as Brahman and finally Ānanda (bliss) as Brahman. These, therefore, are the koshas or five sheaths which are within the body and whose functions should be properly studied to realise Brahman.

Annamaya Kosha: The body is produced from food which gives vitality, and produces semen which sows seed inthe womb for the human body. Therefore the whole of humanity is generated out of food. The human body is nourished on food and is maintained by food. And as one who sustains is Brahman, therefore food, which sustains the body, should be regarded as Brahman and should be so venerated as a form of Brahman. Since the body is composed out of food, food is the physical sheath of human beings.

Prānamaya Kosha: Food so consumed vitalises the prānas (vital airs) and since the body survives if the prānas thrive, they should be regarded as Brahman. With such worshipful regard for prānas, the purity of prānas should be maintained. Prānamaya Kosha covers five kinds of prāna – prāna (drawn from outside), apan (downward moving), saman (digestive), vyan (pervasive) and udan (upward moving) and also five conative organs. This sheath survives the passing of the physical sheath.

Manomaya Kosha: The mental sheath. The vital sheath thrives upon this sheath. Words and mind cannot reach Brahman. But a sage who has purified his mind by identifying it with Brahman and by experiencing the unparalleled bliss of Brahman within the mind, has conquered all fears and attains Brahman. Mind and the five cognitive organs form the manomaya kosha.

Vijnānmaya Kosha.- This is the intellectual sheath, which preserves the purity of the mental sheath. All actions, either sacrificial or mundane, are performed through the intellect. Since the intellect predominates, the five cognitive organs which form this Kosha together with intellect are directed by the intellect with perfect discrimination. Intellect therefore should be worshipped as Brahman, whose pure guidance will make man incorruptible.

Ānandamaya Kosha.- The sheath of total bliss. When intellect identified as Brahman is introverted towards Ātmā (the soul) one experiences absolute bliss in enjoying the Paramātmā, and becomes fully Brahmanised.

Thus one who knows and realises Brahman attains Parabrahman. The existence of Parabrahman is realised by this method of establishing Brahman within.

The Upanishads have very logically put the matter before every sādhak. They say it is like identifying the star of Arundhati (evening star) in the sky, although it is very remote, by pointing at the other star which is nearer and calling it Arundhati. When the gaze is fixed on this star again it is then said 'not that star but the star above that is the star of Arundhati. Again the gaze is fixed on this star. And again, when the gaze is fixed, it is said 'not that but the one above it' and so on until the star of Arundhati itself is spotted by the eyes and the gaze is fixed on it. Similarly, since everything is evolved out of Brahman, Brahman is all-pervasive. But the physical eyes cannot perceive all as Brahman.

So food is called Brahman as food sustains the body, as Brahman sustains the various universes. And as food vitalises prāna and the prānas sustain the body, so the prānas are Brahman. And so on, until one realises the Ānandamaya Brahman which is one's own Ātma. One who so realises Brahman realises Parabrahman. To him the existence of God does not remain a hypothetical question but by divine law becomes a matter of reality.

GLOSSARY

Abhaya	Fearlessness
Abhedya	Unpierceable
Āchārya	Teacher; spiritual guide or preceptor
Achhedya	Uncuttable
Achit	Non-sentient
Ādi	First
Ādi Nārāyan	The Ultimate God
Advaita	Monism
Ahamkār	Ego
Ahimsā	Non-violence, in thought, word or deed
Aishwarya	Divine Power
Akārya	Acts which are prohibited
Akhand	Integral, whole
Akshar	Eternal abode of Lord Swaminarayan. In its personal form, *Akshar* serves *Purushottam* in His abode and manifests as His choicest devotee on this earth
Akshar Deri	Shrine built over the cremation spot of Aksharbrahman Gunatitanand Swami in Gondal
Akshar Mukta	A liberated soul residing in *Akshardham*
Akshar Purush	*Akshar mukta*
Aksharatmak	That which is identifeid with *Akshar* i.e. *Aksharrup*
Aksharbhāv	*Brahmabhav*
Aksharbrahman	*Akshar; Brahman*
Akshardhām	The divine abode of Lord Swaminarayan
Aksharrup	Oneness with *Akshar*; brahmanised state
Alfi	A saffron coloured garment to be worn by a sādhu
Amāyik	Free from *maya*; divine
Amravāti	*Swarga loka*; abode of Indra – God of rain
Amsha	Part
Anādi	Having no beginning; eternal
Anādi Bhed	Eternal entity
Ānand	Bliss
Anant	Endless; infinite
Aprithakasiddhabhāv	Non-dual relation

Anātman	Non-atman
Antahkaran	Aggregate of *Manas, Buddhi, Chitta* and *Ahamkar*
Antaryāmi Shakti	God's divine power of immanence
Antaryāmi Swarup	The divine form of God that dwells within, witnessing consciousness
Ārti	Ritual of waving lighted lamps before the deity as an act of adoration
Archā	Image (worship)
Asat Purush	Evil-minded person
Asat	Untruth
Āshram	Religious community; residence of a religious community; stage of life. *Brahmacharya, Grahastha, Vanprastha* and *Sanyasta* are the four stages
Ashtāng Yoga	Eight steps of *yoga* culminating in the realisation of God
Ashtāng Yogi	One proficient in *Ashtang yoga*
Ashubha	Malevolent
Asura	Man of evil character; demon
Ātmā	The soul
Ātmadarshan	The realisation of the self as distinct from the body
Ātmasattā	The power of Atmā
Ātmānubhav	Spiritual experience
Ātmajnān	Knowledge of one's self as *atman*
Ātman	The pure soul
Ātmanishthā	Faith in the soul's inherent power
Ātmasattā	Soul; soul's inherent power
Ātyantik Pralay	Period of final rest
Avatārs	Incarnations
Avatāri	Cause of all incarnations
Avidyā	Ignorance
Baddha jivas	Souls bound by Māyā
Badrikāshram	Abode of Nar-Narayan
Bandha	Bondage
Bhāgawati Tanu	Divine body
Bhagwadbhāv	Godliness
Bhagwān	God
Bhāgwat Dharma	Devotion to God accompanied by righteousness; *Ekantik Dharma*

Bhajan	Devotional song; worship
Bhakta	A devotee of God
Bhaktas	Devotees
Bhakti	Devotion
Bhakti Mārg	The path of devotion
Bharatkhand	India
Bhaya	Fear
Bhed (drishti)	Vision which perceives differences
Bhumāpurush	One of the demigods
Brahma drishti	Divine vision
Brahmā	Creator of the universe
Brahmabhāv	Consciousness of being one with *Brahman*
Brahmachāri	One who vows to lead a life of celibacy
Brahmacharya	The practice of celibacy
Brahmadhām	*Akshardham*
Brahmahatyā	Sin of killing a brahmin
Brahmajnān	The knowledge of *Brahman*
Brahmajyoti	The divine light of *Akshar*
Brahmamahol	*Akshardham*
Brahmaloka	*Akshardham*
Brahmarasa	The divine nectar
Brahman	*Akshar; Aksharbrahman*
Brahmanised	One who has attained oneness with *Brahman*
Brahmānda	The Universe
Brahmapur	*Akshardham*
Brahmarup	Oneness with *Brahman*
Brahmaswarup	Oneness with *Brahman*; God-realised
Brāhmarandhra	That area of Sushumna (q.v.)which culminates in the head
Brāhmattva	State of Brāhmic awareness
Brahmavettā	Knower of *Brahman*
Brahmavidyā	Spiritual lore
Brahmaswarup ātmā	The soul that has attained Brāhmic bhāv, or awareness of Brahma
Buddhi	Intellect
Chaitanya	Pure consciousness
Chetnā	Sentient
Chidākāsh	The divine space–Akshar
Chidrupashakti	The sentient power
Chit	Sentient

Darshan	Seeing; the sight or beholding of the deity or holy person with reverence or devotion
Desh	Place
Dev	Deity; demigod
Dhām	Abode
Dhāmi	Master of the abode
Dharma	Righteousness; Moral or social duty and law; code of ethical conduct; religion
Dhyān	Meditation
Diksha	Initiation into sainthood
Divya	Divine
Divyabhāv	Divine attributes
Divya Vigrah	Divine body
Drishya	Body
Drashtā	Soul
Dwāpar Yuga	The third age of the world
Ekāntik Bhakta	A devotee in whom *dharma, jnan, vairagya* and *bhakti* are fully developed
Ekāntik Bhāv	Single-mindedness
Ekāntik Dharma	*Bhagwat Dharma*
Ekras	Pure
Gādi	Seat of the Head
Golok	The abode of Lord Krishna
Gopis	Milkmaids of Vrindavan, who were devotees of Lord Krishna
Goval	Shepherds of Vrindavan
Gunas	Qualities referring to *Sattva* (goodness), *Rajas* (passion) and *Tamas* (darkness)
Gunātit	State beyond the three *gunas* or qualities
Guru	A religious teacher, adviser or guide; spiritual preceptor
Guru Paramparā	The unbroken line of gurus in the spiritual hierarchy
Himsā	Violence
Icchāshakti	The power of will
Indra	God of rain
Indriyas	Cognitive and conative organs
Ishwar	One of the five eternal entities; demigods

Jada	Non-sentient
Jagat	Universe
Janmāshtami	Birthday of Lord Krishna; 8th day of the dark half
Jiva	Individual soul (see ktmd)
Jivanmukta	Released soul even although embodied
Jnān	Knowledge of the self or God
Jnān Shakti	The power of knowledge
Jnāni	One who has the knowledge of Brahman
Kainkarya	Service
Kāla	Time
Kali yuga	The fourth and present age of the world
Kāran	Causal
Karma	Actions
Kārya	Things to be done
Kirtan	Religious hymn; devotional song.
Kinkara	Servant
Kriyāshakti	The power of action
Kshar	Perishable
Kshetra	Body
Kshara Purushas	Perishable jivas
Lakshmi	Consort of Vishnu; Goddess of wealth
Loka	World
Mahāmukta	Released soul
Mahā Purush	The primordial self of *Akshar mukta*
Mahāmāyā	Primordial *maya*
Mahāmukta	*Akshar mukta*
Mahant	Head priest of a temple
Mahārāj	Title of respect for spiritual leaders; commonly used on own to refer to Lord Swaminarayan
Mahāttattva	Cosmic intelligence
Mahimā	Glory; greatness
Manas	Mind
Mantra	Revered words or syllable or hymn recited during worship and meditation
Manushya	Human
Manushyabhāv	Human attributes
Māyā	One of the five eternal entities; the power of God responsible for creating attachment towards the body and its relations

Māyik	The doctrine of illusion
Moha	Delusion
Moksha	Release or salvation
Mukta	A released soul
Mukti	Liberation from the cycle of births and deaths
Mul	Primordial
Mul Akshar	Primordial *Akshar*
Mul Māya	Primordial *maya*
Mul Purush	The primordial self of *Akshar mukta*
Mumukshu	Aspirant for salvation
Muni	Seer; sage
Murti	Image of the deity installed in a temple for worship; a picture or statue
Naimishāranya	An important place of pilgrimage near Ayodhya. Kshetra
Nārāyan	God
Nirākār	Formless; devoid of all forms evolved from *maya*
Nirdosh	Free from faults
Nirgun	Devoid of attributes; divine
Nirgun Brahma	Subtlest form of Braliman, without qualities
Nirlobh	Freedom from covetousness
Nirmān	Freedom from ego
Nirvikāri	Immutable
Nirvikalp Samādhi	The highest state of realisation where only the undisturbed bliss of God is experienced.
Nishchay	Conviction of the form of God
Nishkām Bhakta	A devotee desirous of nothing but the service of God
Nishthā	Faith; conviction of the form of God
Nissneh	Non-attachment
Nisswād	Without taste
Nishkām	Without passion
Nishkām bhakta	A devotee having no desires
Nitya muktas	Eternally released souls
Niyam	Moral habit or rule
Niyamya	Controlled
Niyāmaka	Controller
Panch Bhutas	Earth, water, fire, wind and space; the five evolutes of *maya*
Panch Vartmān	Five vows taken at time of initiation into the *Sampradaya* or into sainthood

Panchvishayas	The five sense objects
Parābhakti	Intense devotion
Parabrahma	God
Parā Prakriti	Divine ements of matter
Param	Supreme; greatest
Paramātman	God
Paramhansa	Highest stage of ascetic renunciation
Parampad	Highest position; final beatitude
Parmeshwar	God
Pārshads	Attendants in white garments
Purnatvam	Fullness
Paroksh	Unmanifest
Pātāl	Lowest of the fourteen *lokas* in this universe
Pradhān Purush	'First-produced'; described as lower nature or lower *Brahman*
Pragat	Manifest; present
Pragat Brahmaswarup	Present form of *Brahman* – referring to the God-realised brahmanised *Satpurush*
Prakriti	*Maya*; one of the five eternal entities
Pralay	Destruction
Prānas	Vital airs
Prasād	Sanctified food from that offered to the deity
Pratyaksha	Visible before the eyes
Pujā	Act of worship or adoration; ritual and prayer offered at home or in the temple
Purna	Total; complete; perfect
Purna Purushottam	The Ultimate Reality; the supreme God
Purush	This term is variously used to mean soul, lower *Brahman*, *Brahman* or *Parabrahman*
Purushottam	The supreme God; Lord Swaminarayan
Purushottamrup	Like the form of *Purushottam*
Rajas	Mode of passion; one of the three *gunas*
Rās	A Gujarati folk-dance
Rishi	Seer; sage
Sachchidānand	Truth, consciousness and bliss
Sadāchārya	The True Guru
Sadguru	Senior ascetic; eminent preceptor
Sādhak	An aspirant walking on the spiritual path
Sādhanā	Spiritual endeavour

Sādhu	Holy man who has renounced the world; ascetic
Sagun	With qualities
Sagun Brahman	Active form of Brahman, possessed of qualities
Shaivites	The followers of Lord Shiva
Sakām	Full of desires
Sākār	Personal; with form
Sāmkhya	One of the six chief systems of Indian philosophy attributed to the sage Kapil
Sampradāya	Holy or religious fellowship; tradition handed down from a founder through successive religious teachers
Sāmyavasthā	State of equilibrium
Sanyāsi	Hindu ascetic or renunciate
Sarvagna	Omniscient
Sarvopari	The supreme; transcending all
Sat yuga	The first age of the world
Sat-Chit-Ānand	Truth, consciousness and bliss
Satpurush	The Saint who has established rapport with God; God-realised Saint
Satsang	Holy Fellowship; religious group or gathering; association with sadhus and devotees
Satsangi	Member of the *Satsang*
Sattva	Mode of goodness; one of the three *gunas*
Satyaloka	The *loka* of Brahma
Sevak	Servant
Sākshātkār	Realisation
Sālokya	To stay in the above of God
Samādhi	Trance associated with higher consciousness
Samipya	Nearness
Sankirtans	Singing of hymns
Sampradaya	Fellowship
Sat	Truth
Satpurush	The saiant who has established rapport with God
Satsang	Holy Fellowship Satya
Sankalpa	One whose wishes are always fulfilled
Sāyujya	To merge in God
Sevā	Service
Sevak Bhāv	The spirit of servitude
Sevya-Sevakabhāv	The relation between the Master and the Devotee

Shākshi	Witness
Shakti	Power
Sharir	Body
Shariri	Soul; controller
Shāstra	Scriptures
Shloka	Verse
Shubra	Benevolent
Shushka	False; dry
Shruti	Pramānas Authority of the Shrutis
Shraddhā	Faith
Shuddha Chit	Pure mind
Sinhāsan	Throne
Sthān	Place; position
Sthula	Gross
Sthitapragna	Perfect balance of mind
Sukshma	Subtle
Sushumnā	Channel of subtle force in the human spine, culminating in Brahmarandra, an area in the head. Two other subtle channels accompany Sushumna - Pingala on the right and Ida on the left
Swabhāv	Nature; character; disposition
Swadharma	Ethical rules applying to oneself
Swāmi	Lord; master; saint
Swāmi-sevak Bhāv	Feeling of Master-servant relationship
Swargaloka	Abode of Indra – God of rain
Swarup	Form
Swataha sukhi	Blissful by nature
Swayamjyoti	Self-luminous
Tamas	Mode of darkness or ignorance; one of the three gunas
Tapa/Tapas	Austerities
Tattva	Evolute; element
Tilak	A vertical mark on the forehead symbolic of the footprints of God
Tirth	Sacred place; pilgrimage
Tretā Yuga	The second age of the world
Trigunātit	Transcending the three gunas of prakriti
Upādhi	Adjunct

Upanayana Samskãr	Ceremony of the investiture of the sacred thread
Upãsak	Worshipper
Upãsanã	Way of understanding God; Mode of worship
Upasham	A state of no-mind
Upãsya	To be worshipped
Vaikunth	Abode of Lakshmi-Narayan
Vairãgya	Detachment; indifference or aversion to worldly pleasures
Vairãj Purush	A demigod
Vaishnav	Devotee of Lord Vishnu
Varna	Caste or class;the four main castes are *Brahmin, Kshatriya, Vaishya* and *Shudra*
Vartmãn	Vow
Vãsanã	Worldly desire
Vãsanãmaya	Chitt Mind full of mundane desires
Vãsanã ling sharira	Causal body
Vãsudev	God
Vedanta	One of the schools of Indian philosophy; the final part of the Vedas; the Upanishads
Vedantin	Follower of *Vedanta*
Vibhutvam	Fullness
Vikrutis	Degenerated elements
Virãt	The gross body of *Ishwar*
Visheshana	Adjective
Visheshya	The object
Vishishta aikya	Unitive consciousness
Vishishtãdvaita	Qualified non-dualism of Ramanujacharya
Vishwaswarup	The cosmic form of God
Vivek	Discrimination
Vrat	Holy injunction
Vyãpak	All-pervading; immanent
Vyatireka Swarup	Separate form
Yagna	Sacrifice
Yagna Vedi	Sacrificial altar
Yãtrã	Pilgrimage
Yoga	One of the schools of Indian philosophy founded by sage Patanjali
Yogamãyã	Yogic powers

SCRIPTURES

Bhagvad Gitā
Dialogue between Lord Krishna and Arjun on the *Mahabharat* battlefield; one of the central scriptures of Hinduism.

Bhaktachintāmani
Scripture composed in verse by Nishkulanand Swami describing the life and work of Lord Swaminarayan.

Chosath Padi
A book of *Nishkulanand Kavyam* detailing the attributes of a true Saint.

Haridigvijay
Sanskrit text by Nityanand Swami describing the *lila* of Shriji Maharaj.

Harililākalpataru
Sanskrit work by Achintyanand Brahmachari with *Acharya* Shri Raghuvirji Maharaj describing Shriji Maharaj's supreme glory and divine pastimes; one of the longest scriptures of the *Sampradaya* with 33,000 verses.

Harililāmritam
Gujarati work by *Acharya* Shri Viharilalji Maharaj in verse describing life and work of Lord Swaminarayan.

Kirtans
Devotional poems composed by the saint-poets of Lord Swaminarayan – Muktanand Swami, Nishkulanand Swami, Brahmanand Swami, Premanand Swami, Devanand Swami, etc.

Mahābhārat
The Great Epic of India. With 100,000 verses, it is the world's longest poem revolving around the family feud between the five Pandavas and their cousins, the Kauravas – culminating in the great battle, the *Mahabharat* war.

Mokshadharma
A chapter of the *Mahabharat*.

Nishkulānand Kāvyam
Compilation of 22 books written by Nishkulanand Swami in Gujarati verse to guide the spiritual aspirant.

Purānas
The principle 18 sacred works by Vyasji which contain the whole body of Hinduism.

	Include *Shrimad Bhagvatam, Skanda Purana* and *Vayu Purana.*
Satsangijivanam	A volume of Sanskrit verses composed by Shatanand Swami in the time of Lord Swaminarayan; includes details regarding the rites and rituals of the *Sampradaya.*
Shikshāpatri	Sanskrit text written by Lord Swaminarayan detailing codes of ethics.
Shrimad Bhāgavatam	*Purana* describing the *lila* of the various incarnations of God.
Shruti	Commentary on the *Vedas;* the *Upanishads.*
Smriti	Ethical codes of conduct written by Manu, Yagnavalkya, etc.
Swāmini Vātu	Spiritual talks of *Aksharbrahman* Gunatitanand Swami.
Upanishads	Final portion of *Vedas;* collection of experiences of the ancient seers; includes *Chhandogya Upanishad, Shvetashvatara Upanishad, Katha Upanishad, Mundaka Upanishad, Taittiriya Upanishad, Brihadaranyaka Upanishad.*
Vachanāmritam	Scriptural text compiled by four senior *paramhansas* containing the sermons of Lord Swaminarayan given at at various places; the most sacred scripture of the
Vāsudev Mahātmya	A chapter from the *Skanda Purana* describing *Ekantik Dharma.*
Vedās	Ancient Hindu scriptures containing the knowledge of the sages and seers; the oldest writings in history.
Vedras	A compilation of the letters written by Shriji Maharaj to His *paramhansas* explaining the five *vartmans* to be followed by all renunciates and describing the lofty spiritual ideals to be cultivated by a devotee.

INDEX OF NAMES